Toy Buildings
1880-1980

Patty Cooper & Dian Zillner

4880 Lower Valley Road, Atglen, PA 19310 USA

Dedication

This book is dedicated to our boys,
Caleb, Jacob, and Prather.

Front flap photo:
"Bliss warehouse photograph courtesy of The Wenham Museum, Wenham, MA. Photograph by Rob Huntley."

Cooper, Patty.
    Toy Buildings. 1880-1980 / Patty Cooper & Dian Zillner.
        p. cm.
    Includes bibliographical references.
    ISBN 0-7643-1011-9 (hc.)
    1. Dollhouses--History--19th century Catalogs. 2. Dollhouses--History--20th century Catalogs. I. Zillner, Dian. II. Title.
NK4894.A2C67 2000   99-40538
745.5928--dc21   CIP

ISBN: 0-7643-1011-9

Book Design by Anne Davidsen
Typeset in Americana /Humanst521

Printed in China
1 2 3 4

Published by Schiffer Publishing Ltd.
4880 Lower Valley Road
Atglen, PA 19310
Phone: (610) 593-1777; Fax: (610) 593-2002
e-mail: schifferbk@aol.com
Please visit our website catalog at
www.schifferbooks.com
or write for a free printed catalog.
This book may be purchased from the publisher.
Please include $3.95 for shipping.

In Europe, Schiffer books are distributed by
Bushwood Books
6 Marksbury Avenue
Kew Gardens
Surrey TW9 4JF England
Phone: 44 (0)181 392-8585; Fax: 44 (0)181 392-9876
e-mail: bushwd@aol.com
Please try your bookstore first.

We are interested in hearing from authors
with book ideas on related subjects.

Contents

Acknowledgements

Over a hundred collectors, museums, dealers, and friends helped with the book by answering questions, providing information, and sharing photographs. The authors are grateful to the following individuals and organizations without whom this book would not have been possible: Jane Al-Mashat, Pen Andrishok, Angels Attic, Judith Armitstead, Sharon Barton, Sheryl Bell, Sharon and Kenny Bernard, Linda Boltrek, Lisa Boutilier, Gail and Ray Carey, Jim and Shirley Cox, Jim and Beverly Cox (Sussex Toy Shop), Paul Cumbie, Deborah Davey, Ben DeVoto, Bill Dohm, Chuck Donovan, Jim Ferguson, Richard and Joan Ford, Lois L. Freeman, Kathy Garner, Charles L. Gilbert, Gene Harris Antique Auction Center Inc., Libby Goodman, Rita Goranson, Cynthia Stuart Greene, George Handforth, Linda Hanlon, Mary Harris, John Hathorne, Gloria R. Hinkel, Gene Joseph, Lisa Kerr, Jenny LeMasurier, Eleanor LaVove, Theresa Luttenegger, Jackie McMahan, Gaston and Joan Majeune, Ann Meehan, Marge Meisinger, Carol Miller, Mineral Point Toy Museum, Nancy Moore, Gene and Arliss Morris, Gary D. and Judy Mosholder, Heinz A. Mueller, George Mundorf, Betty Nichols, Don Nix, Becky and Don Norris, Gene and Vicki Olswold, Leslie and Joanne Payne, Ruth Petros, Marilyn Pittman, *Plastic Figure & Playset Collector Magazine*, Marge Powell, Elaine Price, Marianne Price, David Pressland, Geraldine Raymond-Scott, Nancy Roeder, Jack Rosenthal (Toys and More), Sandy Rusher, Joe Russell, Jim Schaut, Roy Sheckells, Louana Singleton, Sibyl W. Smith, Roy Specht, Ben Stevens, Bob Stevens, Carol Stevenson, Werner and Mary Stuecher, Fran Tagesen, Tom Terry, Linda and Carl Thomas, Jr., Beverly J. Thomes, Thrilling Toys of Yesteryear, Toy & Miniature Museum of Kansas City, Toys and More, Anna Tracy, Marcie and Bob Tubbs, Marge Voigt, Bill and Stevie Weart, The Wenham Museum, Diane Whipple, Kirk F. White, and Jim Yeager.

The authors would also like to thank Schiffer Publishing Ltd. and its excellent staff, particularly Anne Davidsen, layout designer, and Brandi Wright, editor, who helped with this publication.

Introduction

Patty Cooper and Dian Zillner are primarily dollhouse collectors and are the authors of *Antique and Collectible Dollhouses and Their Furnishings*. Both have a love of architectural history and are intrigued by the ways that designs of the past were interpreted in miniature form as toys for children. To complement their dollhouse collections, barns, stables, and garages were acquired, much to the delight of the young boys in their families. This led to an interest in fire stations, railroad depots, schools, churches, and other structures that would have been part of any toy community. Both of the authors are former librarians and could not resist researching their new finds. This book is the result of their quest for toy buildings and information about them.

Toy buildings were made for a variety of purposes. Small villages were often used under Christmas trees. Other villages and buildings were intended as scenery for model railroads. Early in the century, many toys were marketed with a serious purpose as if mere play were too frivolous. Toy churches had blocks which taught Bible verses. Dollhouses were intended to prepare little girls for domestic life. Toy stores provided lessons about commerce. Small farms provided an introduction to agriculture and, even in the 1940s, one was advertised as "a true replica of farm buildings which would be helpful to older boys and girls, especially 4-H members." Many buildings were intended as settings for other toys. Although a child might enjoy staging pretend battles with toy soldiers, it was even more exciting for them to have a castle to defend. Toy airplanes needed a place to land and toy cars had to have a place to refuel.

Miniature buildings have been made for hundreds of years, but they were not commercially produced until the mid-1800s. Early companies such as Moritz Gottschalk and Christian Hacker in Germany; J. & G. Lines in England; R. Bliss, W.S. Reed, and McLoughlin in America all began the production of such toys in the latter part of the nineteenth century. Over the years, many other companies made additions to the toy community using a variety of materials. By the 1950s, a child could choose from a barn, house, grocery store, service station, railroad depot, airport, theater, castle, fort, hospital, school, church, firehouse, garage, or almost any other structure. The toy manufacturers of the 1950s, especially the Louis Marx company, probably provided a greater variety of toy buildings than in any other era.

It is hoped that this book will be of use to both toy collectors and students of architectural history. Over 550 photographs of toy buildings and related items are provided as well as information about the companies who made them. This book should enable collectors to identify the products of many different manufacturers.

Because toys are far less likely to be remodeled than their real-life counterparts, this book can also provide a glimpse into the changes in the architecture of residential, municipal, and commercial buildings for over a century.

Whenever possible, the authors have attempted to provide an approximate date for the time a toy was manufactured. Occasionally, they were lucky enough to find a patent date on a toy or its box. But more often, the examples shown were dated through researching catalogs and magazines, including published reprints, originals owned by the authors or other collectors, copies from the Library of Congress, and especially items generously shared from Marge Meisinger's huge collection. However, it should be noted that many companies made the same toys for a decade or more, so the date given may not reflect the exact age of each particular example.

In attributing a particular toy building to a specific company, the authors once again relied on logos printed on the toy itself or box and examples shown in old magazines or catalogs. The last chapter of the book provides information on most of the companies whose products are shown in the photographs.

As with all collectibles, the value of toy buildings depends on the condition, popularity, and rarity of the piece. A collector will pay more for a mint-in-the-box toy than one without the box. Toy buildings in original condition, complete with all accessories, no repainting, or replaced parts will command the highest prices. Missing doors, windows, or other items, including accessories, lower the value. Damage to the toy or insensitive restoration also decreases its value. Playsets with missing pieces are priced considerably lower than those that are complete.

The many pictures in this book are intended to illustrate the wide variety of items which are available to today's collectors. The back of the book contains a list of museums where such items are displayed, as well as dealers who may have toy buildings for sale. The bibliography provides a list of materials used to research this book and may be useful to readers who want to find more information.

A Note On Scale

One of the frustrations in assembling a collection of toy buildings is their inconsistency of scale. Dollhouses tower over airports and the fiercest soldier is barely taller than a box of soap powder in most toy groceries. To further complicate matters, the method of measurement varies according to the kind of toy building.

Collectors of model railroads and their accompanying structures, generally use the width of the train track or gauge as a stan-

In the early 1930s, Milton Bradley produced a Bumpalow Town in a highly stylized, Art Deco design. Labeled "a model village to construct," the pieces were made of four-ply fiberboard and slotted for assembly. The buildings were sold both individually and as a set.

Several block villages were produced during the 1950s. Keystone made a "Wood Block Village" which contained tiny buildings only a little over two inches tall. The buildings were packaged in sets of five, eight, or sixteen buildings, all with wood fences, vehicles, trees, and flocked platforms to be used as lawns. Both Kenner and Keystone made "Paint and Build" villages in the 1950s. These sets consisted of wood buildings that were to be painted and assembled by the child to form a complete town.

The popularity of Western movies and television shows inspired a few toy Western towns. Louis Marx made several variations including a Roy Rogers Mineral City and a Wyatt Earp Dodge City. The German firm, Elastolin, made wood buildings for a western town which was probably meant to be used with the company's composition figures.

In the 1950s, several companies began making plastic buildings for towns and villages. Bachmann Brothers (Plasticville) made a greater variety of such buildings than any other firm. Although intended as train accessories, they were interesting enough to be used individually or grouped without a train. The Plasticville buildings included churches, railroad buildings, houses in a variety of styles, barns, hospitals, airports, stores, motels, diners, banks, schools, fire stations, television stations, and post offices. Because the buildings were sold separately, they have been included in other chapters of the book. A few similar buildings, compatible in scale, were also produced by Marx and Skyline.

In the 1960s and beyond, children began playing more with toy cars and trucks than with trains. Several playsets were made to accommodate small vehicles, some in the form of suitcase-type sets which were easily transported.

Toy villages and towns are fascinating collectibles which reflect the changes in the way we've lived, from the slow-paced time of the blacksmith shop to the fast-lane pace of today. A collection of these toys gives its owner a permanent record of how we've lived over the past century.

Gottschalk Village #4268. This lithographed paper over wood village by Moritz Gottschalk includes three houses and a stable. Like the similar fortresses produced by Gottschalk, the buildings and accessories can be removed and stored in the base. However, this set is much larger in scale than the Gottschalk forts. It was made in Germany circa late 1890s. 21" high x 31" wide x 25.5" deep. ($4000). *Courtesy of Judith Armitstead.*

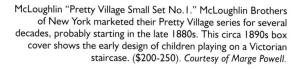

McLoughlin "Pretty Village Small Set No.1." McLoughlin Brothers of New York marketed their Pretty Village series for several decades, probably starting in the late 1880s. This circa 1890s box cover shows the early design of children playing on a Victorian staircase. ($200-250). *Courtesy of Marge Powell.*

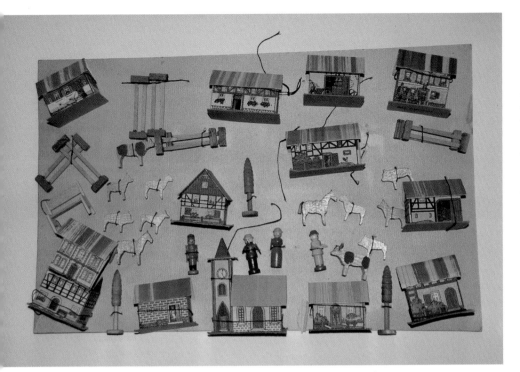

German Wood Village. Small wood villages were made in the southern part of Germany for many decades. This one was probably made circa 1910-1930. It is unusual to find pieces still attached to their original backing. The twelve buildings reflect the architecture of rural German communities. The people are lathe-turned, much like those that came with turn-of-the century toy arks, and somewhat larger in scale than the buildings. ($400-500). Each house is approximately 3" high x 2" deep x 2.5" wide. *Courtesy of Ruth Petros.*

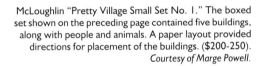

McLoughlin "Pretty Village Small Set No. 1." The boxed set shown on the preceding page contained five buildings, along with people and animals. A paper layout provided directions for placement of the buildings. ($200-250). *Courtesy of Marge Powell.*

"The New Pretty Village Boat House Set No. 545." Another of the four variations available in the smallest size, this set contained the no. 4 boat house, the no. 5 "Little Folks Hotel," and two houses numbered 2 and 14. It also bears a copyright date of 1897. ($175-200). *Courtesy of Marge Powell.*

"The New Pretty Village School House Set No.545." This box is marked "Copyright 1897, McLoughlin Bros. New York." The New Pretty Village series, apparently an updated design, came in three different sizes. This is one of four variations of the smallest set. The School House set, shown here, contained the no. 7 school house (marked "Public School, Founded 1897"), and houses numbered 3, 12, and 15. All four of the small sets were numbered 545 and contained four folding buildings, with trees, people, and a layout sheet. Houses are approximately 5.5" high x 5.5" wide x 4.5" deep. The box is 8.5" x 11.5" x 1". ($175-200). *Photograph by Patty Cooper.*

"The New Pretty Village. Rip Van Winkle Set No. 546." This medium size set is marked "Copyright 1897 by McLoughlin Bros. NY" All of the medium size sets were numbered 546 and came in boxes which measured 11.5" x 15.5". These contained eight buildings which were a combination of two of the smaller sets. This size was advertised in the 1903 Montgomery Ward & Co. catalog for 50 cents. ($250-300). *Courtesy of Mineral Point Toy Museum. Photograph by Carol Stevenson.*

"The New Pretty Village Rip Van Winkle Set No. 546." The medium size sets combined items from two of the smaller sets. This package included all the pieces from the Engine House set (shown) and the Boat House set. The Engine House section contained the no. 16 Rip Van Winkle house, the no. 9 photographer's shop, no. 8 engine house, no. 17 blacksmith's shop, and house no.1. ($250-300). *Courtesy of Mineral Point Toy Museum. Photograph by Carol Stevenson.*

"The New Pretty Village Set No. 547." This is the largest of the McLoughlin village series. It contained all the pieces from the four small sets including 17 buildings and all of the people, trees, flowers, gates, stands and layout sheets. One of the buildings is not pictured. ($700-850). The box is 15" x 20.5". *Set from the collection of Mineral Point Toy Museum. Photograph by Carol Stevenson.*

"Bradley's Toy Village." In 1920, McLoughlin Brothers was purchased by Milton Bradley who continued to make many of the McLoughlin toys including the village sets. This version of the School House set used the same paper layout with the same numbers for the buildings. The size and construction of the buildings remained the same, but the exterior details were changed. The Milton Bradley school is marked "Village School" and the three houses in the set are all different from those in the McLoughlin School House set. Although the lithography was redesigned, it was not updated. The architecture of the houses and the children's clothes remained very much in the style of the late 1800s. (Boxed set $175). Houses are approximately 5.5" high x 5.5" wide x 4.5" deep. The box is 8.5" x 11.5" x 1". *Photograph by Patty Cooper.*

Bradley "Pretty Village." At some point, Milton Bradley updated the cover design of their Pretty Village box. The inside of the box lid has the number 4671 and a copyright date of 1909. The style of the children's clothing has been updated and an automobile is pictured. However, the pieces inside were the same as those in the earlier Bradley sets. The six-piece set combines buildings from all four of the small sets. The building shown second from the right is marked "Bradley's Boat House," unlike the McLoughlin set in which it was named "Friendship Boat Club." (Boxed set $225-250). The box is 15" x 15". *Photograph by Patty Cooper.*

Bradley Church Set. This small set contained the no. 11 church, no. 6 florist's shop, and houses numbered 10 and 13. Note that the lithography on all of these buildings is different from the McLoughlin set, although the numbers of the buildings are the same. The florist's shop is named "Toy Village Florist" which makes it easily distinguished from the McLoughlin greenhouse marked "M.A. Flower, Florist." (Individual buildings $20-25). *Photograph by Patty Cooper.*

"Ready-Cut Village." No manufacturer's name is given on this boxed set. The company made at least two different sets which could be combined. This one includes a church, gas station, grocery store, and two houses. The buildings can be folded flat for storage in the box. The style of the buildings and vehicles suggests that it was made in the early 1930s. ($100). Each structure is approximately 4.25" high x 4.75" wide x 3.5" deep. The box measures 15" long x 5" wide. *Courtesy of Mineral Point Toy Museum. Photograph by Carol Stevenson.*

"Ready-Cut Village." A second Ready-Cut Village set contains an automobile garage, village store, hardware store, fire station, and one house. A wood icebox and a stove on tall legs, with an oven on the side, are displayed in the window of the hardware store, strong indications that this set was made in the early 1930s. Each structure is made of two pieces, one which can be folded to form four side walls and a separate roof. The gables of the buildings fit into sections cut out of the roof. There are no floors. The folding tabs on the ends of the wall sections are marked "printed in U.S.A." ($100). *Photograph by Patty Cooper.*

"Spear's Model Village." According to the box cover, this village was manufactured at the "Spear Works, Bevaria. Designed in England." From the design of the buildings, it appears to be circa 1920s. The set contains 10 buildings including a church, school, store, blacksmith's shop, butcher shop, and houses. ($175-200). The store is 4.25" high x 4" wide x 2.75" deep. The box is 15.5" x 11" x 1.5". *Photograph by Suzanne Silverthorn.*

"Schoenhut's Hollywood Home Builder." This set was advertised in the 1930 Schoenhut catalog as "A most attractive wooden construction toy." Each box contained all the pieces needed to assemble one house. Reflecting the attitudes of the times, the covers depicted an industrious little boy constructing a house for his admiring sister. The buildings were all named after US presidents. In the front row, left to right, are the Madison, the Jackson, and the Jefferson. The house in the back is the Washington. The Monroe and the Adams are not shown. ($150-175 each). Largest house is 6" high x 10" wide x 4.5" deep. *Photograph by Patty Cooper.*

"Schoenhut's Community Store Builder." A set of 8 buildings were listed as "New and Novel" in the 1930 Schoenhut catalog. They were made of basswood with brightly lithographed cardboard fronts. The fronts were perforated so that light could penetrate through the print giving a "realistic appearance of the Show Window when illuminated." The buildings have metal windows on the back and sides. The set included a cigar store, drug store, produce and flower store, five & ten cent store, automobile dealer, bank, grocery, and movie theater. 6.5" high x 6/5" wide x 5" deep. (MIB $150-200 each). *Courtesy of Sybil W. Smith.*

"Schoenhut's Little Village Builder." Also shown in the 1930 Schoenhut catalog, the set contained five buildings to be assembled and painted, with decals of windows, doors, clock faces, etc. The buildings included a house, church, school, railroad station, and freight station. The set was sold through Sears in 1930 for 89 cents. ($250-275). Church is approximately 7" high x 3" wide x 5" deep when assembled. Box measures 16" long x 5.75 high by 2" deep. *Courtesy of Lois L. Freeman.*

Milton Bradley "Bumpalow Town." The original box contains a cottage, school, house, church, store, and garage. These were also sold as individual buildings. (Boxed set $950-1000). The box measures 20" x 12". *Courtesy of Becky Norris. Photograph by Don Norris.*

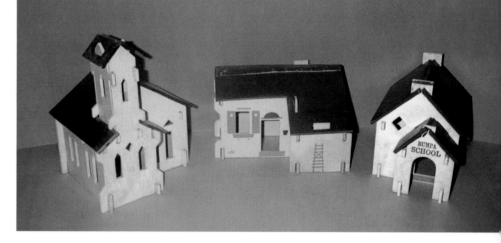

Bumpalow Town Church, House, and School. The circa 1931 buildings by Milton Bradley were made of four-ply fiberboard. They could be assembled and taken apart using tab and slot construction. Church: 7" high x 8" wide x 6.75" deep, house: 6" high x 9.5" wide x 6.5" deep, school: 7" high x 5.5" wide x 7" deep. *Courtesy of Becky Norris. Photograph by Don Norris.*

Bumpalow Town Garage, Store, and House. Three other buildings complete the Bumpalow town set. Store: 5.75" high x 10.25" wide x 4.5" deep, house: 6.75" high x 11" wide x 5"deep, garage: 5.75" high x 7.75" wide x 4.5" deep. *Courtesy of Becky Norris. Photograph by Don Norris.*

"Royalville." The maker of these circa 1930s-40s cardboard buildings is unknown. However, the repeated use of the word "Royal" suggests that these may have been distributed as a premium for a company with that name. It is possible that there were other buildings in the original set, but eight remain: "Municipal Airport," "Hotel Royal," "Royal Theatre," "Royalville Fire Department," a gas station, "Village Grocery Store," "Royalville Railroad Station," and one house. Each of the buildings is made of a single piece which can be folded flat. An exception is the airport which has a separate piece for the roof. The railroad station, grocery, and theater have slots in the front through which part of the roof can be inserted to create an awning. Each building has a small hole in the back and cut-out windows which indicate that they may have been designed to accommodate a string of Christmas lights. Circa 1930-40s. ($12-15 each). The tallest building, the hotel, is 4" high x 3.75" wide x 2.25" deep. *Photograph by Patty Cooper.*

"Main Street set No. 400 Miniature Village." This uncut, boxed set is marked "Skyline Manufacturing Co., Inc. Philadelphia, Pennsylvania." It contains eleven buildings including a "Middletown Town Hall," church, several houses, and a block of stores bearing the names "National Grocery," "Sams," "Roxy Shore Dinners," and "Bonton." The cardboard buildings were to be punched out and glued together. Separate sheets of paper were printed with store windows, doors, and signs which could be cut out and glued onto the buildings. No date is given on the box, but one of the automobiles appears to be from the 1930s. ($200-250). Box measures 12" x 14" x 1". *Photograph by Patty Cooper.*

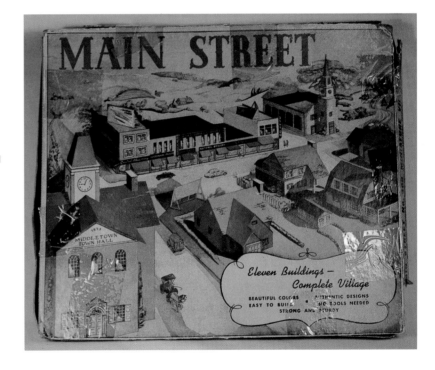

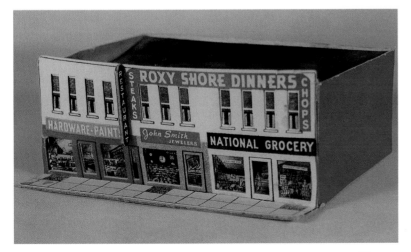

Main Street Commercial Buildings. These assembled buildings from another set appear to be much brighter in color and better in overall quality than those in the previous photograph but all of the pieces match those shown on the cover of the boxed set. It is believed that these are from an earlier version, also produced by Skyline. This section contains three different buildings which display their wares at ground level while a restaurant on the second floor offers "Roxy Shore Dinners." Separately constructed buildings housed the Bonton Department Store, the Central Pharmacy, several houses, and a church. ($35-45 each). *Courtesy of Pen Andrishok.*

"Built-Rite Complete Toy Village Set no. 556." The box for this set by Warren Paper Products Co. of Lafayette, Indiana, contains a large business block, church, school, railroad station, fire station, drug store, and six houses. The buildings are made of cardboard which can be fitted together with slots and tabs. This set was sold for over a decade. It was advertised in the December 1939 issue of *Child Life* magazine for $1.00 and in the October 1949 *Children's Activities* for $1.40. (Boxed set $350). The box is 9.5" x 16" x 1". *Courtesy of Marge Powell.*

Built-Rite Business Block. The impressive, and often elusive, Business Block from the Built-Rite Village included buildings with as many as six stories. There was a hotel, restaurant, bank, hardware store, theater, and meat market. The bottom of the box is used as the base of the business block, much like the construction of larger Built-Rite buildings. The roof of the building was printed with an arrow directing pilots to Wright Air Field. The tallest point of the Business Block is 7" high. *Courtesy of Marge Powell.*

Built-Rite Toy Village Buildings. There were five other commercial buildings in the complete Built-Rite Toy Village, a church, school, railroad station, drugstore, and fire station. Because the buildings have both floors and roofs, they are quite sturdy when properly assembled. (Individual buildings $25 each). The school is 4.25" high x 6.25" wide x 3.75" deep. *Photograph by Patty Cooper.*

Built-Rite Toy Village Houses. The Warren Paper Products set included six residences. (Individual houses $25 each). The larger houses are 4.25" high x 5.25" wide x 3.5" deep. *Photograph by Patty Cooper.*

Jaymar "Railroad and Village Construction Set" buildings. The original black and white envelope identifies this as no.151. The address given on the envelope for the Jaymar Specialty Company is 220 Fifth Avenue, New York, the same address as the related company, Louis Marx. The Jaymar set is made of medium weight cardboard which could be punched out and assembled by means of tabs and pre-cut slots. The set is believed to be circa 1950. It includes a railroad station, watchman's shanty, waiting station, billboard, fire station, shopping center, a garage, and two houses, one a traditional two-story and the other a "modern" flat roof. There are also several trees, billboards, and people, all with slotted cardboard stands. ($50-65). Railroad station is 3.5" high x 7.25" long x 4" deep. *Photograph by Patty Cooper.*

"Keystone Wood Block Village #706." The Keystone block villages were made in three different sizes. The small set included a railroad station, block of stores, and three houses. There were also trees, brick walls, and flocked yards for each of the houses. It is possible that other small boxed sets were available with some of the other buildings such as the garage, school, church, and restaurant. (Boxed set $75). The houses were approximately 2.25" high x 3.5" long x 2" deep. Box measures 16.25" x 8.25" x 3". ($75-100). *Courtesy of Lois L. Freeman.*

"Keystone Wood Block Village #712." The medium size Keystone village contained 8 buildings: a church, "Keystone Garage," restaurant, four houses, and a structure with a cupola labeled "Garrison." There were also platforms for houses, trees, brick walls, and three wood vehicles with wheels. This set is circa late 1950s. (Boxed set $150-175). The box is 10.25" high x 18" long x 3" deep. *Photograph by Patty Cooper.*

"Keystone Wood Block Village #718." The largest Keystone village was twice as large as the medium set. It included sixteen buildings: a railroad station, church, town hall, restaurant, barn, garage, school, supermarket, store, fire station, and six houses. There were also cars, trees, brick walls, and platforms for buildings. ($250). The box is 22.25" x 15" x 3". *Photograph by Patty Cooper.*

In 1957, Montgomery Ward offered a Marx playset in the form of a western town called Dodge City. The lithographed steel town contained a post office, barber shop, bank, hotel, and music hall, all attached when fully assembled. Plastic horses, Indians, cowboys, and wagons were provided for playing Wyatt Earp. Marx also made a "Silver City" using the same blank and lithographed with the same names for buildings. *Photograph by Suzanne Silverthorn.*

Marx "Roy Rogers Mineral City." This lithographed metal town appears to be identical to the Dodge City set shown in the 1957 Montgomery Ward catalog, except that it is named "Mineral City." ($300-400). *Courtesy of Marilyn Pittman.*

The lithographed interior of the Marx Mineral City includes a two-story hotel, with saloon on the first story, complete with the expected swinging doors. A bank is housed in the middle, just waiting to be saved by Roy Rogers from the bad guys. The room shown on the left serves as both a post office and barber shop. Plastic furnishings were provided for all the businesses, along with plastic figures of cowboys and their horses. *Courtesy of Marilyn Pittman.*

Sears sold a variation of the Marx western town in their 1958 catalog. The Sears version was named Roy Rogers Mineral City. It contained 95 pieces and sold for $4.99. Although the metal blank appears to be the same as the one shown above, the lithography is different. This version provides a jail, newspaper office, hardware store, and feed store in place of the hotel, bank, and post office. The plastic figures appear to include horses, cowboys, cows, and fencing, but no Indians. *Photograph by Suzanne Silverthorn.*

The facade of this version of the Marx western town has a General store on the right, a newspaper office in the middle, and a jail on the left. The two sets, used together, make an impressive display with endless opportunities for play. This model, labeled merely "Western Town" was advertised in the 1953 Alden's catalog for $5.69. According to the catalog description, it contained 84 pieces including 23 pieces of furniture ("such as printing press, dry goods counter, sheriff's desk, etc."), nineteen outside accessories, twenty-two cowboys, five horses, two calves, six saddles, plus fences, trees, cacti, and wagons. Kilpatricks of Omaha advertised this set in their 1957 catalog. The Kilpatricks set was packaged with the Roy Rogers ranch house shown in the "Down on the Farm" chapter of this book. Together, they sold for $7.98. ($300-400). 9" high x 27.5" wide x 6" deep. *Courtesy of Marilyn Pittman.*

"Milton Bradley Tru-Model Toys New England Village #4835." The boxed set by the Milton Bradley Company of Springfield, Massachusetts, contained blocks which could be assembled to form eight buildings. The original sticker price, circa 1960, was $4.75. ($45). The box is 16.75" x 10.25" x 1.75". Barn is 3.5" high x 5" wide x 3.25" deep. *Photograph by Suzanne Silverthorn.*

II. Home Life

Like other toy buildings, dollhouses were designed as a reflection of the real-life architecture of their times. Admittedly, commercially produced dollhouses were more caricatures than copies, but this serves to emphasize those elements considered most essential to their designers and young owners. Even to serious students of architecture, dollhouses can provide information about the history of residential design. Unlike their full-size counterparts, dollhouses are much less likely to have been remodeled and are often found with their original colors, architectural details, and possibly even furnishings, intact. Some of the dollhouses were conservative in style, appealing more to the comfort zone of parents than contemporary fashion. Many models remained on the market for some time, so they were out of style by the time they were replaced with the next innovation. Others, however, were on the cutting edge of technology and design. Dollhouses have been made with elevators, electric lights, running water, garages, and bomb shelters.

Companies which made dollhouses often produced other toy buildings and it is interesting to note how an individual manufacturer interpreted various structures. Dollhouses were usually produced in a larger scale than other buildings, perhaps to allow for greater detail in furnishing. Children (or collectors) who envision a whole community of buildings are often frustrated when the dollhouses tower over the service stations or airports. The latter buildings were often designed to accompany a collection of toy vehicles, much too small in scale for a doll. One has only to picture an airplane large enough to accommodate an inch to the foot scale doll, then imagine the size of an airport (with runways) that would be needed to welcome that plane, to get an idea of the need for a difference in scale.

The earliest dollhouses were usually artisan-made for wealthy families. It wasn't until the latter part of the 19th century that dollhouses began to be mass-produced. Some of the earliest ones still had hand-crafted details that made them very expensive, both at the time they were manufactured and now. Among these are the houses produced by the German firm of Christian Hacker. Many of their houses were very large with decorative pieces of turned wood and hand-painted details.

However, around this same time, advances in the process of color lithography allowed manufacturers to design dollhouses which appeared to have all of the color and detail expected of a Victorian house but could be manufactured at a price affordable to the middle class. Both Moritz Gottschalk of Germany and R. Bliss in America produced such houses in great quantity. The early lithographed paper over wood dollhouses by Gottschalk are usually referred to as "Blue Roofs" since this is a name used by collectors before the manufacturer was identified. The Gottschalk houses came in a size for every pocketbook. Some of their houses contained many rooms, lathe-turned finials and balusters, and hand-painted details. However, they also made tiny structures with all of their exterior details merely printed on paper. The Bliss company did not offer as wide a range of dollhouses, but their line varied in size from ones less than a foot tall to an elaborate Queen Anne, complete with turret, which stood approximately 28" tall. Other companies, such as W.S. Reed, Converse, and McLoughlin Brothers also produced lithographed dollhouses.

By the 1920s, Gottschalk discontinued the use of lithographed papers and began painting the exteriors of their dollhouses. The roofs of these later models were usually painted red. By this time, Bliss was no longer in business, but the A. Schoenhut company began producing wood dollhouses which were quite similar to the Gottschalk "Red Roofs." The early Schoenhut dollhouses were notable for their lithographed interiors which provided trompe l'oeil glimpses into bathrooms, stairways, and butler's pantries which made the houses seem much larger than they really were.

In England, the firm of J. and G. Lines made wood dollhouses from the late 1800s through the early part of the twentieth century. Lines Brothers, a company created by three sons of one of the original owners, produced dollhouses under the name Triang until the 1970s. The dollhouses manufactured during the long span of these two related companies reflected the enormous changes in residential design over a century, from Victorian and Tudor through Art Moderne and Ranch style.

Very high quality dollhouses were introduced in the 1920s by the Tynietoy company of Providence, Rhode Island. They were commercially produced, but hand-crafted, and expensive even at the time they were made. Some were sold through upscale retailers but many of the dollhouses had to be custom-ordered.

The early 1930s saw a boom in the commercial production of dollhouses. Even with the economic depression, furnished cardboard houses could be purchased for less than $3.00 and catalogs of the time advertised a wide variety of choices, including those by Dowst (Tootsietoy), Built-Rite (Warren Paper Products), and others.

With the post World War II baby boom, the popularity of dollhouses continued. Many of the German toy manufacturers were out of the picture and the void was quickly filled by American companies such as Rich, Keystone, and Marx. Both Rich and Keystone made houses of heavy Masonite or pressed wood, with lithographed details. The De Luxe Toy Corporation made similar Tekwood houses, usually sold through Sears.

The Louis Marx company was one of the most prolific dollhouse manufacturers. They first entered the field in the 1920s with the small metal "Newlywed Rooms" which were similar to their Hometown series of stores and other buildings. These rooms consisted of three sides and a floor. The exteriors were plain but the interiors were brightly lithographed with wallpaper, roaring fires, draped windows, and pictures. In the 1930s, Marx produced a "Modern Metal Bungalow," again in a small scale, furnished with "Midget Tootsietoy" furniture. However, it was in the 1950s that Marx really hit their stride in the production of dollhouses. These structures reflected solid, slightly retrospective, middle class tastes. The most common ones had two stories, five rooms, and were Colonial in style. More elaborate ones featured garages or recreation rooms. Lithographed metal dollhouses were also produced by other companies including Frier Steel, T. Cohn (Superior), Wolverine, and Playsteel.

Although the rare, artisan-made houses are beyond the reach of most collectors, it is still possible to find the mass-produced dollhouses of the 1930s through 1950s at reasonable prices. Dollhouses from the late 1800s and early 1900s are difficult to find but still available through auctions or dealers who specialize in antique toys. No matter the size of the budget, dollhouses can be found ranging in price from under $100 to more than $25,000.

The history of dollhouses is covered more thoroughly in the authors' previous books; however, some representative examples are included here to place them in the context of the world of toy buildings.

Stirn and Lyon "Combination Doll House." The Stirn and Lyon company of New York produced at least two similar dollhouses, in different sizes, circa 1880s. The houses were made of thin wood and were to be assembled using tongue and groove construction. Part of the box was used as the base of the house. The houses were very fragile and not many are found in excellent condition. (Boxed $1000-1200). *Courtesy of Ruth Petros.*

Christian Hacker Dollhouse. The mansard roof is characteristic of many of the houses made by the Hacker firm of Nuremberg, Germany circa 1900. The house is made of wood and comes apart in three stackable sections. The front opens for play access and the roof can be removed. This model contains three rooms. ($1600-2000). 21" high x 19" wide x 11" deep. *Photograph by Suzanne Silverthorn.*

Gottschalk "Blue Roof" No. 4450. Although this house actually has a litho-graphed paper roof, it would be considered part of the Gottschalk "Blue Roof" series because of its lithographed exterior papers. The printed faux stucco finish was apparently a transition to the painted exteriors of the later Red Roof series. Similar designs were used for Gottschalk warehouses, stables, and a village. ($1600-1800). 18.5" high x 14" wide x 9" deep. *Photograph by Patty Cooper.*

Gottschalk "Blue Roof." The lithographed paper over wood dollhouses by the German firm of Moritz Gottschalk are often called "Blue Roofs." The number 24?6 on the bottom of this house identifies it as an early one, circa 1890s. It is front opening and contains two rooms. ($3000-3500). 25.5" high (including chimney) x 16.5" wide x 13.25" deep. *Photograph by Suzanne Silverthorn.*

Gottschalk "Red Roof." The later houses produced by Moritz Gottschalk had painted, rather than lithographed exteriors. The roofs were usually red, providing a convenient nickname for collectors. The number penciled on the bottom is 5869, indicating that it was made circa mid-1920s. The house contains four rooms and an attic. There is a built-in toilet in the closet of the entryway. ($2000-2500). 25" high x 18" wide x 12" deep. *Photograph by Patty Cooper.*

22

Whitney S. Reed Dollhouse. The W. S. Reed Toy Company was located in Leominster, Massachusetts. This small, two-room house is made of lithographed paper over wood. It has cut-out windows and an opening door. The inside is papered with a small print. Reed dollhouses are often confused with the Gottschalk "Blue Roofs." A distinctive clue is the presence of a series of "X's" usually found on the doors or gables of Reed houses. ($1000-1200). 11.5" high x 7.5" wide x 7" deep (at base). *Photograph by Patty Cooper.*

Bliss Dollhouse #204. This lithographed paper over wood dollhouse was made by the R. Bliss Manufacturing Company of Pawtucket, Rhode Island. Although unmarked, it was pictured in their 1911 catalog as "A two room Colonial" said to be "entirely new this season." The one-story house opens from the front and contains two rooms. ($2000-2500). 17.5" high x 16.5" wide x 15" deep. *Photograph by Patty Cooper.*

Above: McLoughlin Brothers Bungalow. The folding cardboard dollhouse was made circa 1911 and contains two rooms. The front of the house folds down to form a garden. The one-story version shown here is much more difficult to find than the similar two-story one also made by McLoughlin. The interior is brightly lithographed in high Victorian style. ($700-900). 8" high x 16.5" wide x 6.5" deep. *Courtesy of Linda and Carl Thomas, Jr.*

Right: G. & J. Lines Dollhouse. One of a series known to collectors as "Kit's Coty," this large dollhouse was made by the English firm of G. & J. Lines circa 1910. The wood front opens in two sections to reveal four rooms. Some distinctive features of this house are the two chimneys with chimney pots, the widow's walk, and the two bay windows. ($2000-2500). 32" high x 24.5" wide x 17" deep. *Photograph by Suzanne Silverthorn.*

Converse Bungalow. The wood house is attributed to the firm of Morton E. Converse and Son of Winchendon, Massachusetts. Other houses of similar design have been found with the company name printed on the floors. The architectural details on the outside and inside walls were lithographed directly on the wood. The circa 1914 house opens from the front and contains only one room. ($450-500). 10" high x 11" wide x 8" deep. *Photograph by Suzanne Silverthorn.*

Schoenhut Dollhouse. The two-room, two-story house was advertised in the 1923 A. Schoenhut catalog. It has a wood base and vertical supports. The sides of the house are made of heavy fiberboard embossed to represent brick and the roof is made of the same material in a tile pattern. Pressed cardboard frames surround the glass windows. The interior has printed wallpaper and borders. Earlier versions of this house had trompe l'oeil architectural features with views into other "rooms." Many different variations of this house, both one- and two-story, with as many as eight rooms, were made through the 1920s. ($1200-1400). 18" high x 12" wide x 15" deep. *Photograph by Patty Cooper.*

Schoenhut Colonial. Pictured in the 1930 catalog of the A. Schoenhut Company of Philadelphia, this house was made of wood and fiberboard. The shutters and window frames were made of pressed cardboard. These houses were made for several years in sizes ranging from one room to eight rooms and in a variety of scales. This four-room version is in the smallest scale, approximately 1/2" to 1 foot. The front can be removed to provide access to the house. ($650-800). 15" high x 17" wide x 12" deep. *Photograph by Suzanne Silverthorn.*

Marx "Newlywed" Rooms and Dollhouse. The lightweight cardboard dollhouse was marketed during the 1920s to hold four furnished, metal rooms. The rooms, which were also sold separately, were made of lithographed steel and included a kitchen, bathroom, bedroom, dining room, parlor, and library. The house was printed on the exterior with a brick pattern and oversized windows which opened to provide access to the rooms. The completely furnished four room house was sold by Sears for 48 cents in 1929. (Furnished house $600-800; Boxed room $175-200). 8.5" high x 10.25" wide x 2.5" deep. *Photograph by Patty Cooper.*

Wayne Paper Company Dollhouse. The 1928 Sears catalog advertised this cardboard house for $1.89. It was designed to be used with metal Tootsietoy furniture by Dowst. The house contained six rooms and opened, from the front, in two hinged sections. It was manufactured by the Wayne Paper Products Company of Ft. Wayne, Indiana. This company may also have been the maker of similar cardboard houses marked "Tootsietoy" or "Daisy." ($400-500). 19" high x 21" wide x 15" deep. *Photograph by Suzanne Silverthorn.*

Frier Steel "Cozytown Manor." The heavy, lithographed steel dollhouse is marked "Frier Steel Co./106 Washington Blvd./St. Louis, Mo./Pat. Appl'd For." According to the company's 1928 advertising, two other models were available, the "Cozytown Cottage" in a scale of 1/2" to the foot and the "Cozytown Mansion" which was 1" to the foot. Unlike most other metal dollhouses, the Frier Steel models could be completely closed. The fronts opened in two sections for play access. The Cozytown Manor contained four rooms and had a metal stairway. ($400-450). 18" high x 20.5" long x 16.5" deep. *Photograph by Suzanne Silverthorn.*

Tynietoy New England Town House. The Georgian style house was made by Tynietoy, a small company in Providence, Rhode Island, which also produced high quality, wood dollhouse furniture. The Town House contained six rooms plus two hallways and an attic. ($5000-7000). 29.5" high x 47" long x 16.25" deep. *Courtesy of Gail and Ray Carey.*

"New Modern Home Seven Rooms Doll House." Similar in style to Built-Rite, this cardboard house was made by the O.B. Andrews Company of Chattanooga, Tennessee. The circa late 1930s house included seven rooms complete with fireplace and stairway. Sets of cardboard furniture were supplied for the kitchen, dining room, parlor, bathroom, sun parlor, and two bedrooms. (Boxed set $200-250). 16" high x 30 "wide x 13" deep. *Photograph by Patty Cooper.*

Built-Rite "Toy House Set No. 9." Warren Paper Products of Lafayette, Indiana made many different designs and sizes of cardboard houses in the 1930s and 1940s. The houses ranged in size from one room to six rooms and came in both one and two story models. This house contains only one room and, like all Built-Rite houses, is open in the back. The bottom of the box is used as the base of the house and has a carpet printed on it. ($50-65). 9.25" high (to top of chimney) x 10" wide x 6.5" deep. *Photograph by Patty Cooper.*

Good Cooks Start Young

BUNGALOW INTERIOR FURNITURE INCLUDED

98c

MODERN METAL BUNGALOW—14 Pieces FURNITURE
The last word! All set up on metal base, 17x11 in. 4 room house with colorful awnings and arched doorway. Removable roof. Nicely furnished with sofa, 2 tables, lamp, 3 arm chairs, easy chair, 2 beds, table, vanity table, chest, piano. Garage, 5½x3⅛x2½-in. Auto.
49 V 2148—Shipping weight, 3 pounds 3 ounces................**98c**

The 1938 Sears Christmas catalog pictured a "Modern Metal Bungalow" by Marx, priced at 98 cents. The package also included 14 pieces of metal "Midget Tootsietoy" furniture (sofa, two tables, lamp, 3 arm chairs, easy chair, 2 beds, table, vanity table, chest, and piano.) Although the house contained four rooms, the pieces of furniture were only for a bedroom and a parlor. A separate garage, on the same metal platform, housed an automobile. *Courtesy of Marge Meisinger. Photograph by Suzanne Silverthorn.*

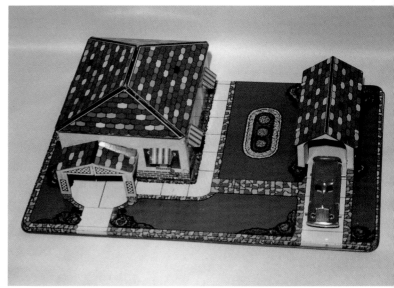

Marx "Modern Metal Bungalow." The house and garage were mounted on a metal base which formed a landscaped yard. The roof of the house could be lifted to provide access to the interior. The automobile was also made of metal. ($500-700). Base measures 17" x 11". *Courtesy of Ben DeVoto.*

Tri-ang Dollhouse No. 93. The English firm of Lines Brothers introduced this model in their 1939 catalog. It continued being sold into the 1950s. Known to collectors as the "Stockbroker Tudor," this rather large house contains five rooms, a garage, service porch, and central hallway with staircase. Access to the house is provided by four opening sections on the front. The house is scaled for the smallish 1" to the foot furniture made by Tri-ang. ($1800-2000).
24" high x 47" wide x 17" deep.
Photograph by Patty Cooper.

A Gypsum board house made by the Kiddie Brush and Toy Company (Susy Goose) of Jonesville, Michigan was advertised in the 1939 Montgomery Ward catalog. The house sold for $1.79. *Courtesy of Marge Meisinger. Photograph by Suzanne Silverthorn.*

Roomy Gypsum Board Doll House
Extra Strong—Extra Big—More Fun
$1 79 The partitions are movable, so you can make a few big rooms or five smaller ones. 2-story house 29½ by 13 by 18 in. high. Open back. First story looks like cobble stone, second like frame. Shades and curtains are printed on windows. Printed trees, flowers. Heavy ⅛-in. Gypsum board, a hard, non-warping pressed wood. Smoothly finished. No furniture. Ship. wt. 8 lbs.
448 T 802—Shipped flat, easily assembled...**$1.79**
48 T 807—41 Pieces of Furniture
Same as with No. 48 T 801 at top of page. Ship. wt. 1 lb. 12 oz..............**$1.29**
56ᶜ

Kiddie Brush and Toy Company Dollhouse. The Gypsum board dollhouse contains two rooms downstairs and three rooms upstairs, with movable partitions on the second floor. The house is printed on the outside only with no interior decoration. It is marked with the company name. ($65-75). 19" high x 30" wide x 12" deep. *Photograph by Suzanne Silverthorn.*

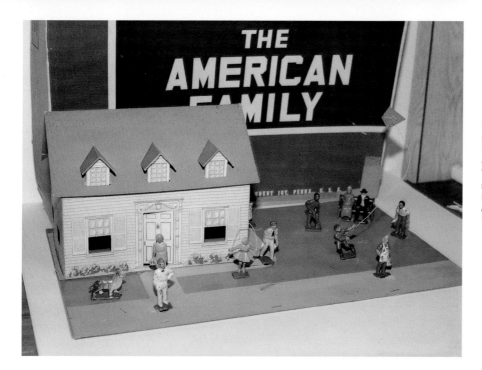

Grey Iron "The American Family Home." This boxed set was made by the Grey Iron Company of Mount Joy, Pennsylvania circa 1940. The house is made of cardboard and the people (and animals) are cast iron. The people are 2.25" to 2.50" tall. Other sets in this series were The American Family On the Beach, On the Farm, and The American Family Travels. (Not enough examples to determine price). *Courtesy of Keystone Toy Trader. Photograph by Bob Stevens.*

Rich Toy Company Colonial Dollhouse. Rich Toys of Clinton, Iowa made dollhouses and other buildings out of Gypsum board. This circa 1940s house is open-backed and contains six rooms. The house has four round columns on the front porch and features printed shrubbery and shutters. The windows in the example shown have been replaced. Rich made dollhouses from the 1930s into the early 1960s. ($175-200). 22" high x 32" wide x 21" deep (including porch). *Courtesy of Becky Norris. Photograph by Don Norris.*

Keystone Dollhouse. This Keystone house is made of Masonite and contains six rooms. The Boston company made many other sizes and styles of dollhouses during the 1940s and 1950s. Their houses were usually printed both inside and outside. The larger houses included staircases. This house was sold with a turntable on the base. ($175-200). 17.75" high x 28.5" wide x 12.5" deep. *Courtesy of Becky Norris. Photograph by Don Norris.*

De Luxe Game Corporation Dollhouse. The house is one of a series of Tekwood houses sold by Sears from 1945 until 1948. Tekwood was a three-ply material made of thin wood at the center with cardboard outer layers. The De Luxe company also made other toy buildings out of the same material. This house contains five rooms, appropriate for furniture in 3/4" to the foot scale. It is colorfully printed both inside and outside. The windows made as part of the house, then scored and folded open. They were easily torn and are often missing. ($85-100). 17" high x 35" long x 10" deep. *Courtesy of Becky Norris. Photograph by Don Norris.*

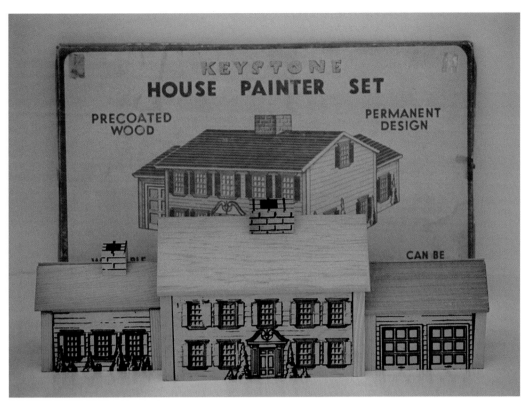

"Keystone House Painter Set" Model No. 202. The circa 1950s boxed set contained wood pieces to be assembled into a house, along with directions and paint for finishing it. The Boston company also made similar painter sets with churches, schools, and barns. The size was appropriate for O scale train layouts. ($40-50). *Photograph by Suzanne Silverthorn.*

Ohio Art "Midget Manor" No. 95. The tiny lithographed metal dollhouse was introduced by Ohio Art of Bryan, Ohio in 1949. The house is open-backed and contains four rooms. The illustration on the back of the box shows the 28 pieces of tiny plastic furniture which came with the set. (MIB $250). 5.25" high x 6" wide x 2" deep. *Courtesy of Marilyn Pittman.*

Skyline "Metal House M." The lithographed metal house was intended as a model train accessory. A similar airport by Skyline was advertised in the November 1950 issue of *Children's Activities.* ($40-50). *Courtesy of Ben DeVoto.*

T. Cohn Dollhouse. This two story, lithographed metal dollhouse was produced by T. Cohn (Superior) of Brooklyn in several different colors including blue, pink, and green. The early houses included a door and one window that opened. The windows and doors were lithographed on later houses and not operable. The example shown was made circa 1950s. It was open-backed and had a brightly lithographed interior with five rooms. ($50- 75). 13.5" high x 23" wide x 9.5" deep. *Photograph by Suzanne Silverthorn.*

Eagle Dollhouse and "Super Garage." The lithographed metal dollhouse and matching garage were made in Montreal, Canada by the Eagle Toy Company. The firm produced several different models of dollhouses throughout the 1950s. The pair shown are approximately 1/2" to one foot in scale. (House $85-100, garage $50-75). House measures 15.5" high (to top of chimney) x 18.5" wide x 7" deep. *Courtesy of Mary Harris.*

"Cheerio Doll House." Another Canadian firm produced fiberboard dollhouses circa 1950s**.** ($200-250). *Courtesy of Sharon Barton.*

Pyro "Design a House." The original box also says that this is a "Scale Model Designer Construction Set." The set included plastic parts to assemble a house that could be constructed in many different designs. This house could have been used as part of a railroad layout when finished. ($40-50). *Courtesy of Ruth Petros.*

Wolverine "Town and Country Dollhouse" No. 805. The metal lithographed house by The Wolverine Supply and Manufacturing Company was first introduced in 1970 and remained part of their line for ten years. A distinctive feature of the house was the plastic bay window. The other windows and doors were also plastic. The house was available in variations containing four to six rooms with interesting lithography throughout. It was sold furnished with soft plastic furniture. ($50-75). 17.5" high x 22.5" wide x 12" deep. *Photograph by Suzanne Silverthorn.*

Ideal Petite Princess Dollhouse. The vinyl suitcase type house was designed to be used with the Ideal Petite Princess furniture in the mid 1960s. The front of the suitcase drops down to form a patio. The furniture shown is Petite Princess but not all is original to the house. Later, Sears sold this house furnished with twenty pieces of furniture. Several items included in the Sears set were the cheaper pieces made in Hong Kong and labeled Redbox. (Unfurnished $50-65). Open measurements: 18" high x 22" wide x 23" deep. *Photograph by Suzanne Silverthorn.*

Marx Dollhouse. This circa 1960s lithographed metal dollhouse is typical of those made by the Louis Marx Company. This model has five colorfully lithographed rooms. The chimney, bay window, and door are made of plastic. ($75-85). 15.5" high x 30" wide x 10" deep. *Courtesy of Nanci Moore. Photograph by Roy Specht.*

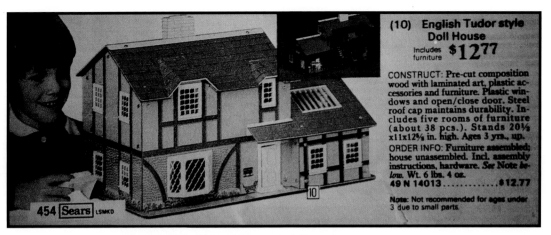

An advertisement for an English Tudor style dollhouse by Brumberger appeared in the 1978 Sears Christmas catalog. The house was furnished with five rooms of plastic furniture in approximately 1/2" to one foot scale. It sold for $12.77. *Photograph by Suzanne Silverthorn.*

Brumberger "English Tudor Style Doll House." The house was sold unassembled by Sears in 1978. The pre-cut composition wood pieces were brightly printed on both sides and laminated. The windows and opening door were made of plastic. The house was open-backed and contained five rooms. ($65-75). 12.5" high x 20.5" wide x 11" deep. *Courtesy of Becky Norris. Photography by Don Norris.*

III. Down on the Farm (and Back at the Ranch)

In 1910, half of the American people lived on farms or in rural areas. By the 1980s, the numbers had declined to less than 20%. The popularity of farm toys has followed the demographics of the real world. In the early part of the twentieth century, mail order catalogs offered five or six different sizes and styles of barns and stables each year. By the end of the century, few toy barns were being made and most of those were targeted at preschoolers.

Many of the commercially produced barns made a century ago came from Germany. The firm of Moritz Gottschalk made lithographed paper over wood stables from the late 1800s through the early twentieth century. The Gottschalk stables were produced in an amazing range of sizes and styles. Many included living quarters for farm hands. By the 1910s, the Gottschalk stables began to have painted, rather than lithographed, exteriors and red roofs. As automobiles became more common, the company began producing structures that were a hybrid of automobile garages and stables, with double doors for the cars and a stall with metal hay racks for the horses.

It should not be assumed that all such German stables were made by Gottschalk. Other German companies, including Wagner and Christian Hacker, were making stables at the turn of the

century and *The Universal Toy Catalog 1924-1926* shows stables made by at least two other unidentified German companies. The same catalog shows several different farm sets by O. M. Hauser (Elastolin), some complete with walled barnyards, barns, outbuildings, and farmhouses. These were sold with the composition type animals for which the company was noted.

The R. Bliss company of Pawtucket, Rhode Island made a large variety of stables from the 1880s through 1914. They were made of lithographed paper over wood or cardboard in a scale fairly consistent with their dollhouses. Their earliest barns included brightly colored cardboard animals with wood stands. Later stables were made of wood and sometimes came with papier mâché or composition horses that were probably imported from Germany.

Another American company, Morton E. Converse and Son, made sturdy wood stables with the printed details applied directly to the wood. Their Roosevelt Stock Farms were advertised in catalogs as early as 1907. The Converse barns came in several sizes. The simplest were open-fronted and contained only one room while more elaborate ones featured sliding doors, many stalls, and a cupola on the roof. Some of the Converse barns were marked Red Robin Farm. The animals which came with the

Lithographed Stable. This lithographed paper over wood stable has many features characteristic of the R. Bliss Company. Each doorway reveals a detailed farm scene. The gabled end bears the name "Sunny Hill Farm" over the doorway, with two lithographed children looking out from the hayloft. One section of the barn is removable to provide access to the interior. There are many lithographed cardboard animals with stands, including two chickens, two pigs, one sheep, two cows, and one horse plus four duplicates. ($1600-1800). 10.25" high x 13" long x 7.25" deep. *Courtesy of Fran Tagesen, Kinney Pioneer Museum. Photograph by Rita Goranson.*

Bliss "Woodbine Farm." The wood and lithographed cardboard stable was advertised in the 1895 Butler Brothers catalog. It was shown with thirty animals, people, and fencing. The people and animals are made of cardboard, lithographed in four colors, with wooden stands. As with the similar variations of "The House that Jack Built," the figures all have names printed under their feet, such as a pig named "Squoddy" and a cow named "Tibbie." ($1800-2000). 15.5" high (to top of cupola) x 19.75" wide. *Courtesy of Linda and Carl Thomas, Jr.*

"Rockyway Stable" No. 244. Two different versions of this stable were shown in the 1896 Bliss catalog. The smaller version, No. 244, contained two small stalls on the left, with a larger stall on the right. It sold for 25 cents. One of the partitions is missing in the example shown. The 50-cent size, No. 245, had three small stalls on the left and a large one on the right. Both were said to contain "horses and golf carts, saddle horses and jockeys." ($800). 9" high x 9.5" wide x 6" deep. *Photograph by Patty Cooper.*

Converse farm sets were made of wood printed in black ink. Converse also sold a farm set which included a house, barn, garage, greenhouse, and fenced yard.

Even as people migrated to the cities during the 1930s, their fond memories of the rural life they had left behind led them to continue to purchase toy farm sets for their children. Perhaps they still expected to fulfill a dream and eventually return to the rural life of their childhood.

As might be expected, Sears Roebuck and Company, the mail order retailer who catered to rural families, offered many different kinds of farm sets over the years. During the 1930s, they sold several different wood barns which were quite similar to the Converse barns. They had exterior details printed directly on the wood, often showing chickens or pigs on the back wall of the outbuildings or a Model T Ford in a garage. The animals that were sold with the earliest sets strongly resembled the Converse animals. They were made of wood with details printed in black ink. By the mid-1930s, the animals sold with the Sears barns were lithographed in full color on cardboard. These same animals continued to be sold with the Sears sets even after the company's wood barns were replaced by cardboard ones. In the 1940s, Sears offered several heavy cardboard sets that included farmhouses and outbuildings. The designs of these sets were updated each year to reflect the modern changes taking place in agriculture.

The Montgomery Ward catalogs of the 1930s advertised cardboard stock farm sets that were based on real farm designs. These sets not only included barns, but outbuildings, animals, and equipment as well. The largest set covered an area 54" x 32" when completely assembled. It was made by Built-Rite (Warren Paper Products) who produced many other cardboard

barns and farm sets over the next two decades. Other companies, such as Judy Toys and D.A. Pachter, also made cardboard farm sets during the 1940s.

Both Keystone and Rich Toys made barns of Masonite in the 1940s and 1950s. The Keystone farm came with plastic animals that had working features, such as a cow that could be milked and chickens that laid eggs. The Rich Toys barns had cardboard animals with wood stands.

By the 1950s, several companies made barns of lithographed metal. The Friendly Acres Dairy Farm by Kiddie Brush and Toy Company of Jonesville, Michigan included a mixed herd of plastic cows painted to resemble Guernseys, Holsteins, and Jerseys. Both Ohio Art and T. Cohn (Superior) made metal barns. But, as with other toy buildings, the most extensive producer of metal barns was the Louis Marx Company. Their barns were often marked "Lazy Day Farm," "Happi-Time," or "Garden Mark," depending on the retailer for whom they were made. Like other Marx playsets of the 1950s, they came with an extensive array of accessories. Marx also made ranch sets with a lithographed metal bunkhouse and various combinations of horses, cowboys, cows, and fencing.

In the years following World War II, the dream of life on the farm receded for most Americans and they no longer envied their rural neighbors. Toy barns and stables were replaced by newer products, such as airports or gas stations, which reflected contemporary life or more modern fantasies of space exploration. Although farm stores still carry a barn or two each Christmas, the current generation of children does not seem very interested in playing with farm toys. But collectors still enjoy the great old barns and stables of yesterday with their memories of days gone by.

Bliss "House That Jack Built." Three different versions of this toy, which appears to be more of a stable than a house, were offered in the 1896 Bliss catalog. The largest, No. 189, shown here, had three front gables. A smaller version, No. 189, had only two gables. A third version, with the same name, was numbered 187 and said to have been designed as a companion piece for the two larger ones. The catalog lists a patent date of March 12, 1895 for all three models. Like the Bliss Woodbine Farm, this structure is made of lithographed paper over wood and cardboard. The animals and people, all with names, are printed on cardboard and have wood stands. Originally, it included sixteen figures. ($1800-2000). 15" high x 20" wide x 10.5" deep. *Courtesy of Linda and Carl Thomas, Jr.*

Bliss Stable. Like many other Bliss buildings, this lithographed paper over wood stable is clearly marked with the company's logo. There are two stalls and a hay loft with opening door. The finial atop the cupola is lathe-turned as are the three posts in the front of the stable. The wood chickens are not Bliss. Circa 1905. ($850-1000). 14" high x 10" wide x 6" deep. *Photograph by Patty Cooper*

Bliss Stable #593. A larger Bliss Stable was advertised in the 1909/10 A.C. McClurg & Company catalog. It is made of lithographed paper over wood. The lithographed, rather than turned, posts and pierced metal side rails are typical of the company's later products. It is marked Bliss over the smaller stall. ($1000-1200). 17" high x 12" wide x 7.75" deep. *Photograph by Patty Cooper.*

Bliss Stable. Probably the largest stable made by Bliss, this model has many stalls with opening gates of pierced metal. There are three different loft sections, two of which have opening double doors. The supporting posts are made of lithographed paper over wood as opposed to the turned posts found on earlier models. ($2000-3000). 29.5" high x 30.5" wide x 12" deep. *Courtesy of Angels Attic Museum. On loan from private collector.*

Bliss Stable No. 105. Bliss advertised this lithographed paper over wood stable in their 1911 catalog. It was shown with "imported" horses and a dog cart or carriage. A larger stable, with a hay loft on each end, was shown in the same catalog as number 106. This version has two large stalls and hay-loft on the left with double doors. It is marked Bliss above the opening to stall on the right. ($1700-2000). 17.25" high x 11/5" wide. *Courtesy of The Toy & Miniature Museum of Kansas City.*

Bliss Stable No. 100. This was the lowest priced of four variations shown in the 1911 Bliss catalog. Simple in construction, all of the details were lithographed with no opening doors or turned posts. It was sold with a horse on wheels and a hay wagon. Of the three larger variations, with consecutive numbers 101-103, two had hinged doors to the hayloft. Like the dollhouses in the same catalog, this stable is not marked with the Bliss logo. It has a price of 25 cents penciled on the back. ($500-750). 9.5" high x 8" wide x 5" deep. *Photograph by Patty Cooper.*

Christian Hacker Stable. This stable exemplifies the quality of toys produced by the German firm of Christian Hacker. Because it is approximately 1" to the foot in scale, it would make a perfect companion to a Hacker dollhouse. It is made of painted wood with gold and silver metallic accents. The roof and shingles are lithographed paper. The windows are made of glass with painted mullions. All of the doors are operable. There is an apartment for the farm hand or groomsman on the right. ($2800-3500). 15.75" high x 29" wide x 13.5" deep. *Courtesy of Lois L. Freeman.*

Gottschalk Stable. The German firm of Moritz Gottschalk produced many different toy stables. This wood stable is unmarked but its lithographed papers are consistent with those made by the Gottschalk company circa 1890. It has double doors leading to a first-floor stall. There is a hay loft, above, with opening door. The two outer finials have been replaced. ($1200-1800). 15.75" high x 8.75" wide x 5.75" deep. *Courtesy of Marilyn Pittman.*

Gottschalk Stable #4331. This large stable, with bell tower, is made of lithographed paper over wood. It has a penciled number underneath, indicating that it was probably made by the Moritz Gottschalk company circa 1900. The lithographed paper over wood buildings made by Gottschalk are known to collectors as "Blue Roofs" and this stable has all those characteristics. ($4500). 25.5" high x 18" wide x 10.5" deep. *Courtesy of David Pressland.*

Gottschalk Stable #3256. This stable is representative of a transitional period for Gottschalk. Its lithographed papers would define it as a "Blue Roof" however the roof is actually painted red. Its number indicates that it was probably made at the end of the 19th century. It contains two small stalls with a metal hay rack and space for a wagon on the right. There is a hay loft above with an opening door. ($800-1200). 10.5" high x 9.25" wide x 5.5" deep. *Photograph by Patty Cooper.*

Gottschalk Stable. Believed to be an early Gottschalk, this stable has a penciled number under its base which appears to be 2937. It is made of lithographed paper over wood with glass windows in a scale of approximately 3/4" equals a foot. ($1200-1500). 12" high x 16" wide x 5.5" deep. *Courtesy of Lois L. Freeman.*

Gottschalk Stable #4423. Although its roof is actually covered with lithographed paper, this stable would still be considered part of the "Blue Roof" series. The number is marked under the base along with a "G.A. Schwarz, Philadelphia" label. It was probably made circa 1910 and is similar to some of the faux stucco, lithographed dollhouses made by Gottschalk during this period.

In addition to the single stall and non-accessible loft, the left front opens to reveal a one-room apartment, making it something of a combination dollhouse and stable. ($1200-1600). 11.25" high x 12.5" wide x 8" deep. *Photograph by Patty Cooper.*

German Stable #4794. The penciled number suggests that this stable is a Gottschalk "Red Roof" circa 1920s. However, the trapezoidal shape of the front gable is similar to those found on dollhouses believed to have been made by another German company, possibly Wagner.

The lower section contains two stalls for horses, with hay racks embossed with the names "Zampa" and "Kastor." A larger area on the right provides a sheltered space for a wagon. There is an opening door to the loft with two shuttered windows. The horse is a papier mache candy container, not original to the stable. ($800-1000). 14.5" high x 16.5" wide x 9" deep. *Courtesy of Lois L. Freeman.*

Gottschalk Stable. This stable combines the pressed cardboard mullions which partially define a Gottschalk "Red Roof" with the faux half-timbered lithograph paper found on earlier "Blue Roof" dollhouses. There are two stalls on the right as well as room for a wagon behind the opening double doors. The spacious upstairs could be perceived as either a loft or living quarters. ($1000-1400). 18" high x 16.25" wide x 9.75" deep. *Courtesy of Marilyn Pittman.*

Gottschalk Stable #5200. This stable by Moritz Gottschalk has lithographed paper on the front. There are two stalls and an opening door to the hay loft. ($1200-1500 with horse and wagon). 9.5" high x 9.75" wide x 4.75" deep. *Courtesy of Ray and Gail Carey.*

38

An advertisement from a 1924 Montgomery Ward catalog pictures a German stable with two horses and a cart. It was available for $1.98 plus 14 cents postage. Part of a Gottschalk "Red Roof" dollhouse can be in the same illustration. *Photograph by Suzanne Silverthorn.*

Gottschalk Stable/Garage #5360. This combination stable and garage also provides living quarters above for a groomsman/chauffeur. The number penciled under the base probably dates it to the early 1920s. The second floor apartment has two rooms, accessible through the door and window sections in the dormer. A stairway provides access for dolls to the upstairs. ($1200-1600). 15.5" high x 18.5" wide x 9" deep. *Courtesy of Lois L. Freeman.*

Gottschalk Stable #5872. This lithographed paper over wood stable appears to be the same as the one shown in the 1924 Montgomery Ward catalog. There are stalls for two horses, with a metal hay rack, and space to house the wagon. The second story has a loft with an opening door and two windows with pressed cardboard mullions. Under the base are the words "Made in Germany" along with the model number. The stable still has its original two horses and wagon. ($1200-1800 with original horses and wagon). 13.5" high x 13.75" long x 7.25" deep. *Courtesy of Rita Goranson.*

Gottschalk Stable #5935. This elaborate stable includes living quarters on the second floor as well as a third story hayloft. Play access is provided to the apartment by opening doors on each side. There are two horse stalls on the main level and a space for a wagon. The window mullions and porch rails are made of pressed cardboard. ($1300-1600). 23.25" high x 20.25" wide x 11.75" deep. *Courtesy of Marianne Price.*

German Stable/House. This Bavarian style building opens in front to reveal a stable below with living quarters on the second floor. The upper windows are made of glass with painted curtains. The roof has been repainted, but was originally light blue. There are stenciled details on the wood including a tree on the side. The building was purchased in Germany. ($1000-1400). 14.25" high x 17.75" wide x 8" deep. *Courtesy of Linda Hanlon.*

German Stable, probably Gottschalk. This large stable is wood with lithographed details. The roof is now red, but the original color was a bright blue. The door to the loft is missing. It was purchased in Germany. ($1200-1500). 20.75" high x 27" wide. *Courtesy of Linda Hanlon.*

German Stable. Some of the German stables were quite elaborate. The windows on this large stable are decals, a device sometimes used on later Gottschalk dollhouses. There are opening doors to the storage areas on each side. The large, center loft probably had a pair of doors originally. The railings on the second floor are made of pressed cardboard. ($1200-1500). 19.5" high x 28.5" wide x 8.5" deep. *Courtesy of Lois L. Freeman.*

Elastolin Farm. This house and barn with walled farm yard is believed to have been made by O. & M. Hausser. The German company is best known for toys made in a composition material trademarked Elastolin. This set was probably made circa 1930s. ($750-900). 10" high x 25" wide x 17.5" deep. *Courtesy of Ruth Petros.*

German Stable. The maker of this German stable is unknown. It is made of painted wood with stenciled windows. The animals are believed to be original. The building was originally purchased in Germany. ($350-450). 15" high x 14.5" wide x 7.5" deep. *Photograph by Suzanne Silverthorn.*

F.A.O. Schwarz Farm. A similar farm set with fenced farm yard may have also been made by O. & M. Hausser (Elastolin). This one was sold by F.A.O. Schwarz, circa 1930, and still retains part of the original label under the gable. The roof of the house is hinged to provide access. The four stalls slide in and out of the stable and the door above the ladder opens into the hayloft. A wooden bracket in the shape of a horse head decorates the front of the house and defines this as a horse farm. ($750-950). House is 11.5" high. Farm is 18.5" wide x 24.25" deep. *Courtesy of Sharon and Kenny Bernard.*

Converse "Roosevelt Stock Farm." The Converse barns had the architectural details printed directly on the wood. This version has its name printed on the blue "shingled" roof. It features a cupola and sliding doors. The diamond-shaped mullions in the printed windows are a more old-fashioned looking design than those found on the company's later barns. The horse-drawn cart is an especially appealing, and hard to find, accessory.

Similar Converse farms, marked "Roosevelt Stock Farm," were advertised in the 1907 L.H. Mace catalog. The 1912 Sears Roebuck catalog showed another model, marked "Stock Farm." ($1800-2200). 17" high x 19.5" wide x 11" deep. *Courtesy of Sybil W. Smith.*

Converse "Red Robin Farm." A page from the 1912 Converse catalog, reproduced in *Antique Toy World*, shows a "Red Robin" Stock Farm, with sliding doors, in three different sizes. The one shown here is the largest and contained six stalls. The catalog illustration showed a rooster weather vane atop the cupola. ($1500-2000). 17" high x 19.5" wide x 10" deep. *Photograph by Patty Cooper.*

Converse "Red Robin Farm." By 1919, Sears was advertising Converse barns, like this one, with sliding doors, but no cupola. They were offered in two sizes, one described as "medium size," 8" high x 10.5" long x 6.5" deep and a larger one, shown here, approximately 11" high x 13.5" long x 10" deep. ($1000-1200). *Courtesy of Ruth Petros.*

Converse Farm. The 1912 Sears Roebuck catalog pictured a Converse farm set which included a farm house, barn, garage, greenhouse, fencing, and seven wooden animals. The buildings were printed with colored ink directly on the wood. The roofs are removable allowing the buildings to nest inside each other for storage. ($750-1000). House: 9" high (to top of roof) x 11" wide x 8.75" deep. Barn: 9.75" high (to top of cupola) x 8" wide x 6.25" deep. Garage: 5" high x 4.75" wide x 6.25" deep. *Photograph by Patty Cooper.*

Converse Stable. Typical of other Converse buildings, this small stable is made of wood with details printed in ink. A similar, open-fronted stable with three stalls was advertised in the 1914 Butler Brothers catalog. It came with six lithographed wood animals (horse, mule, pig, cow, sheep, and rooster) and was available in two sizes, 10.25" high x 10" wide x 6" deep and 8.75" high x 8" wide x 5.25" deep (shown here.) ($200-250). *Courtesy of Marilyn Pittman.*

The Fall/Winter 1934 Sears catalog advertised a wood farm set with three outbuildings and 14 wood animals and figures for $1.00. *Photograph by Patty Cooper.*

Sears Barn. This open-backed wood barn appears to be identical to the one shown in the 1934 Sears catalog. Like buildings made by the Converse company, this barn has the windows and siding printed directly on the wood. The tool shed is not one of the outbuildings shown in the catalog photograph. The animals are made of wood and are printed only in black, unlike the full color, cardboard animals found with later barns. ($200). 13" high x 12" wide x 8.5" deep. *Courtesy of Libby Goodman.*

"Anchor Toys" Wood Barn. Although different in design, this barn also has the windows and siding printed directly on the wood. It features sliding doors and two outbuildings. The outbuildings, although in the same style as the previous barn, have different details. The building on the left is a pig pen with hogs printed in blue ink on the back wall. On the right is a chicken coop with several printed hens sitting on their roosts. The heavy cardboard animals are printed in four colors. Although mostly obscured by the wood stands, they each have the name of their breed printed under their feet. They appear to be identical to the animals pictured in the 1934 Sears advertisement.

A boxed set marked "Anchor Toys" has been found with this barn and three outbuildings, including a garage with a circa 1930s car printed on the back wall. It is not known if Anchor was a manufacturer or retailer. ($150-250). 9" high x 12.75" long x 8.25" deep. *Photograph by Patty Cooper.*

"Mohawk Stock Farm." This cardboard farm set does not have a manufacturer's name, but is very similar to the "New Modern Home Dollhouse" made by the O.B. Andrews Company of Chattanooga, Tennessee. Both are made of the same weight cardboard and have the same shades of red and green. Both are assembled with round tabs and precut slots that have an oval in the center.

The Mohawk Stock Farm was probably made in the mid to late 1930s. It is open-backed and has a loft. In addition to the shed-roofed wing on the left side, there are three other outbuildings and a silo with the set. ($50-65 in condition shown.) Barn measures 15" x 20" long x 11" deep. *Photograph by Patty Cooper.*

The 1934 Montgomery Ward Christmas catalog advertised a 48-piece "Purebred Stock Farm" for $1.19. Smaller sets were available with the 21-piece medium size set priced at 50 cents and the small 10-piece set at 25 cents. The barn was made of wood and had an open front.

Although very similar to some of the other wood barns shown, this one does not have vertical lines to represent siding. There were three wood outbuildings. The tool shed had an automobile printed on the back wall; the chicken coop had a roost, and the pig pen had a picture of pigs. The people, animals, and farm equipment were made of heavy cardboard, lithographed in full color, and mounted on wood bases. These appear to be identical to the figures sold with the Anchor Toys barn and those advertised in the 1934 Sears catalog. *Photograph by Suzanne Silverthorn.*

44

"Honor Bilt Farm." The set, which originally had 64 pieces, was advertised in the 1937 Sears catalog, for $1.00. The sides of the barn are Tekwood, a three ply material with a wood center. The roof of the barn is made of wood as are the three outbuildings, a tool shed, chicken coop, and pig pen. The chicken coop and pig pen have appropriate animals printed on the back walls. The barn is also printed on the inside. The animals and farm family are printed in full color and are made of Tekwood.

Missing from this set are two wood ventilators, two silos, a windmill, and a green cardboard fence. It is possible that this barn was made by the De Luxe Game Corporation, a company that made other buildings of Tekwood that were sold by Sears in the 1940s. ($75-100). 10.5" high x 16.75" long x 9" deep. *Photograph by Patty Cooper.*

Grey Iron Farm. The Grey Iron Company of Masontown, Pennsylvania produced this farm set as part of their "American Family" series, circa 1930s. The cast iron figures are enameled in bright colors. The people are approximately 2.25" tall. The barn appears to be made of cardboard. ($1200-1500). *Courtesy of Bob Stevens, Keystone Toy Trader.*

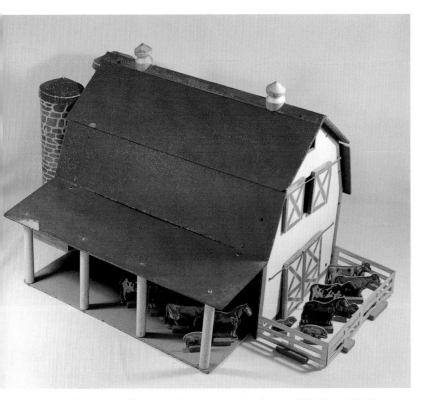

Marshall Field & Co. Barn. This barn, which was advertised in the 1939 Marshall Field catalog, bears several characteristics which suggest that it was made by the Rich Toy Company. Other buildings by Rich were made of a similar heavy Masonite. Attached to the barn are two cardboard silos which are printed in a stone pattern much like the chimneys of Rich dollhouses. The corners of the barn are reinforced with metal strips like those found on early Rich dollhouses.

The barn includes a loft which is accessible by removing the front part of the roof. The main level is open in the front. There are sets of doors on both levels which open on a wire glide. The building is held together with screws and circular metal fasteners much like those found on clipboards. The silver ventilators on the roof are made of painted wood. Masonite partitions are provided to create movable stalls. The animals and fence pieces are made of printed cardboard with wood stands.

Although similar in construction to the printed cardboard animals shown with Anchor Toys barn (and others), these are obviously drawn by a different artist and made by a different company. ($150-200). 15" high x 21" long by 17" deep. *Photograph by Patty Cooper.*

The 1939 catalog of the Chicago based Marshall Field & Co. advertised a wood barn with 18 animals and 2 silos. It was white with a red roof. Shipped unassembled, it sold for $3.95. *Courtesy of Marge Meisinger. Photograph by Suzanne Silverthorn.*

"Borden's Golden Crest Farm." Obviously made as a promotion for the Borden milk company, this Masonite barn bears marked similarities to the previous one. Both of the silos are printed in the same stone pattern much like the early Rich dollhouse chimneys. The Rich Company is known to have made other products which advertised Bordens, such as a milk wagon pull toy sold in 1938. ($125-150). 11" high x 11" wide x 9.5" deep. *Courtesy of Sýbil W. Smith.*

The 1939 Sears Roebuck catalog advertised a "Tekwood" dairy barn with rubber cows and vehicles for $1.00. The barn was 7.75" high x 13" long x 8.25" deep. *Courtesy of Marge Meisinger. Photograph by Suzanne Silverthorn.*

Rich "Sunny Brook Farm" #727. The original box identifies the manufacturer and number of this large farm set. It is made of heavy fiberboard with wood trim pieces and wood fencing. The tractor and wagon are also made of wood and have rubber wheels. The animals are punch-out cardboard figures, printed in full color, with wood stands. The barn doors slide open along wooden runners. No date is given, but it was probably made in the 1940s. (MIB $250-300). The barn is 14" wide. *Courtesy of Lois L. Freeman.*

46

Sears "New Stock Farm." The 1939 farm, shown in the following photograph, was made of "Tekwood" and could be folded flat for storage. The sturdy buildings are assembled by tabs and slots. They are open-backed with no floors. ($150-200). Barn is 9" high x 16" long X 9" deep. House is 7 " high x 10.75" long x 10" deep. *Courtesy of Sheryl Bell.*

The 1939 Sears catalog advertised a "New Stock Farm" for $1.98. Made of "Tekwood," the set included a barn, farm house, hen house, dog house, cattle shed, water trough, silos, windmill, and fencing with 24 rubber implements and animals. *Courtesy of Marge Messinger. Photograph by Suzanne Silverthorn.*

Above::The 1939 Montgomery Ward Catalog advertised an elaborate cardboard "All New Model Stock Farm" said to have been built to scale and developed with the cooperation of 15 colleges and the Bureau of Agricultural Engineering of the U.S. Department of Agriculture. It was described as "more than a toy—a true replica" of farm buildings which would be helpful to "older boys and girls, especially 4-H members, and even adults, to study the theories of scientific farming."

When completely assembled, the farm covered an area 54" by 32". Both the interior and exteriors of the buildings were printed. The main structures included a barn, hog shed, sheep shed, and granary. A galvanized metal windmill was also included. Although the buildings may have been "all new," the animals are a smaller version of the color lithographed ones sold with the wood barns in the Fall/Winter, 1934 Sears Catalog. *Photograph by Suzanne Silverthorn.*

Right:The black and white booklet which accompanied the Ward's Stock Farm was copyrighted 1939 and the text stated that "this farm stead has been planned for the typical livestock farms common to the Middle West." The buildings were said to be in 3/4" to the foot scale and precise measurements were given for each building if built in full size.

The booklet also pictured various "blue ribbon winning" farm animals with detailed descriptions of each breed. The farm appears to have been made by Built-Rite (Warren Paper Products), a theory confirmed by the presence of one of that company's dollhouses advertised on the back cover as a "Ward's Doll House" to accompany the farm. ($300-350). *Photograph by Suzanne Silverthorn.*

Ward's Stock Farm. The barn of the cardboard Ward's set was an impressive three story structure, which, unlike many other Built-Rite buildings, required both the box bottom and lid to form the base. According to the accompanying booklet, the barn was to provide accommodation for the dairy herd and horses. 14" high x 20.5" long x 13" deep. *Photograph by Suzanne Silverthorn.*

Ward's Stock Farm. The sheep barn also made use of both parts of the box to provide "shelter and feed accommodations for a herd of 25 to 30 sheep." 6.5" tall x 20.5" long x 12" deep. *Photograph by Suzanne Silverthorn.*

Ward's Stock Farm. The hog house had a gable roof with fenced yards on each side. Several different hog breeds were provided, including Chester Whites, Spotted Poland Chinas, Hampshires, Yorkshires, and Duroc Jersey pigs. 5" tall x 21" long x 12.5" deep. *Photograph by Suzanne Silverthorn.*

Built-Rite Farm Set. This marked Warren Paper Products farm set was advertised in the 1939 Montgomery Ward catalog on same page as the "All New Model Stock Farm," along with an "Authentic Scale Model Poultry Farm." Some of the animals are missing from the set. ($150-200). Base is 22" wide x 16" deep. The barn is 10.5" high x 15.5" long x 8.5" deep. *Courtesy of Becky Norris.*

UILT-RITE FARM SET Barn and Lot: Set up, 21x14x12. Open in back. ealistically printed inside and out, including stalls in barn and lot fences. Red barn, een roof, white fence. Machinery and Tools: Tractor, Wagon, Plow and Seeder, Fork, ovel, Milk Can, Oil Drum, 4 Sacks of Food, Wire. Tractor 5¾" long, with other eces in proportion. Farm Animals: 38 Authentic Farm Animals in full color, both les, on heavy stock. Animals stand upright, include horses, cows, sheep, hogs, steers, llie dog, Shetland pony, and Palomino saddle horse and rider. Packed flat th instructions in sealed box. *At dealers everywhere.* **$1.19**

The October 1946 *Children's Activities* magazine advertised a Built-Rite farm set for $1.19. When assembled, barn and lot were 21" x 14" x 12". The barn was open-backed and printed inside and out. It came with a variety of fence, farm implements and animals. The animals appear to be the same as those sold with the Montgomery Ward Model Stock Farm. *Photograph by Patty Cooper.*

Built-Rite Farm Set. Warren Paper Products also made a farm set in the same small scale as their Built-Rite Village. ($100-150). The barn is 4.5" high x 6.5" long x 4" deep. *Photograph by Patty Cooper.*

The 1945 Spiegel Catalog advertised the Build-a-Set Stock Farm as part of a special offer that included a Donald Duck Coloring Set. Together, the two sold for $1.29. The Stock Farm had 58 units and was made of colored, heavy cardboard. The set included a barn, corn crib, silo, windmill, L-shaped house, and various animals and people. *Photograph by Patty Cooper.*

Build-a-Set Farm Set. The cardboard farm was made by the D.A. Pacter Company of Chicago, Illinois, circa 1945. It was similar in construction and scale to Built-Rite. The individual pieces are unmarked, unlike Built-Rite pieces which almost always have a model number.

The farmhouse was one-story with a printed clapboard exterior in an L-shape. The original set contained 173 die-cut pieces which included an almost excessive number of split rail fences. The set also included 2-dimensional cut-outs of four farmers, two sheep, two horses, two cows, and two pigs with cardboard stands. The farm vehicles had parts that moved on spokes made of dowels. The barn, shown in the advertisement above, is missing from this set ($75). Farm house is 5" high x 8" wide x 8" deep. *Photograph by Patty Cooper.*

An advertisement from the October, 1946 *Children's Activities* magazine offered a cardboard farm by Judy Toys for $2.50. According to the ad, Deluxe Farm No. 206 contained over 90 pieces, including 20 sections of fence rail and 40 red wooden fence posts. The "bright plastic" figures were said to be able to stand on their own feet and included a Happy Farm Family. *Photograph by Patty Cooper.*

Judy Farm #206. This circa 1946 cardboard farm set was made by the Judy Company of Minneapolis. The set included a house, barn, machine shed, silo, corn crib, fencing (missing), water trough (missing), windmill, and chicken coop. A similar set, with the same box and barn, has been found with the small wooden animals shown in the following picture. Accessories included a car, truck, tractor, four people, and 16 brightly colored rubber animals. Neither the buildings nor the animals are marked. ($125-150). Box measures 18" x 12" x 2". Barn is 6.75" high x 10" wide x 7.5" deep. The house is 7" high x 8" wide x 7" deep. *Photograph by Patty Cooper.*

"Keystone Farm." Keystone made a farm set with attached barnyard and outbuildings, circa 1952. This set also had animals designed with special features which allowed children to "milk" the cow or get eggs from the chickens. A similar Keystone farm has been seen with a plastic "pond" in place of the chicken house. ($300-350). 16" x 24" base. *Courtesy of Lois L. Freeman.*

An advertisement from the December 1950 *Children's Activities* magazine pictured the Friendly Acres Dairy Farm by Kiddie Brush and Toy Company of Jonesville, Michigan. For $2.89, a child could purchase the lithographed metal barn along with 12 plastic cows, metal milk cans, and 12 movable sections of fence with gates. The same barn was sold through Montgomery Ward in their 1948 Christmas Catalog. The Ward's barn had a picture of a cow in the gable of the barn, instead of the words "Friendly Acres." It came with fewer accessories, only eight fence sections and 9 cows, three each of the breeds Guernsey, Holstein, and Jersey. *Photograph by Patty Cooper.*

"Friendly Acres Dairy Farm." Kiddie Brush and Toy Company (also known as Susy Goose) made the barn on the left with natural colored metal trim and a white interior. There were cow stanchions inside to facilitate milking the plastic herd. The cows are distinguishable from those made by other companies because they are made in the realistic colors of their particular breed and have rectangular bases. The barn on the right is also marked "Friendly Acres" on the back, but the side promotes "Golden Guernsey Milk," suggesting that Kiddie Brush and Toy may have made this as an advertising premium. The quonset style roof is lithographed instead of being plain metal, but the interiors are the same. (Barn with animals $100; barn only, $45). 6.5" high x 13" wide x 7" deep. *Photograph by Patty Cooper.*

Ohio Art "No. 195 Lifelike Farm Set." The barn is marked with the logo used by Ohio Art, circa 1945-58. It was advertised in the 1956 Ohio Art catalog. The set originally came with 9 soft plastic animals and 4 pieces of fence. The size of this farm makes it an appropriate companion to the Ohio Art dollhouse known to collectors as "Midget Manor." ($80). Barn is 5.75" high x 10" wide (including silo) x 4.25" deep. *Photograph by Patty Cooper.*

Ohio Art "Play Time Farm Set" No. 194. The pieces appear to be the same as those in set No. 195, but the packaging is different, with a cardboard backdrop and a cardboard "farmhouse" to hold the plastic animals. The roof of the barn is also a different color. ($80-100). Barn is 5.75" high x 10" wide x 4.25" deep. *Photograph by Patty Cooper.*

Ohio Art "Rolling Acres Farm" Set #198. This set appears to be quite similar to the one advertised in the 1961 catalog of the Cullum & Boren company in Dallas. The assembled Ohio Art barn featured two cupolas with weather vanes and sliding doors. This set contains 83 pieces. (Boxed set $125-150). *Photograph by Suzanne Silverthorn.*

Ohio Art "Valleyview Farm." This barn was made in the same scale but in softer colors and with a blue roof. It was lithographed both inside and out. Apparently, most Ohio Art barns were made without a floor to the loft. ($35-55). *Courtesy of Sheryl Bell.*

Ohio Art "Sunnyfield Farm." Another very similar barn had a sliding door, attached silo, and was open-backed. It was apparently available in sets of different sizes with 18 to 33 animals and several sections of fence. ($50-65). 11" high x 15.75" x 9" deep. *Courtesy of Gene and Arliss Morris. Photograph by Gene Morris.*

Ohio Art "Meadow Lane Farms." This metal set was offered in the 1969 Montgomery Ward catalog for $4.77. It was open-backed and had two dormers lithographed on the roof. The farm came with a tractor, fencing, and a variety of animals. This barn was probably made for many years because it has been found with the logo used earlier by Ohio Art, circa 1959-62. Like other Ohio Art farm sets, Meadow Lane was made in sets of varying sizes, including one with as many as 40 plastic animals. ($100). 11" high x 16" long x 8.5" deep. *Photograph by Suzanne Silverthorn.*

55

Marx "Magic Barn." The left side of the brightly lithographed metal barn pictures a farmer with a horse and the right side shows a cow. It is similar to a garage made by Louis Marx during the 1950s. ($75). 10.5" long. *Courtesy of Gene and Arliss Morris. Photograph by Gene Morris.*

In 1950, the Louis Marx Company sold a "Magic Barn" through Alden's for $1.97. The tractor with farmer was part of the set. A clockwork mechanism allowed the rubber treaded tractor to open the door while emitting harmless sparks. The same barn and tractor were sold through Sears and Montgomery Ward in 1952. *Photograph by Suzanne Silverthorn.*

Two different sizes of the Lazy-Day Farm by Marx were advertised in the 1957 Alden's catalog. The 88-piece set sold for $4.69. It had a two-story, lithographed metal barn and came with plastic fencing, farmers, animals, and vehicles. The original barn had a device for lifting plastic bales of hay into the loft. The $2.98 version had a smaller, 1-story barn, farm tractor with wagon, mower, plow, fifteen animals, four barn accessories, and fencing—a total of forty-four pieces. A set of fourteen additional farm animals could be purchased for 87 cents. *Courtesy of Marge Meisinger. Photograph by Suzanne Silverthorn.*

Marx "Lazy-Day Farm." The barn was all metal, with lithographed doors which did not actually close. Note that the roof is printed in a different color than the one shown in the Alden's advertisement. ($50-65). 9.5" high x 14" wide x 10" deep. *Courtesy of Ruth Petros.*

Marx "Lazy-Day Farm." The interior of the barn was lithographed inside on the first floor while the slanted walls of the hay loft were blank. Unlike the Ohio Art barns, the Marx barns had floors for the lofts which provided additional space for play. The same blank was used for a barn with yellow siding and a blue roof. *Courtesy of Ruth Petros.*

A Marx farm set was sold by Sears in 1952. The barn was lithographed with the "Happi-Time" name often used for Sears toys. The set, which included a metal silo and plastic fencing, vehicles, implements, and animals, sold for $4.99. The doors of the barn appear to be made of plastic and operable. *Photograph by Suzanne Silverthorn.*

In the 1959 Sears catalog, Marx introduced a large dairy farm with over 220 pieces. The price was $9.98. The barn had an attached tool shed and two silos. The whole structure was elevated on a lithographed metal base which housed the dairy operation. The set also included two lithographed metal chicken coops. Plastic farm accessories included a stile, scarecrow, feed bags, milk cans, fodder shock, storage tank, pitchfork, and milking stool. There were also 54 plastic animals, 8 people, a variety of farm produce, and 24 sections of fence. *Courtesy of Marge Meisinger. Photograph by Suzanne Silverthorn.*

Marx "Happi-Time" Dairy Farm. The 1959 dairy barn, with silos marked "Happi-Time," is an impressive structure with its dairy facility base and convenient ramp. Like the other Marx barns, this one is open-backed for play. The scale is approximately 1/2" equals a foot. ($175-200). The barn itself is 10.5" high x 25" long x 9" deep. *Courtesy of Mary Harris.*

The 1954 Sears Catalog offered a 45-piece Roy Rogers Rodeo Ranch for $3.94. It was made by the Louis Marx Company. The lithographed steel bunkhouse was 6" high x 11" long x 7" deep. In addition to Roy Rogers, it housed 8 cowboy figures approximately 2 3/8" high. Plastic accessories included a hitching rail, grinding stone, chopping block, anvil, hitches, and fencing. *Photograph by Suzanne Silverthorn.*

Marx "Roy Rogers Ranch Set." A slightly different version is illustrated on the cover of this boxed set. The bunkhouse appears to be the same as the one shown in the 1954 Sears Catalog, but the accessories are different. Low fencing is provided, but not the tall fence pieces needed to form corrals. Plastic furniture for the bunkhouse included a hutch, table, chair, barrels, and bunk beds. ($300-350). 6" high x 11" long x 7" deep. *Photograph by Suzanne Silverthorn.*

Marx "Western Ranch Set." The same bunkhouse was also used for the Western Ranch Set shown here. A similar set, by Marx, has been found with the name "Bar-M Ranch" and in 1956, Montgomery Ward sold a version called the "Lone Ranger Ranch." (MIB $300-350). *Courtesy of George Handforth, Catskill Toys.*

Auburn "Large Farm Set." The Auburn Rubber Company was well-known for their toy animals, many of which were sold with farms made by other companies. This boxed set includes Auburn animals, people, and vehicles, as well as a plastic barn and silo. ($75-100). Box is 14" x 11". The barn is 7.5" high x 10" long x 6" deep. *Courtesy of Gene and Arliss Morris. Photograph by Gene Morris.*

Plasticville Barn. Bachmann Brothers, Inc. made at least two different barns, each in a variety of color combinations. This one was probably made in the mid-1950s and has an unusual metallic top on the silo and ventilators. These barns were appropriate in size for train layouts. ($20-25). 4.75" high x 6" wide x 4.25" deep. *Photograph by Suzanne Silverthorn.*

Tote-a-Toy "Super Deluxe Farm" by Ideal. The concept of providing a self-contained, portable toy has obvious appeal. Ideal made several dollhouses in the 1960s and 70s which used this concept. This boxed farm set included a vinyl, suitcase type barn which opened to create a farm yard. The opened Tote-a-Toy barn reveals a highly detailed interior as well as row crops and a driveway for farm vehicles. When not stored in the plastic silo, animals could be housed in the built-in stalls and chickens could roost in the hayloft. ($75-100). 9.5" high x 14.5" wide x 19" deep (when opened). *Courtesy of Roy Specht.*

IV. Church and State

Every town of any size needs a church, school, hospital, post office, fire station, police station, and city hall. As might be expected, most of these buildings have, at some time, become models for children's toys. Many were sold as part of village sets, but a significant number were larger in scale and sufficiently detailed to stand alone.

Churches

Churches were most frequently produced as "Sunday Toys," playthings that were deemed appropriately spiritual to be used on church days. Toy churches from Victorian times were made as building toys with verses of scripture printed on the blocks in the hope that the child might get a religious lesson while playing. R. Bliss and Whitney S. Reed each produced block churches of this type.

"Reed's Sunday Toy." This circa 1880s building, by the Whitney S. Reed Company, is formed entirely of blocks. The storage box is marked "Reed's Sunday Toy" on the sides and "Church and Sunday School" on the top. Unlike some of the other Reed toys, the designs of this church are printed directly on the wood instead of lithographed on paper. The blocks which form the sides are printed with stained glass windows on the outside and Bible verses on the inside. The finials are missing from this set. ($1000-1200). Box measures 16" x 7" x 3.5". Assembled church is 15.5" high x 11" wide x 11" deep. *Photograph by Patty Cooper.*

W.S. Reed Cathedral. Although this lithographed paper over wood church bears a strong resemblance to Bliss, it is believed to have been made by the W.S. Reed company. It was advertised in the 1894 Montgomery Ward catalog for 75 cents. The lidded box was designed to form the base of the church. The blocks were printed with illustrations of the Noah's Ark story, a Book of Prayer, the Ten Commandments, and the alphabet. ($1500-1800). 16" high x 7.5" wide x 9.5" deep. *Courtesy of Linda and Carl Thomas, Jr.*

Bliss Church. Like the Reed church, this is a block building toy. An 8.5" square box forms the main part of the church and also serves as a storage container. The box is marked "Church & Sunday-School Blocks" and "Published by R. Bliss Mfg Co. U.S.A." In addition to the blocks which form the building, there are flat blocks, 2.5" x 4.5", which are printed with the names of books from the Bible on one side and a scene from each book on the other. All of the pieces are made of lithographed paper over wood. This set was advertised in the 1895 Bliss Catalog. Some of the finials are missing from the buildings. ($1200-1500). 20.5" high x 8.5" wide x 8.5" deep. *Photograph by Patty Cooper.*

Chiming Cathedral. The wood church has lithographed paper on all sides with no access to the interior. On the back of the building is a set of eight keys. When a key is pressed down, a hammer hits the wooden chimes to simulate the bells of a church. ($200-250). 14" high x 8" wide x 12.5" long. *Photograph by Patty Cooper.*

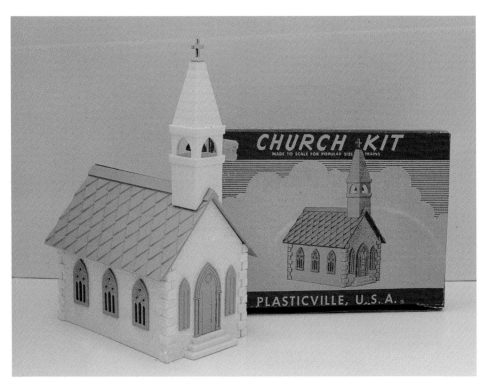

Plasticville "Church Kit CC-8." Ten plastic pieces snap together to complete this circa 1950s church by Bachmann Brothers. The box still bears the original S.S. Kresge price tag of 98 cents. Plasticville made several other church models including ones with paper inserts to represent stained glass. ($18-25). 8.75" high x 4" wide x 5" deep. *Photograph by Patty Cooper.*

Schools

Children have always enjoyed playing school. Like churches, toy schools were probably seen as having some value beyond mere recreation for Victorian children. The most collectible of these were made around 1900, in Germany, and were open-fronted structures, with three walls and a floor, and few, if any, exterior architectural details. Many were made for the French market and are sold, today, as "French school rooms." The furnishings usually consisted of desks, often connected, cabinets, blackboards, and maps, as well as a teacher and pupils.

Perhaps the earliest commercially produced American toy school was made by Crandall. Their "District School" was advertised in an 1879-80 wholesale catalog. The set was made of wood and consisted of several students, some seated at desks, a teacher, a lamb, and even a dunce. The R. Bliss Company made at least one lithographed paper over wood school desk. The Strombeck-Becker Company of Moline, Illinois marketed a boxed set which did not include a building, but provided a wood teacher's desk, four student desks, and cardboard accessories. A set of school desks was also made by the German Erna Meyer company and was sold with their bendable cloth dolls. F.A.O. Schwarz sold a similar set, complete with a classroom box, furnished with wood desks and peopled by Caco dolls from Germany.

By the 1950s, at least three different companies, Marx, Renwal, and Thomas, were selling schools with plastic furniture. It is interesting that all of these were designed in the form of one-room school houses despite the fact that most of the baby boomers were attending the modern schools rapidly built after the war. As with dollhouses, perhaps the styles were intended to provide more of a comfort zone for parents than the children. As late as the 1970s, the popular Play Family School by Fisher Price still used the one-room schoolhouse theme. Plasticville (Bachmann Brothers) was one of the few companies to produce a toy school which resembled those actually being built at the time.

German School Room. This circa 1920s school room was made of wood with three walls and floor. The school room is furnished with a wood cabinet, easel, school master's desk, and eight student desks. The teacher is marked "Elastolin" and it is likely that the twelve students are also made of this plaster-like material by the O. & M. Hausser co any of Germany. ($1600). 11.25 high x 22.5" wide x 13.5" deep. *Private collection.*

German or French School Room. The room includes three student desks and a desk for the head master. 14" high x 35.5" wide x 15.5" deep. *Courtesy of Angels' Attic Museum. On loan from private collector.*

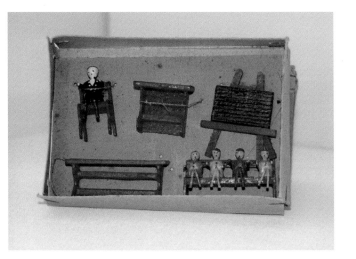

Small German School Set. Still tied in their original box, four students and their teacher await an appropriate school room. ($75-100). 4" high x 6" high. *School from a private collection. Photograph by Ruth Petros.*

Milton Bradley "Toy Town Library." The original box describes this toy as "A game in which the books are issued in exchange for wit and humour." The circa 1910 wood library shelf contains books made of paper over wood which have silly sounding titles. ($150-175). 7" high x 9" wide x 3" deep. *Courtesy of Lois L. Freeman.*

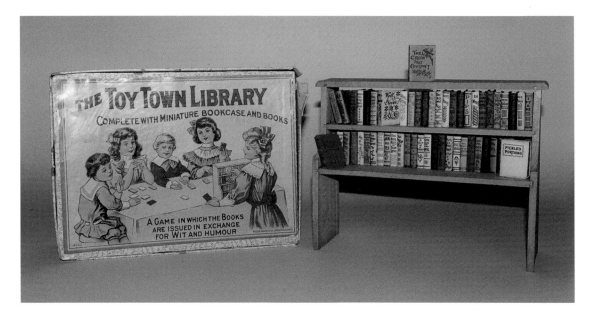

"Public School." Made of Masonite, covered with very thin paper, the purpose of the building is clearly printed over the main entry. The entrance/tower section can be pulled out. The roof lifts off for access to the interior which is not papered or decorated in any way. No manufacturer's mark has been found. 12.25" high x 19.25" wide x 12.5" deep. *Courtesy of Gene and Vicki Olswold. Photograph by Rita Goranson.*

63

Strombecker School Room. Set No. 547. Although advertised in the 1938 Strombecker catalog as being in a "scale 3/4-inch to one foot," the actual scale (considering that the desks are sized for child-dolls) was closer to 1" equals a foot.

The set included a wood teacher's desk with opening drawers, a swivel chair for the teacher, and four student desks with seats that could be folded up. The cardboard insert for the box contained pieces that could be cut out and folded to form a set of books, a waste basket, and a blackboard with which to furnish a school room. ($200-250). The box is 10" x 14" x 2.5". *Photograph by Patty Cooper.*

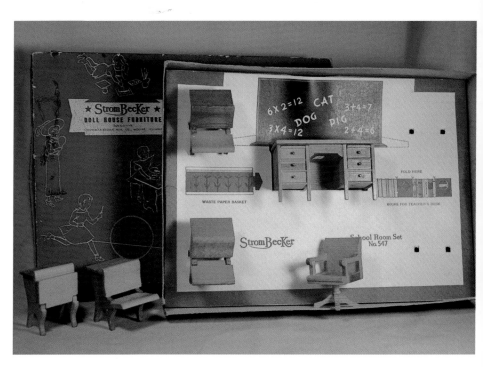

"Little Red School." Made of wood by an unknown manufacturer, the school has details printed directly on the wood and a bell that can be rung to summon the doll children to class. ($100-150). 14.25" high x 14.75" wide x 8.5" deep. *Courtesy of Marcie Tubbs. Photograph by Bob Tubbs.*

"Little Red School." The wood school by an unknown manufacturer is open-backed. Inside, it has a blackboard printed on the wall and windows on each side. *Courtesy of Marcie Tubbs. Photograph by Bob Tubbs.*

"Renwal Little Red School House and Furniture Set." The No. 1200 set was introduced by Renwal in 1947 as a complement to their Jolly Twins dollhouse furniture. (Boxed set $300-350). *Courtesy of Ray and Gail Carey.*

Renwal School. The folding cardboard school had cut out windows on the side which dropped down for play. Details were printed both inside and out. 10.5" high x 8.5" wide x 14" deep. *Courtesy of Ray and Gail Carey.*

Renwal School. The side of the building opened for play access. The original set contained six #33 plastic school desks with molded inkwells and folding seats, a #34 teacher's desk with opening drawer, and a #35 desk chair which swiveled. There were four #8 Renwal babies. The teacher was printed on one of the walls, therefore no doll was provided. *Courtesy of Ray and Gail Carey.*

65

Marx "Little Red Schoolhouse." The Louis Marx Company produced this
lithographed metal school in 1956 as part of their Main Street USA series which
also included the Babyland Nursery and Pet Shop. All were approximately 1/2" to
the foot in scale. The #3381 school building had a metal bell on top and clear
plastic windows. (Boxed set $400-450. Building with accessories $150-300). 8"
high x 16.5" long x 7" deep. *Courtesy of Marcie Tubbs. Photograph by Bob Tubbs.*

Marx "Little Red Schoolhouse." The inside was lithographed with a blackboard,
pull-down map, clock, shelves, and a coat closet. Accessories for the set
included a teacher, eight students, six student desks, teacher's desk with chair,
reading table with chairs, table with film projector, globe, and a waste basket.
All were molded in a beige hard plastic which has the dolls frozen in one
position so that the pupils standing at the blackboard can never resume their
places at desks. *Courtesy of Marcie Tubbs. Photograph by Bob Tubbs.*

Campbell School Room. In 1955, the Thomas Toy Company was licensed by Campbell Soup to manufacture a school room set as part of their Campbell Kids promotion. The set included eight plastic flip-top desks, eight students, and a teacher, all in a scale of approximately 3/4" to a foot. The items were packaged in a box with a cellophane window. The back of the box provided pieces which could be cut out and folded to create books, maps, a dunce cap, a report card, and a stool to accessorize the school. Inside, the box was printed with a blackboard, bulletin board, clock and pop-out desk for the teacher. ($200-250). *Courtesy of Marcie Tubbs. Photograph by Bob Tubbs.*

Vinyl Suitcase School. This vinyl school may also have been made by the Thomas Toy Company or its successor Banner Plastics, circa 1960s. It has details printed on the exterior with opening double doors. ($100-150). 8.5" high x 14.5" wide x 8" deep. *Courtesy of Ruth Petros.*

Vinyl Suitcase School. The vinyl suitcase still has its original Thomas school desks tied in to the floor. In this set, the teacher has a plastic table for a desk. The dolls are German Caco dolls, not the dolls made by Thomas. 8.5" high x 14.5" wide x 8" deep. *Courtesy of Ruth Petros.*

Plasticville "School House Kit SC-4." Bachmann Brothers, Inc. of Philadelphia, Pennsylvania produced this school as part of their line of model railroad buildings. The plastic pieces snapped together to make a building with an opening front door but no play access. The school was introduced in 1951 and sold during the 1950s with several different colors for the roofs, but always with red walls. ($45-50). The box is 10.5" x 4.5" x 2". The school is 5.75" high (to top of weather vane) x 10.25" wide x 4.5" deep. *Courtesy of Gary Mosholder.*

"Liliput Puppen-Schule." The German firm of Erna Meyer produced this boxed set circa late 1960s, to accompany (and educate) their dolls. The dolls had flexible bodies, painted features, and rather intricate outfits which included book bags. The dolls sold during this period had cloth covered cardboard feet and were approximately 1" to the foot in scale. The set included a teacher, six pupils, three two-person desks with attached seats, a teacher's desk with chair, and a free-standing blackboard. The box illustration shows a slightly different teacher's desk and a male teacher. Perhaps this set was made at a different time or the population of each class was unique. ($200-250). The box is 6" x 12.25" x 4.25". *Photograph by Patty Cooper.*

F.A.O. Schwarz "School Room." The famous New York toy store sold this German school room in the early 1960s for $15.00. The wood room had a floor and three walls. The exterior of the school was brown stucco. Inside, there was simulated carpet on the floor. The side walls were printed with a blackboard and a wall map. The back wall contained three celluloid windows and the words "School Room." Four German Caco students and their teacher sit at maple desks with separate chairs. ($200-250). 8.25" high x 17.75" wide x 9" deep. *Courtesy of Marcie Tubbs. Photograph by Bob Tubbs.*

Hospitals

Plasticville provided a realistic looking hospital during the 1950s. Unlike many of their other model railroad type buildings, it was furnished with miniature hospital equipment which provided added play value. Mettoy, of England, made a lithographed metal "Emergency Ward 10" which included an extensive array of plastic accessories and is now highly collectible. Both Kenner and Fisher Price produced plastic hospitals in the 1960s, mostly designed for preschoolers.

Renwal and Marx made nursery sets obviously intended to be hospital nurseries. The three known variations of the Renwal nursery consisted primarily of furniture, although the box of one was printed to look like the interior of a hospital nursery. The Marx "Babyland Nursery" was a free-standing lithographed metal building which contained all the latest isolettes, incubators, and other equipment for a modern nursery. In the 1950s, F.A.O. Schwarz sold a "Tiny Tots Nursery" which was described as "imported." It was furnished with German Caco dolls and was probably manufactured in Germany.

Mettoy "Emergency Ward 10." The Mettoy company of England was one of the few manufacturers to offer a toy hospital. According to the original box, the set came with 24 people and over 60 pieces of hospital equipment. There were two floors with an elevator which provided access to each level and to the roof-top parking area. Each floor contained one room with lithographed details on the floors and walls. An article in *Plastic Figure and Playset Collector* said that this set was based on a British television show, *Emergency-Ward 10,* which was aired in the 1960s. The base is 24" x 11". *Courtesy of Plastic Figure & Playset Collector Magazine c1995.*

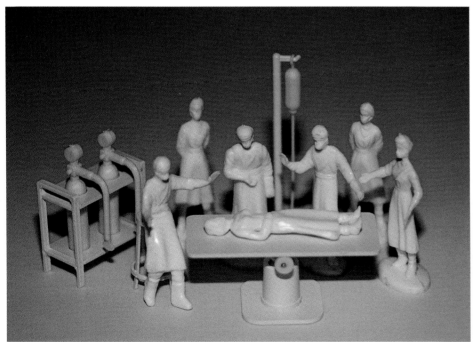

Mettoy Hospital figures and accessories. The 54 mm people of the Mettoy hospital were made of plastic and molded permanently into their medical roles. The extensive array of hospital furniture and accessories were also plastic, primarily in white and pink. *Courtesy of Plastic Figure & Playset Collector Magazine c1995.*

Marx "Babyland Nursery" #3379. Although this is a free-standing structure, it is obviously meant to be a hospital nursery. The baby beds are more like hospital isolettes than baby cribs and there is an incubator along with other medical equipment. The metal building is made with the same blank as the School House and Pet Shop, but the lithography is completely different, both inside and out. The door is non-opening and the windows are clear plastic with red trim. A lithographed metal counter is attached to one side wall. ($250-300). 8" high x 16.5" wide x 7" deep. *Courtesy of Marcie Tubbs. Photograph by Bob Tubbs.*

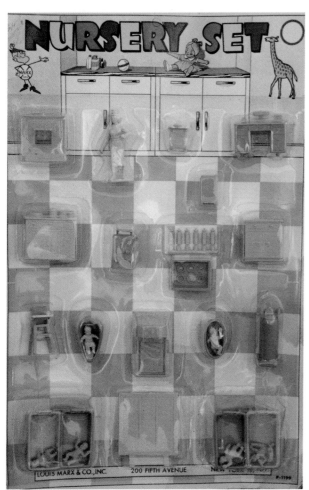

Marx Babyland Nursery. The lithographed metal building came with many off-white plastic accessories including four isolettes, an incubator with clear plastic cover, several tables and counters, a screen, a high chair, desk with chair, oxygen bottle, bathtub, diaper pail, scale, and tray with bottles. There are six babies, all cast in different positions, and one nurse. *Courtesy of Marcie Tubbs. Photograph by Bob Tubbs.*

Above: Marx "Nursery Set." The accessories for the Babyland Nursery were also sold separately in a bubble pack. ($100-125). *Courtesy of Ray and Gail Carey.*

Right: Plasticville "Hospital Kit # HS-6." Bachmann Bros., Inc. made this hospital in the mid-1950s. The plastic pieces snap together to form a two-story structure. Although small in scale, appropriate for a train layout, the hospital is remarkable because it actually contains furniture. The tiny furnishings include hospital beds, desks, chairs, nightstands, toilets, and carts. The beds are a little over 1" long. The second floor is printed with a rather serious looking diagram (more reminiscent of a blueprint than a child's toy) showing where each item should be placed. The doors of the hospital are all operable. The box measures 9" x 7.75" x 3.25". ($35-45). The building is 6" high x 8.5" wide x 6.5" deep. *Courtesy of Gary Mosholder.*

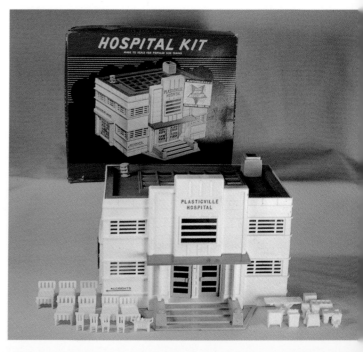

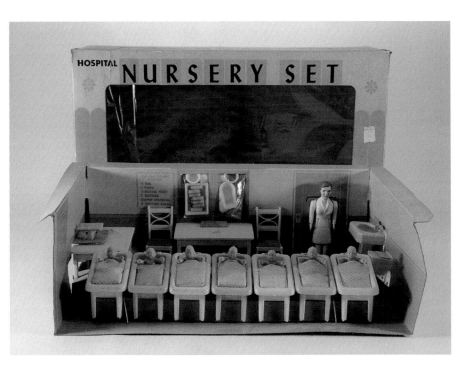

Renwal "Hospital Nursery Set" #214. The Renwal Company produced nursery sets in two sizes. The larger, introduced in 1954, had a cellophane display window through which the nursery could be viewed. The inside of the box was printed with "tile" on the floor and hospital charts on the back wall.

The set contained seven cribs with rubber-like babies snugly tucked into a cardboard insert and covered with cloth blankets. Each of the beds had a baby's name cast into the plastic at the top. Although there were seven beds, only five (apparently popular) names were used: John, Alice, Peter, Mary, and Irene...then a repeat of two names. The plastic cribs have been found primarily in ivory and pink, although other colors have been reported. A typical Renwal-type woman, with a molded white nurse's uniform and cap, watched over the babies.

Also included with the set were two chairs (which were the same as #63 Renwal kitchen chairs), two #76 (kitchen) tables, a #84 night stand, a #96 bath sink, a scale, tube, pans, bottle tray, seven bottles, 5 cotton balls, and diapers. ($275-325). *Courtesy of Chuck Donovan.*

Renwal "The Little Hospital Nursery Set" #279. A smaller version was introduced in 1956. The fold-back lid provided a hospital backdrop with two busy nurses who took the place of an actual doll. Only five cribs were included with the small set. Aside from the isolettes and accessories, no other furniture was provided. ($175-200). 5.5" x 12" x 2.25". *Photograph by Patty Cooper.*

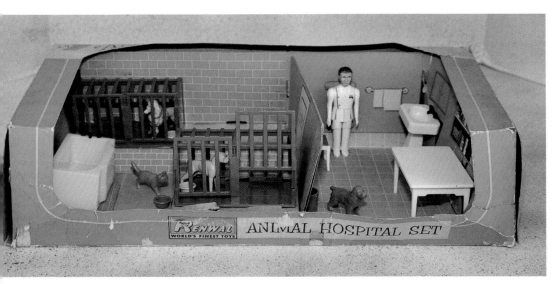

Renwal "Animal Hospital Set" #272. The Renwal Animal Hospital was introduced in 1956. It is included in this section because animals are so often accorded equal status to humans in the world of children. The set was advertised as a "Sales Producers, because it's both for Girls and Boys." It contained several pieces that were identical to those sold as dollhouse furniture, including a table, bath sink, and bathtub, the latter in an unusual yellow color. There were also cages with sliding gates, dogs and cats, feeding dishes, and a veterinarian doll. ($350-450). 4.5" high x 18" long x 9.5" deep. *Courtesy of Marcie Tubbs. Photograph by Bob Tubbs.*

Fire Stations

Fire stations were a vital part of the community when most buildings were made of wood and heated with combustible fuels. Bliss manufactured at least three different fire stations, complete with horse drawn pumpers.

The German *Universal Toy Catalog for 1926* shows a lithographed metal fire station with two bays. The simple structure is very similar to the automobile garages advertised by the same unidentified company, probably Bing. The Louis Marx Company made lithographed metal stations beginning in the 1930s, as did Wyandotte and Courtland in the 1950s.

Schoenhut manufactured several different fire stations in a scale more consistent with the company's train stations than their dollhouses. These buildings included one to three bays and came with wheeled vehicles, spring-loaded to shoot out the doors when a lever was released. A bell, which rang at the same time, contributed to the excitement. In the 1920s, a variation was introduced with a decal on one side which read "Ed Wynn, Fire Chief." This one-bay, firehouse came with a wooden cart driven by a miniature version of the famous comedian.

The Keystone Company of Boston made two different firehouse designs, with variations, out of printed Masonite. The Keystone models even included burning buildings. Most of their fire stations were originally equipped with a fire truck or two, but many of these have been lost over the years. The De Luxe Game Corporation made a fire station out of Tekwood which is easily confused with those made by Keystone. It also included a two-dimensional burning building with hinged "flames" in the windows which could be knocked over with the toy fire hose. F.A.O. Schwarz offered a pressed board fire station in the early 1970s of sufficient quality to compete with those made much earlier.

Bliss Fire Station. According to Flora Gill Jacobs, in *Dollhouses in America*, the 1901 R. Bliss catalog offered fire stations in three different sizes. All three used the same lithographed paper. On this version, there are opening double doors below and a projecting, squared bay window on the second story. ($2500-3000). 19.5" high x 10.5" wide x 8" deep. *Courtesy of Linda and Carl Thomas, Jr.*

Bliss Fire Station #509. A slightly smaller Bliss fire station makes use of the same lithographed papers in a different way. The number 509B is barely discernible on the edges of the fire station shown here. The presence of a pierced metal rail on this version indicates that it was probably made circa 1914. ($2000-2500). 14.5" high x 9.75" wide x 7.5" deep. *Photograph by Patty Cooper.*

German Firehouse. The maker of this early twentieth century German firehouse is unknown. Made of painted wood, it may have been hand-crafted. The structure features an impressive total of eight bays, all with various types of fire-fighting equipment. 6" high x 14" long x 3.5" deep. *Courtesy of Sybil W. Smith.*

Bliss Fire Station #508. A completely different Bliss fire station has a clock in the bell tower. Horses look out of the lithographed windows. Above the center window is the company's logo with the word "Bliss" inside an elongated "C" with an "o" at the end. This logo indicates that the fire station was probably introduced circa 1900-1905. The station is open-backed with operable double doors. ($1200-1400). 12" high x 10" wide x 6" deep. *Courtesy of Linda and Carl Thomas, Jr.*

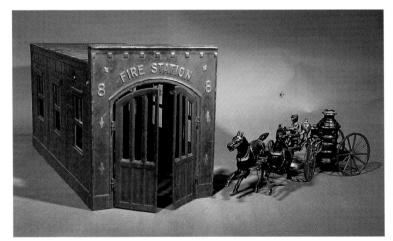

Wilkins-Kingsbury Metal Fire Station #8. This metal fire station has opening doors and includes a horse drawn pumper with bell. ($1500). 10" high x 8.75" wide x 19.25" deep. *Courtesy of Toy and Miniature Museum of Kansas City. Photograph by Tom Moulis.*

Marx "Hometown Fire House." The lithographed metal building was sold as part of a series that included a bank, police station, and several different stores. Eight buildings were advertised as a set for 59 cents in the 1931 Sears catalog. The buildings were also sold separately. The fire house had two trucks with fire fighters lithographed on the back wall. A telephone booth, two-dimensional firemen, and two other vehicles were also part of the original set. ($200-250). 3.25" high x 5" long x 2.75" deep. *Courtesy of Kathy Garner.*

"Happiwork Pastime Package for Little Folk." The Gibson Art Company of Cincinnati, Ohio, made this lithographed cardboard fire department, circa 1920s. ($75-100). *Photograph by Suzanne Silverthorn.*

Schoenhut "Fire Company No. 9." Like the company's dollhouses, this fire station was made of wood with an embossed fiberboard roof and heavy cardboard sides. The fire station does not contain a manufacturer's mark, but can be identified by its similarity to other Schoenhut buildings, such as the "Ed Wynn Fire House" advertised in the 1933 catalog. Both fire houses were designed so that a fire truck could be shot out, through the doors, by releasing a rubber band. There are three ejection levers in the back of this firehouse, so apparently it came with three, now missing, vehicles. The two opening doors were released by the same mechanism. A bell on the side clanged as the fire trucks were ejected. ($300-350). 8.5" high x 8" wide x 8" deep. *Photograph by Patty Cooper.*

Arcade "Engine Co. No. 99." Arcade made this wood fire station circa 1930s. The large door opens to admit the two cast iron fire trucks which came with the structure. (Building only $700-1000. With fire trucks $1600-2000.). *Courtesy of Bill and Stevie Weart.*

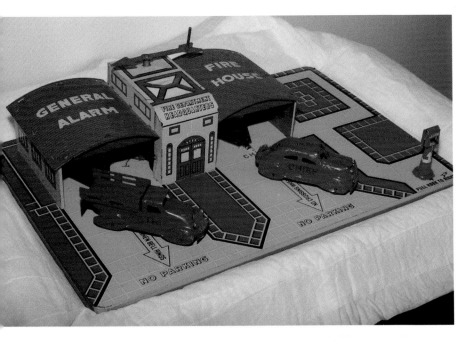

Marx "General Alarm Fire House." The red and yellow lithographed metal building came with two vehicles, a heavy steel car (marked "chief") and a fire truck (marked "patrol."). Both were red with black letters. The General Alarm Fire House used the same basic shape as the Marx City Airport, Grand Central Station, and Greyhound Bus Terminal. ($700-900). 4.5" high x 17" wide x 11" deep. *Courtesy of John Hathorne.*

The 1938 Sears catalog advertised the Marx "General Alarm Fire Station" for 94 cents. On top of the building, a key winder, cleverly disguised as a weather vane, could be turned to make the fire cars shoot out of the bays when a lever was released. An alarm bell rang simultaneously. *Courtesy of Marge Meisinger. Photograph by Suzanne Silverthorn.*

Courtland "Fire Dept." The lithographed metal building by Courtland USA was made circa 1946. The door automatically folds open when nudged by the fire chief's car. A ladder truck can be viewed through the lithographed windows. ($100-150). 5.5" high x 7.5" wide x 10" deep. *Photograph by Suzanne Silverthorn.*

Marx "Automatic Fire House." The lithographed metal toy was designed to eject the friction car while an alarm sounded. It was made by Louis Marx circa 1950. ($400-425). *Courtesy of Don Nix.*

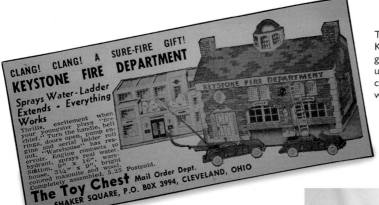

The 1948 issue of *House Beautiful* contained an advertisement for a Keystone Fire Department. The lithographed Masonite building had two garage doors through which the plastic fire trucks could be ejected, using spring-loaded levers, at the rear of the station. The fire trucks could be filled with water to spray the two-dimensional burning warehouse. *Photograph by Suzanne Silverthorn.*

"Keystone Fire Department." The 1948 Keystone fire station is shown with its "burning" building and two fire trucks. This model was also available in a three-door version. The knob which opened the doors also activated an alarm bell. ($200-250). 9" high x 16" wide x 9" deep (at base). *Courtesy of Jim and Beverly Cox, Sussex Antique Toy Shop.*

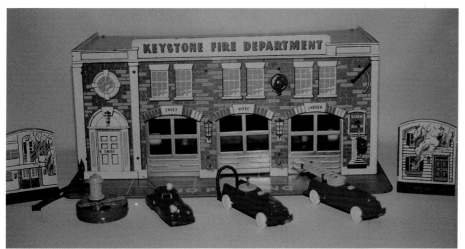

"Keystone Fire Department." A larger, perhaps updated, version by Keystone had three doors. The "burning houses" were originally punch-outs of the fire bay doors. Both of the trucks shown are marked "KEYSTONE MADE IN U.S.A." The fire chief sedan is made by and marked "Thomas" underneath. Unbroken vehicles are very difficult to locate. ($300-350). The burning houses are 3" x 4". The station is 7.25" high x 17" wide x 10" deep (including platform). *Courtesy of Charles Donovan.*

"De Luxe Fire Department." At first glance, this station would appear to have been made by Keystone, but closer examination reveals differences. It is made of Tekwood, the three-ply material used by the De Luxe Game Corporation. And, of course, the name on the front is an indisputable clue. This structure has three bays for fire trucks, but there are only two spring-load devices at the back for ejecting the (now missing) trucks. All three doors open together when a crank on the right side is turned. The building is set on a .75" high base which includes a ramp at the front to speed the fire trucks to their destination. The fire department came with a Tekwood facade of a burning house. The "flames" shown through the windows are mounted on dowels which allow them to drop out of sight when hit by a fire hose. ($200-250). The fire department is 10.5" high and sets on a base 18.75" wide x 15" deep. The house is 10.5" high and stands in a wood base. *Photograph by Patty Cooper.*

Wyandotte "Toytown Fire Dept." This lithographed metal building was advertised in the 1951 Sears catalog for $1.19. It originally came with a 5.5" long plastic fire truck that had a revolving aerial ladder on top. The station is made of lithographed steel. ($85-95). 4.75" high x 6.5" wide x 8" deep. *Photograph by Suzanne Silverthorn.*

"Fire Dept. No. 9." The Gaston Manufacturing Company of Cincinnati, Ohio made these "Changeable Building Blocks" of lithographed paper over wood. The blocks could be assembled to make four different buildings including this fire department. The set of twenty blocks was copyrighted 1953. In addition to the blocks, there were roof pieces, chimneys, and gables. The blocks could also be reassembled to make a service station, log house, or colonial home. ($50-75). When assembled as a fire station, the blocks formed a structure 5" high x 5.5" wide x 9" long. *Courtesy of Gene and Arliss Morris. Photograph by Gene Morris.*

Marx "Vol. Fire Dept." In the 1950s, the Louis Marx Company made a series of plastic buildings which were very similar to Plasticville. Like the Plasticville buildings, these were in a scale appropriate for train layouts. The fire house shown came with a plastic fire engine, three fire fighters in different positions, and a Dalmatian. ($45-65). 6" high x 8.5" wide x 4.5" deep. *Courtesy of Ruth Petros.*

77

Plasticville "Fire Dept. Kit FH-4." The Bachmann Brothers fire house had two red, opening doors. It was made in the mid-1950s and some of the sets included a fire truck. The plastic walls and roof snapped together to form a building with no floor. ($35-40). Box measures 7" x 6.5" x 2". The building is 5" high x 7" wide x 6.5" deep. *Courtesy of Gary Mosholder. Photograph by Jacob Dohm.*

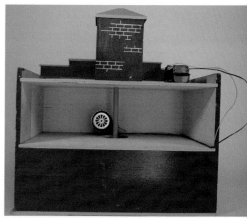

F.A.O. Schwarz "Fire Department." The 1963 F.A.O. Schwarz Christmas catalog described the inside of their fire station as having "a fire pole and furnished second floor: table and four chairs, refrigerator, stove, rocking chair, and four cots." *Courtesy of Lois L. Freeman.*

F.A.O.Schwarz "Fire Department." The high quality and detail of this wood fire department make it seem older than it actually is. It was advertised in the 1963 F.A.O. Schwarz Christmas catalog for $24.75. The fire station was described as "complete with battery-powered electric siren and flashing alarm light." The "friction-powered fire fighting fleet" included a metal ladder truck, pumper, chief's car, and ambulance, with sirens. ($500-600). 16" high x 16" wide x 12.5" deep. *Courtesy of Lois L. Freeman.*

Police Stations

The toy community must have been extremely law-abiding for very few police stations, jails, or courthouses were manufactured. Marx made a small, box-like police station of lithographed metal as part of their circa 1920s Hometown series. It depicts a cut-out metal officer looming over a small man at a desk. A 1953 Alden's catalog advertised a lithographed metal "Dick Tracy police station" apparently made by Marx. It was a simple, garage-like structure with a hipped roof. Like the "Magic" barn, garage, and fire station produced by Marx, the police station included a vehicle (in this case, a "riot car") which shot through the doors when a crank was turned. The set sold for $1.95.

Above: Marx "Home Town Police Station." The circa 1930s police station was sold as part of a series that included a lithographed metal bank, fire house, and several different stores. The exterior of the buildings were not lithographed. In addition to the uniformed officer looming over a small man lithographed at a desk, the movable accessories included a policeman on a motorcycle and two other flat metal people. ($125-150). 3.25" high x 5" long x 2.75" deep. *Photograph by Patty Cooper.*

Left: "Plasticville Police Dep't. Kit PD-3." Bachmann Brothers made almost every type building needed to create a realistic community for a train layout. The police department kit included colored plastic pieces which snapped together to form a station with four walls and a hipped roof. The roof antenna and lights on each side of the opening front door are often missing. The police station was sold during the 1950s. ($40-50). Box measures 6.5" x 7" x 2". Station measures 4.5" high x 7" wide x 6.5" deep. *Courtesy of Gary Mosholder. Photograph by Jacob Dohm.*

Post Offices

A post office toy offers unlimited potential for educational play but, surprisingly, few were made. Milton Bradley offered at least two versions of the Toy Town Post Office in the early 1900s, but they were little more than nicely boxed sets of envelopes, post cards, and stamps with no architectural interest. The Wolverine Company made a folding metal post office with play envelopes, stamps, and other accessories in the 1940s. Plasticville provided the only known example that actually resembled a post office building of its time, circa 1950s.

Milton Bradley "Toy Town Post Office." The Milton Bradley Company of Springfield, Massachusetts made one of the few known toy post offices. This boxed set has no architectural interest but provided postcards, envelopes, stamps, and rubber stamps "For Busy Boys and Girls." The interior of the box has a copyright date of 1909. It also contained the warning that letters must not be dropped in real letter boxes: "we must not forget that we are only playing at Post Office." ($150). Box measures 10.5" high x 7.5" wide x 1" deep. *Photograph by Patty Cooper.*

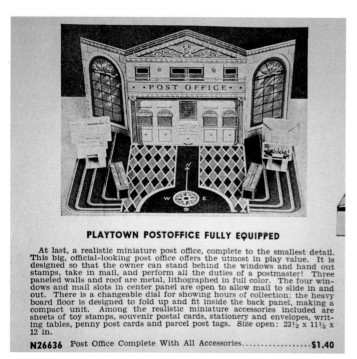

PLAYTOWN POSTOFFICE FULLY EQUIPPED

At last, a realistic miniature post office, complete to the smallest detail. This big, official-looking post office offers the utmost in play value. It is designed so that the owner can stand behind the windows and hand out stamps, take in mail, and perform all the duties of a postmaster! Three paneled walls and roof are metal, lithographed in full color. The four windows and mail slots in center panel are open to allow mail to slide in and out. There is a changeable dial for showing hours of collection; the heavy board floor is designed to fold up and fit inside the back panel, making a compact unit. Among the realistic miniature accessories included are sheets of toy stamps, souvenir postal cards, stationery and envelopes, writing tables, penny post cards and parcel post tags. Size open: 22½ x 11½ x 12 in.

N26636 Post Office Complete With All Accessories..............$1.40

The 1940 John Plain catalog advertised a "Playtown Post office Fully Equipped" for $1.40. Although not named, it is obvious that the set is a Wolverine product, very similar to the grocery stores manufactured during the same period. The catalog copy states that the post office was designed so that the owner could stand behind the windows and "perform all the duties of a postmaster!" *Courtesy of Marge Meisinger. Photograph by Suzanne Silverthorn.*

Plasticville "U.S. Post Office Kit PO-1." This set by Bachmann Brothers bears a patent date of June 17, 1952. Plastic pieces snapped together to form a building with four walls and a roof. There are paper inserts for the windows. The two porch lights and the flag are separate pieces often missing from the set. ($25-35). 3.5" high x 9" wide x 4" deep. The box measures 10" x 4.25" x 1.75". *Courtesy of Gary Mosholder.*

 Wolverine "Post Office." Made of lithographed metal, the post office could be folded for storage. It featured a changeable dial for showing business hours, four windows, and mail slots. The original accessories included sheets of toy stamps, post cards, stationery, envelopes, writing tables, and parcel post tags. The post office is a difficult piece to find. ($300-350). 12" high x 22.5" wide x 11.5" deep. *Courtesy of Ray and Gail Carey.*

V. Goods and Services

Stores and Banks

Children have always loved to "play store" whether it was a commercially manufactured toy or one constructed of orange crates and tin cans. The lessons to be learned from the experience were many. Counting skills were enhanced by using play money to make change and writing skills practiced by making signs. Most children didn't think of these advantages, they just knew they were imitating grown ups—and that it was fun.

However, the commercial potential of a miniature store was clear to manufacturers who began producing them in Germany in the late 1800s. These stores are mainly of two types: Roomboxes, similar to the German kitchens produced at the same time, with three sides, a floor, and an open front or simple structures consisting of a set of shelves filled with goods. Like the toy kitchens, the German stores were often larger in size than the standard dollhouse scales. The shops were modeled on the retail establishments of the period including general stores, milliner's, bakeries, grocery stores, butchers, drug stores, and drapers. Many German firms produced shops of this type, most notably Moritz Gottschalk and Christian Hacker.

Although all of these shops have charm and interest, it is often difficult to know whether the contents are original or not, a factor which makes them difficult to price. If a shop has changed hands many times in the last seventy-five to a hundred years, it is likely that pieces have been lost and were replaced by items available at the time. Those shops that have remained in a museum or in the possession of the same family are more likely to be in original condition. It should also be noted that some of the shops advertised in *The Universal Toy Catalog*, such as those offered by Paul Leonhardt, are depicted without accessories. Such a toy, sold empty, might still be accurately described as "original." These shops have gotten very expensive, often ranging from $3,000-7,0000 or more.

By the late 1800s, toy manufacturers in the United States had also begun producing retail stores of various kinds. Stirn and Lyon of New York patented a grocery store in 1892. Whitney Reed of Leominster, Massachusetts added shops to their line, circa 1900, including a meat market, grocery store, and coal yard. R. Bliss Manufacturing Company of Pawtucket, Rhode Island patented a toy grocery store in 1895 which was still being sold in 1901.

N.D. Cass of Athol, Massachusetts offered a grocery store, circa 1914, that consisted of a few shelves filled with oversized

products. This simple toy was sold by Butler Brothers for a wholesale price of $1.00 per dozen. Similar "Toy Town" grocery stores were made by Parker Brothers in a variety of sizes. The groceries which were sold with these stores were based on real products of the period, including Dunham's Coconut, Arm & Hammer baking soda, and Post Toasties.

In the 1930s, the Louis Marx Company made several different commercial establishments as part of their Hometown series. These tiny structures were lithographed metal boxes with three walls and a floor. They were sold furnished with simple, lithographed counters, customers, and other accessories appropriate to the type of business. The series included a drug store, meat market, and various department stores, probably named after the retailers who sold them.

Wolverine produced several different grocery stores and a drugstore in the 1930s. They were made of metal with three sections which could be folded for storage. Depending on the model, either the two side pieces or the back held shelves with boxes of goods modeled after real products. Some of the products were large enough for a human rather than a doll. The stores came with metal counters, cash registers, and other accessories which are often missing when found by collectors.

A series of folding cardboard stores was produced in the 1940s, apparently as premiums for large grocery chains. These stores have been found with the following names: A&P, Acme, Albers, Colonial, Fisher Foods, Grand Union, Safeway, Super Valu, and Wegmans. The opened stores offered four square feet of play space. They came with coupons which could be used to order additional accessories.

In the 1950s and later, Playtown manufactured a series of stores made of wood. Most of these were simple structures with only a section of shelves and possibly a counter, although Playtown also produced larger, room-box type stores. The company also made food, of cardboard or plaster, to be sold in the stores. These items can still be found on the original cards and can make a nice collection by themselves or be used with dollhouses.

In the 1950s, the Kiddie Brush and Toy Company of Jonesville, Michigan produced a grocery store of lithographed metal, which is now highly collectible. "Susy's Superette" reflected the modern grocery stores of its day and included lots of plastic display cases, shopping carts, check out counters, and other accessories which gave it great play value.

German Store. This circa 1890-1900 store was probably made by the German firm of Moritz Gottschalk for the American or English market. The red drawers on the back wall have porcelain labels with English words identifying their contents, e.g. macaroons, sugar, rice, coffee, tea, and chocolate. Above the drawers, a clock forms the center-piece of an elaborate pediment. *Courtesy of Joan and Gaston Majeune, Toys in the Attic. Photograph by Renee Majeune.*

German Store. Possibly made by Christian Hacker, this store resembles one advertised in the 1902 Gamages catalog. It is notable for the natural oak which has mellowed to a golden patina. There are two glazed display windows with wooden blinds that can be raised and lowered. Porcelain labels identify the contents of drawers. ($5200-5800). 14" high x 33" long x 14" deep. *Courtesy of Joan and Gaston Majeune, Toys in the Attic. Photograph by Renee Majeune.*

Christian Hacker Grocery Store. This grocery shop, marked with the Hacker logo under the base, was made for an English-speaking market, circa 1900. Elaborate transfer designs decorate the drawer fronts and the display cases which flank the opening. ($5000-6000). *Private collection.*

German "Rolf-Ute Wasch." An unusual laundry is made of wood and retains its original blue and white paint. A blue metal money box with German coins is on one of the shelves. There are boxes of detergent and labeled drawers. ($1000-1200). 15" high x 20.25" wide x 6.75" deep. *Courtesy of Linda Hanlon.*

German Pastry Shop. This German shop, circa 1900, has lace-trimmed shelves to hold plaster cakes and pastries. *Courtesy of Joan and Gaston Majeune, Toys in the Attic. Photograph by Renee Majeune.*

German "Kaufhaus." This German emporium is made of wood and retains its original paint. It was purchased in Germany. ($1200-1600). 14.5" high x 20" wide x 7.25" deep. *Courtesy of Linda Hanlon.*

German Apothecary Shop. The maker of this German shop has not been identified. The central opening is flanked by glazed display cases with engaged, turned columns. The nine drawers on the back wall are made of heavy zinc and painted blue. The movable counter has a wood top with a slot to receive coins which can be retrieved from the drawer below. The doll in the photograph is from the 1930s. ($5600-6000). 14" high x 25" wide x 18" deep. *Courtesy of Joan and Gaston Majeune, Toys in the Attic. Photograph by Renee Majeune.*

German Apothecary Shop. Another German store, which appears to be an apothecary shop, features a unusual stairway on the left side, perhaps leading to the unseen laboratory or residence of the proprietor. *Courtesy of Joan and Gaston Majeune, Toys in the Attic. Photograph by Renee Majeune.*

Christian Hacker Shop. Marked with the maker's name on the bottom, this shop is simple in construction, but features an elaborate lithographed mural on each side of the center opening. An oversize scale dominates the center counter and may indicate that it was intended to be an apothecary shop. The drawers are labeled in German, French, and English. *Private collection.*

Gottschalk Butcher Shop. A circa 1890 "Blue Roof" butcher shop still has its original plaster meats. The lithographed paper over wood shop has no number or markings on its base. ($1500-1800). 7.5" high x 6.5" wide x 3" deep. *Courtesy of Lois Freeman.*

Christian Hacker "Butcher's Shop." This German store was obviously made for the English-speaking market. Under the base, it is marked 155/2, "Made in Germany" with the Christian Hacker logo. ($10,000). 15.5" high x 19.5" wide x 12.5" deep. *Courtesy of David Pressland.*

F.A.O. Schwarz "Groceries." This slightly larger grocery store is apparently part of the same series as the Toy Shop produced by Christian Hacker for the American market. *Courtesy of Toy and Miniature Museum of Kansas City. Photograph by Tom Moulis.*

F.A.O.Schwarz "Toy Shop." This is believed to be part of a series of shops made by the German firm of Christian Hacker. Similar stores are discussed in *Dollhouses in America* by Flora Gill Jacobs. Mrs. Jacobs found the stores in a 1918 F.A.O. Schwarz catalog where they were advertised in several different sizes. The shop has papered walls and flooring. The lettering is reverse painted on the window. ($1500-2000). 14.5" high x 13" wide x 10.5" deep. *Courtesy of Lois L. Freeman.*

German Store. A more modern-looking store, circa 1930s, has drawers with wood fronts and metal pulls. The maker is unknown but the metal labels are printed in German. ($750-900). *Courtesy of Ruth Petros.*

German Store. This store appears to have been made by the same manufacturer as the one in the previous photograph. The front of the store is open for play, but dolls enter through the two swinging doors on right side.

The wood-fronted drawers have German labels which read salz (salt), zucker (sugar), bonbon (candy), mehl (flour), tee (tea), and griess (groats).

The rounded celluloid windows of the display cases and the shape of the clock give the store a modernistic look, typical of the 1930s. The store is made of a floor and three walls which can be assembled by dowels and pre-drilled holes. The movable counter holds a wood scale and cash register made of a plastic material. ($800-1000). 10" high x 24" wide x 11.5" deep. *Photograph by Patty Cooper.*

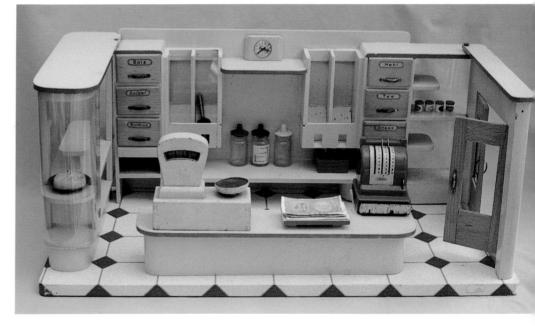

Pet's Grocery. Several variations of the Pet's Grocery were made by Ralph Dunn, of London, circa 1910. The exterior is a rather unimpressive crate, but when the front is folded down, a grocery is revealed with lithographed floor, built-in shelves, and sales counter. *Courtesy of Gaston and Joan Majeune, Toys in the Attic. Photograph by Renee Majeune.*

"Pet's Toy Grocery Store." A slightly different Pet's Grocery, circa 1900, is also a fold-down room made of wood. This model has a beaded wood trim, lithographed flooring, and many tins of foodstuffs. 20" high x 24" wide x 16" deep. *Courtesy of Gloria Hinkel and Beverly J. Thomes, Delaware Toy Museum.*

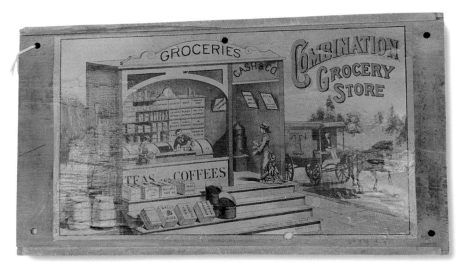

Stirn & Lyon Combination Grocery Store. The grocery came unassembled in a wood box, circa 1894. The box was used to form the base of the store. Other pieces of unpainted wood were made to fit together with dowels and pegs. Some of the pieces are stained with a reddish pigment. ($1500). The assembled store is 21" high x 18" wide x 14" deep. *Courtesy of Linda and Carl Thomas, Jr.*

W.S. Reed Meat Market. Although this store is not marked, it was probably made by the Whitney S. Reed Company of Leominster, Massachusetts. The pattern of brick and stone is obviously by the same artist who designed several of the known Reed dollhouses. According to Flora Gill Jacobs, in *Dollhouses in America*, the Reed company advertised a "'well-furnished' meat market" in their 1897 catalog. It featured block-like meats and poultry and had a cloth awning that could be operated by turning a knob on the side of the buildings. It was 12" high x 12" wide. *Courtesy of Jim Yeager.*

Bliss Grocery Store #347. The number on the edges of the lithographed papers suggests that it was introduced circa 1897. The store originally had a striped cardboard awning and overhanging roof edges. Although made by Bliss, the Bakery counter is not original to the store. It is marked 243, a number which coincides with the three-piece Dollyville set shown in the 1896 catalog. The Dollyville set included a grocery, opera house, and drug store. The opening front door has a sign which reads "Fresh Dried Beef." Lithographed children peer out of the second and third story windows (although it is only a one story structure inside) giving the impression of a residence above the shop. ($450-600 in condition shown). 9.5" high x 8.25" wide x 6.5" deep. *Photograph by Patty Cooper.*

"66" by the "Flemish Art Co. Flemish Quality, New York." The side of the boxy store has lithographed windows with fishscale shingles above them. The windows advertise "Fine Grocery" and "Vegetables." ($1200-1400). 9.5" high x 10" wide x 3.25" deep. *Courtesy of Marge Powell.*

When the double doors on the front of the Flemish Art Co. store are swung open, part of the floor drops down to create a room. The movable lithographed counter has a lithographed proprietor waiting to serve and one shelf which holds groceries. *Courtesy of Marge Powell.*

"Little Toy Town Grocery Store." Parker Brothers Inc. of Salem, Mass., New York, and London made this set circa 1900-1910. When the lithographed box cover is removed, the bottom of the box becomes the simple store with two shelves containing products from the period. These include Dunham's Cocoanut, Post Toasties, and Fleischmann's Yeast. ($200-250). 8.75" high x 11" wide x 2.5" deep. *Photograph by Patty Cooper.*

Toy Town Grocery Store. A larger version, also by Parker Brothers, contains many of the same products. This version appears to be older, perhaps circa 1900. ($650-800). *Courtesy of Gaston and Joan Majeune, Toys in the Attic. Photograph by Renee Majeune.*

Libby's Food Store. This cardboard store was offered by the Libby's Food Company as an advertising promotion circa 1923. ($200-250). 13.25" high x 17.75" wide x 5.5" deep. *Courtesy of Marcie Tubbs. Photograph by Bob Tubbs.*

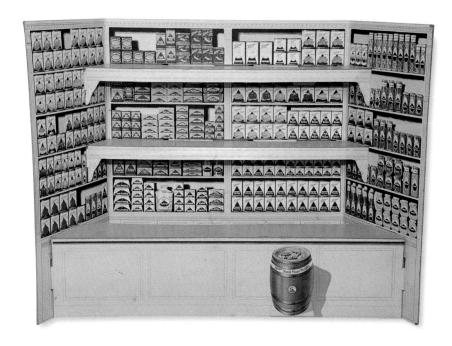

Marx "Home Town Drug Store" and "Home Town Meat Market." Both stores were lithographed metal boxes with three walls and a floor. The stores were sold individually, in sets of four, or as an 8-piece village. Sears advertised the village set for 59 cents in 1931. They are similar to the Marx Newlywed rooms also sold during the 1930s.

The Drug Store has an apothecary cabinet and pharmacist lithographed on the back wall. The movable counter shows a variety of potions and three eager clerks. There is a lunch counter lithographed on one of the side walls. Originally, the separate metal pieces for the Drug Store would have included a table and stools, as well as the counter shown. The Meat Market has a butcher and various cuts of meat lithographed on the back wall. In addition to the metal counter, with the three aproned butchers, the set contained metal stools, a refrigerator, and possibly some customers. ($150-200). 3.5" high x 5" long x 2.5" deep. *Courtesy of Marge Powell.*

Marx "F.W. Woolworth Co." and "Savings Bank." The Home Town series by Marx included several variety stores with different names. In addition to the Woolworth's shown, some were marked "Kresge" and "S.H. Kress & Co." Although the names on the top were changed, all of the variety stores had a sales counter lithographed on the back wall with four columns in the background, giving the illusion of a vast shopping space. A removable metal counter included a sales clerk behind signs which say "toys" and "candy." Some lithographed, flat, metal customers probably were included with the original set.

The Savings Bank has a counter with several tellers and customers lithographed on the back wall. The movable metal counter has two teller windows, one for "paying" and one for "receiving." It is likely that the bank also included metal customers. ($150-200). 3.25" high x 5" long x 2.75" deep. *Courtesy of Marge Powell.*

"Pillsbury Play Bakery Action Cutouts." The paper bakery set was made as an advertising promotion for Pillsbury Flour Mills Co. of Minneapolis, circa 1936. It was produced for Pillsbury by the American Advertising & Research Corp. of Chicago. This set is marked "Form No. 2342." *Courtesy of Mineral Point Toy Museum. Photograph by Carol Stevenson.*

The Pillsbury Play Bakery included six pages of cutouts with a separate sheet showing a diagram of how to assemble the bakery. There were also booklets entitled "How Bread is Baked & Sold, a Step-by Step Story of Baking," and "Little Lessons in Salesmanship." *Courtesy of Mineral Point Toy Museum. Photograph by Carol Stevenson.*

TOY GROCERY STORE WITH MERCHANDISE

A large toy grocery store for girls and boys. As realistic as an up-to-date grocery store! Strong metal construction, enameled in colors. The shelves are filled with miniature packages of popular grocery merchandise, the counter is metal, with a miniature scale, a dial telephone, and an order pad. There is a wrapping roll with real paper to wrap up bundles. Supply of metal money for making change! Counter 16 in. long. Overall size open 31 in. wide, 14½ in. high. (Base illustrated not included.)

G26072   PRICE..$2.25

The 1937 John Plain catalog advertised a "Toy Grocery Store with Merchandise" with the name "Corner Grocer." It was made of metal and enameled in bright colors. The sides of the toy opened out and held a variety of miniature packages which used real brand names. A separate metal counter was provided with a scale, dial telephone, paper dispenser, order pad, and play money. It sold for $2.25. *Courtesy of Marge Meisinger. Photograph by Suzanne Silverthorn.*

Wolverine "Corner Grocer." The box of the Corner Grocer identifies it as No. 182, made by the Wolverine Supply & Mfg. Co., of Pittsburgh, Pennsylvania. The box measures 16" x 12" x 3" and depicts 19 food items. *Courtesy of Mineral Point Toy Museum. Photograph by Carol Stevenson.*

Wolverine "Corner Grocer." When the sides of the Wolverine Corner Grocer were opened out, it created a store with shelves large enough to house some nearly full-sized products. The doll is not original to the set. (Boxed store $750-900). The opened store measures 14.5" high x 31" wide. *Courtesy of Mineral Point Toy Museum. Photograph by Carol Stevenson.*

Wolverine "General Grocery." This set was advertised in the 1941/42 catalog of the N. Shure Company of Chicago. A similar drugstore by Wolverine was shown on the same page. The General Grocery was a variation of the Corner Grocer, with the shelves at the back of the store and lithographed people on the opening "wings."

Separate pieces included a counter, dial telephone, scale, paper dispenser, play money, and packages. The products to be sold in the store were modeled after real brands. There is a movable metal awning beneath the "General Grocery" sign. The counter is missing from this set. (With counter $600-800). The store is 11.5" high x 10.5" wide x 2.5" deep when folded for storage. *Courtesy of Jim and Shirley Cox.*

"Wolverine Super-Service Market." While still using the same basic construction, Wolverine updated the design of their store. The well-stocked, wide aisles lithographed on the back wall are more modern than the earlier general stores and reflect the supermarkets of the 1940s and beyond. The packaging of the products was also updated. Some, like the Lava soap and Good and Plenty candies, are nearly full-sized. Although the lithography has been simplified, there is still a counter with a paper dispenser, dial telephone, and scale. ($400-500). 14.5" high x 25.5" wide x 8.5" deep. *Courtesy of Marcie Tubbs. Photograph by Bob Tubbs.*

Left: A generic envelope, like this one, held folding cardboard "playstores" printed with a variety of retailers' names. The stores were intended as promotions for several different grocery chains including A&P, Acme, Albers, Colonial, Fisher Foods, Grand Union, Safeway, Super Valu, and Wegmans. The same company is also believed to have produced a cardboard Rexall drugstore.

Accessories for the folding playstores could be ordered by mailing in labels from twelve specified products, along with coupons supplied with the set, to the manufacturer in Brooklyn, New York. Available accessories included a store manager's apron, toy turnstiles, hand truck, Swift delivery truck, cardboard people, shopping carts, personalized hand stamp, play money, cleaning equipment, baked goods, store manager's hat, and an accessory kit with scale, cash register, and clock. *Photograph by Suzanne Silverthorn.*

Below: "Acme Super Markets" Playstore. The folding playstore was made of cardboard, printed inside and out. It was sold circa 1940s. ($175-200). 11" high x 23.75" wide x 20" deep. *Photograph by Suzanne Silverthorn.*

The Acme Playstore had a brightly printed interior which showed various departments with groceries on the shelves. Accessories could be ordered by using coupons provided with the set. The many accessories included signs, displays of groceries, customers, and play money. Most of the items were made of flat pieces of printed cardboard, rather than being three-dimensional. ($175-200). 11" high x 23.75" wide x 20" deep. *Photograph by Suzanne Silverthorn.*

"A&P." A nearly identical folding playstore was made for the A&P grocery chain circa 1940s. ($175-200). 11" high x 23.75" wide x 20" deep. *Courtesy of Marcie Tubbs. Photograph by Bob Tubbs.*

The 1947 Sears catalog offered a "Super Market" for $3.98. According to the catalog copy, it was made of "Tekwood" (3-ply wood-centered fiberboard). The front of the store could be lifted to provide play access. The store was also open from the top. It is possible that this store was made by the De Luxe Game Corporation, a company which produced Tekwood dollhouses and gas stations, also sold through Sears. *Photograph by Suzanne Silverthorn.*

"Super Market." The Tekwood "Super Market" was made in a scale of a little less than 1" equals a foot. There was a cloth awning which could be rolled up and a transparent window in the front. The facade was printed with a brick pattern. ($200-250). 14" high x 19" long x 16" deep. *Courtesy of Lois L. Freeman.*

The entire front of the "Super Market" could be removed to allow the young shopkeeper to stock the shelves. The transparent window in front of the dairy and frozen foods case could be raised and lowered. The display cases, scales, and cash register were all made of cardboard over wood. Cardboard hams were hung from the wall on the right side of the store. 14" high x 19" wide x 16" deep. *Courtesy of Linda Boltrek.*

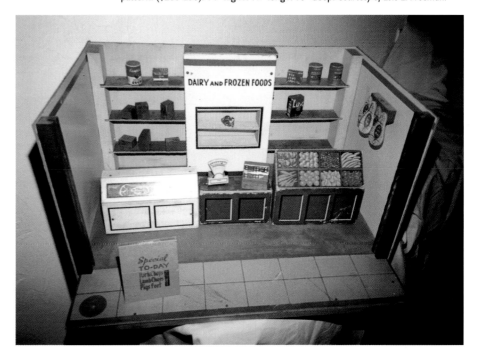

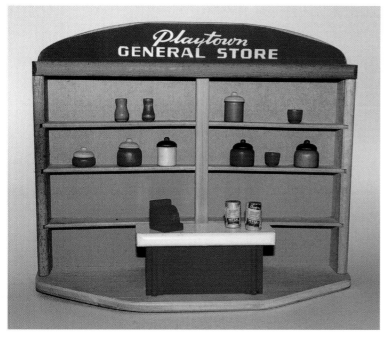

Above: "Playtown General Store." This variation offers twice the shelf space of the previous stores. It is made of wood with a cardboard back. The wood cash register and wood containers appear to be similar to those sold by Grandmother Stover. ($75-100). 8.75" high x 10.75" wide x 3.75" deep. *Courtesy of Lois L. Freeman.*

Right: "Playtown Grocery Store." The original box enhances the value of this simple Playtown Grocery Store. Apparently, it never had a counter or cash register, but the graphics of the box and printed sale signs make it an interesting toy. ($100-125). 15" high x 23" wide x 7.75" deep. *Courtesy of Ray and Gail Carey.*

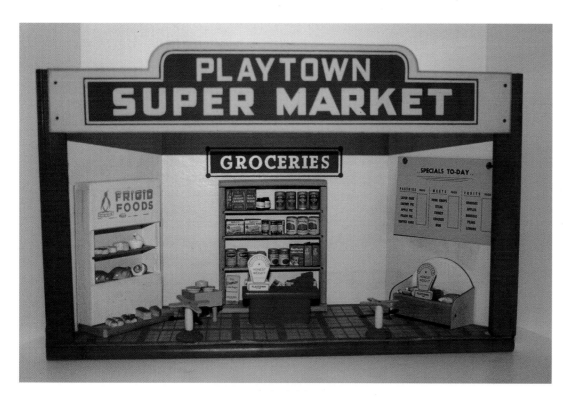

"Playtown Super Market." It is believed that this large Playtown Super Market was sold by Sears in the 1950s. Unlike the Playtown stores previously shown, this is a self-contained room box, reminiscent of the German grocery stores from the early 1900s.

This set contains two sections of shelving, one for "Frigid Foods" and one for "Groceries." There is also a counter with cardboard scale and a vegetable case. The "specials today" sign on the wall provides space for a child to set the prices. ($200-250). *Courtesy of Ray and Gail Carey.*

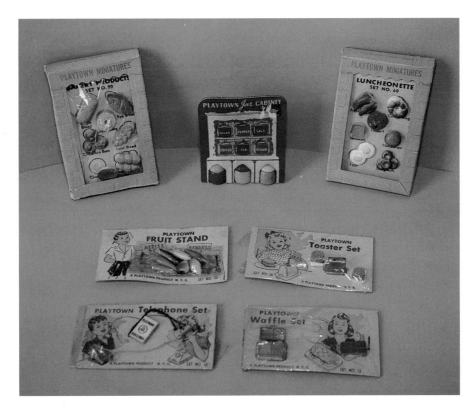

Playtown sold a wide variety of accessories for the late 1940s stores. The boxed sets have cellophane windows. The cards are either wrapped in cellophane or have cellophane bags attached. All are marked "A Playtown Product. N.Y.C." ($15-30 each). *Courtesy of Marcie Tubbs. Photograph by Bob Tubbs.*

"Tri-ang Stores." Tri-ang, the English firm owned by Lines Brothers, advertised two different stores in their 1951/52 catalog. The larger one, shown here, included a flat above the shop. There are two curved display windows in front and a revolving door. The metal windows on the second store actually open. ($900-1200). 21.5" long. *Courtesy of George Mundorf.*

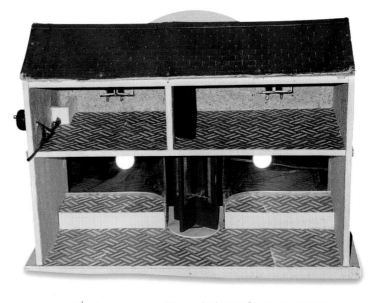

The interior of the Tri-ang store has lithographed paper flooring in a parquet pattern and electric lights. There is one large room on the first floor for the sales area and a two room flat upstairs. The Tri-ang store came fully furnished with display cases. Originally, it also had a mail box and a telephone booth. *Courtesy of George Mundorf.*

For "Grown-up" Play
GIFTS TO WIN A LITTLE GIRL'S HEART

SUSY'S SUPERETTE ... STOCKED WITH "FOOD" 2.69

A FOR A LITTLE GIRL'S SHOPPING PLEASURE. Cardboard "store," beautiful
tailed plastic produce case, check-out stand, cash register, shopping carts, b
polyethylene "people", produce, meats, canned goods. Nationally-known food
to fold, labels to paste on cans; price tags, display cards for the day's "best buys
48 T 4511—All in realistic colors. Store, 13½x8½x6 in. Ship. wt. 2 lbs.........

TRUE-TO-LIFE DOLL HOUSE ACCESSORIES 89c

B MINIATURE TABLEWARE, assorted color
plastic: Set of dishes for 3; plus knives,
forks, spoons; tray, tea set, vases, candle-
sticks, cradle 'phone, books in bookends.
48 T 4512—Ship. wt. 4 oz....31-Pc. Set 89c

C MINIATURE UTENSILS, APPLIANCES, as-
sort-color plastic. Wee kettle, boiler with
removable lid, mixer with removable bowl

D "FAMILY" fits furniture in F
opp. pg. Tinted plastic. Father,
er, Brother, Sister can sit, kneel,
jointed at waist, knees, shoulder. B
arms, legs move. Father, 4¼ in.
48 T 4480—Wt. 5 oz.......5-Pc. S

E MINIATURE TABLE LAMPS
light when you turn shade. P

The Montgomery Ward Christmas catalog for 1956 featured a "Susy's Superette" which appears to have been made by Kiddie Brush and Toy Company, also known as Susy Goose. The Ward's store sold for $2.69 and was made of cardboard with a plastic produce case, check-out stand, cash register, shopping carts, people, and groceries. It also included "nationally-known" food boxes which could be folded, with labels to paste on them. *Courtesy of Marge Meisinger. Photograph by Suzanne Silverthorn.*

"Friendly Folks Super Market." This lithographed metal supermarket by Kiddie Brush and Toy Company of Jonesville, Michigan, may be one of the most difficult to find playsets. The company, better known as Susy Goose, also made a "Friendly Folks" motel and a dairy barn. According to *Plastic Figure & Playset Collector*, Susy Goose produced several small sets which included pieces from the complete Friendly Folks store. It was introduced in the mid-1950s. 20" high x 33" wide x 18.25" deep (at base). *Courtesy of Plastic Figure and Playset Collector Magazine. c1997.*

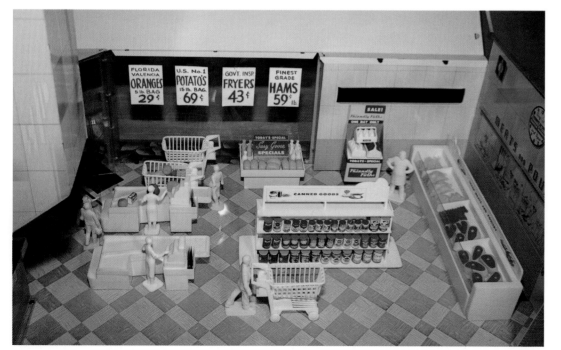

The interior of the Friendly Folks Super Market was highly detailed from the yellow and orange tiled floor to the signs advertising specials in the windows. The set included numerous display cases, bins, and counters along with plastic shoppers with shopping carts. *Courtesy of Plastic Figure and Playset Collector Magazine c1997.*

A close-up of the "Meats and Poultry" case of the Susy Goose Friendly Folks Super Market begins to convey the detail with which the store was designed. The busy butchers lithographed on the back wall capture the feeling of a modern, sanitary 1950s supermarket and the plastic meats in the display case can all be rearranged to suit the young store managers. *Courtesy of Plastic Figure and Playset Collector Magazine c1997.*

Marx "Pet Shop." Part of the Marx Main Street USA series, the brightly lithographed Pet Shop was introduced in 1952 and retailed for $3.89. It featured transparent windows in which the thirty-one plastic pets could be displayed. Also included were eighteen accessories, fencing and four figures. ($400-450). 9" high x 15.75" wide x 8" deep. *Courtesy of Marcie Tubbs. Photograph by Bob Tubbs.*

"Keystone Lumber Yard." The Boston firm of Keystone may have been the only company to produce a lumber yard. The circa 1950s toy was made of pressed board and included pieces of lumber and a wood truck. ($275). 9" high x 16" wide x 12" deep. *Photograph by Patty Cooper.*

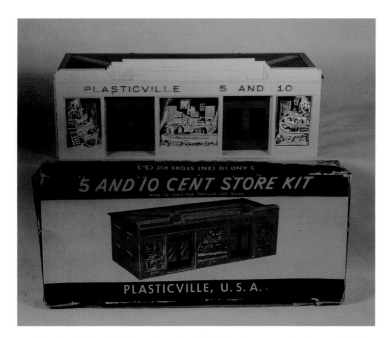

Plasticville "5 and 10 Cent Store Kit CS-5." The box states that this was "Made to scale for popular size trains" by Bachmann Bros., Inc., Philadelphia, PA. It also supplies the patent date of June 17, 1952. Plastic pieces snapped together to form the store and three paper inserts were supplied for window displays. ($25). 3.5" high x 9" wide x 4" deep. *Courtesy of Gary Mosholder. Photograph by Jacob Dohm.*

Plasticville "Supermarket Kit SM." Bachmann Bros., Inc. of Philadelphia patented this set June 17, 1952. The original price tag on the box says 89 cents. The set contains plastic pieces which snap together to form the store. There is also one paper insert for the front window. ($30-35). 7. 5" high x 9" wide x 5" deep. *Courtesy of Gary Mosholder. Photograph by Jacob Dohm.*

Plasticville "Bank, set number 1901 149." The Bachmann Brothers bank featured a "Car Banking Service" window on the side. It was made in the mid-1950s. ($40-50). 6" high x 8" wide (including teller window overhang) x 6" deep. Box measures 7" x 6.25" x 2". *Courtesy of Gary Mosholder. Photograph by Patty Cooper.*

Warehouses and Office Buildings

Several companies made warehouses to store the goods which supplied the toy community. At the beginning of the twentieth century, the American companies R. Bliss and Whitney S. Reed made warehouses of lithographed paper over wood. Similar warehouses were produced in Germany. *The Universal Toy Catalog of 1924-1926* shows warehouses by Moritz Gottschalk and another German firm, possibly Wagner.

In the late 1950s, Keystone, of Boston, manufactured a simple pressed board warehouse which consisted mainly of open shelves onto which a toy forklift could place boxes. Much more impressive was the lithographed metal skyscraper produced by Marx during the same period. The multi-storied building was nearly three feet tall and included offices, retail space, and warehouse storage, all printed in great detail.

German Warehouse. This three story warehouse is made of lithographed paper over wood, probably by Moritz Gottschalk. Although unmarked, the boxes which furnish the set appear to be the same as those found with warehouses known to have been made by Gottschalk. ($1500-1800). *Courtesy of Joan and Gaston Majeune, Toys in the Attic. Photograph by Renee Majeune.*

Above: Gottschalk Warehouse # 4082. This tiny warehouse has printed papers which represent a transitional period for the Moritz Gottschalk company. Like the dollhouses, stables, and village from the same period, this structure is made of wood with exterior lithography intended to represent stucco. The roof is printed in a faux tile pattern. Each of the two stories has a set of opening doors. ($200-250 in condition shown). 13.5" high x 8" wide x 6" deep. *Photograph by Patty Cooper.*

Right: Gottschalk Warehouse #3634. Part of the series known to collectors as "Blue Roofs," this warehouse has the expected roof color and lithographed papers. A knob on the side can be used to lift packages. There is an opening door on each of the three levels and the corner posts are lathe-turned. ($1100). 15" high x 10" wide x 7.5" deep. *Photograph by Suzanne Silverthorn.*

Gottschalk Warehouse with Attached Stable. The roof color and presence of pressed cardboard window mullions indicate that this is part of the series known to collectors as "Red Roofs." It was made by the German firm of Moritz Gottschalk circa 1920s. The three-story, wood structure has a hinged front which opens to provide access to interior. ($1200-2000). 21.5" high x 16" wide x 7.25" deep. *Courtesy of Bill and Stevie Weart.*

Gottschalk Warehouse #3162. Another warehouse, marked Gottschalk on the bottom, is an amazing five stories tall. It has four sets of double doors and a single door in the gable. There is a pulley under the peak of the roof to lift boxes. The exterior is made of lithographed paper and there is a hinged front. ($2500-3000). 41.5" high x 17" wide x 12" deep. *Courtesy of Leslie and Joanne Payne.*

Bliss Warehouse. The lithographed paper over wood warehouse by Bliss has a patent date of March 12, 1895. There are opening doors on each of the three levels. The wood boxes and barrels, many of which are marked Bliss, can be loaded into the warehouse using the pulley attached under the front gable. 19" high x 18" wide x 5" deep. *Courtesy of The Wenham Museum, Wenham, MA. Photograph by Rob Huntley.*

Price Cut! Warehouse with Lift and Truck

Operation "Fun" . . loading and unloading 18-piece open-face warehouse set with rubber-tired mobile fork lift . . clicker crank, 3 pallets, 3 barrels, 2 blocks and 7 decorated fiberboard boxes . . plus realistic rubber-tired platform truck! Drawbar on truck attaches to fork lift. 15x3¾x14-in. high building of 3-ply board on wood frame with 12x16-in. Masonite Presdwood base. Easy to assemble.

49 N 5926—Shipping weight 6 lbs. Was $4.47. . . . . .Now **$3.77**

1958 Sears catalog advertised a wood and pressed board warehouse by Keystone. The toy included a fork lift which could be used to load and unload the 18 boxes in the set. It sold for $3.77. The same set was also advertised in the 1957 Sears catalog. *Photograph by Suzanne Silverthorn.*

"Keystone Warehouse." Although structurally little more than a set of shelves with a front yard, the lithographed boxes on the back wall give it the appearance of greater depth. The set included three pallets, three barrels, two blocks, and seven boxes, marked Keystone, which could be loaded onto the open shelves with the forklift. The platform truck could be attached to the forklift. ($200-250 with forklift). 14" high x 16" wide x 12" deep (at base). *Courtesy of Patty Cooper*

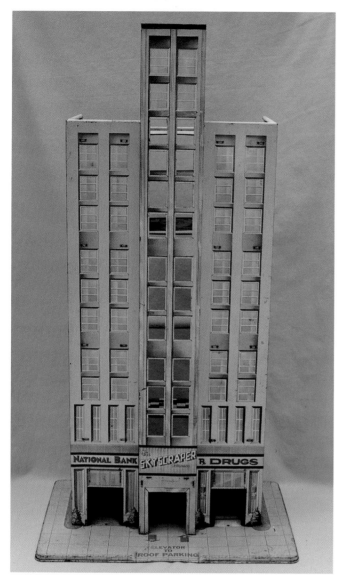

Marx Skyscraper. The 1957 Aldens Christmas catalog advertised this impressive building for $7.98. It was also sold by Wards in 1959. Towering more than three feet in height, the lithographed tin building featured a battery operated elevator to take the office workers from the roof-top parking to their offices. A working doorbell could be used to call the elevator. The building originally had two revolving doors on the main floor, metal awnings, and a plastic tower piece with radio/television mast. ($200 in condition shown). 32" high x 17" wide x 11" deep. *Photograph by Patty Cooper.*

Marx Skyscraper. Although the exterior lithography of the Marx Skyscraper gave the impression of a twelve story building, the interior contained only four playable levels. The first floor housed a bank and a drug store. The center portion was the lobby of the building which provided access to the elevator. The second floor contained two offices; the third had a gymnasium, called "Club rooms" in the catalog; and the fourth floor was a storage room or "Warehouse." In addition to the parking area, there was a helicopter pad on the roof. Original accessories included two cars, sixteen plastic figures approximately 2.25" (54mm) tall, and furniture for each of the businesses. *Photograph by Patty Cooper.*

Restaurants, Diners, and Motels

With the invention of the automobile, people began to travel more and this was reflected by an increase in the number of restaurants, diners, and motels. Inevitably, toy companies began making miniature versions. In the 1930s, the Louis Marx Company marketed a combination gas station and diner of lithographed metal called the "Roadside Rest Service Station." One of the T. Cohn (Superior) gas stations also included a lunch counter. In the 1950s, the Rich Toy Company offered a Masonite barbecue which included stools at a counter for patrons. Playtown made a wood hot dog stand, which was similar to their simple stores. Both Ideal and Bachmann Brothers (Plasticville) made small scale plastic diners. Remco made a diner as part of a larger playset in the 1970s.

One of the few known toy motels was issued in 1953 by the Kiddie Brush and Toy Company. It was called the "Friendly Folks Motel." Like their grocery store, the motel came with an extensive array of accessories which made it fun for children in the 1950s and exciting for collectors today. Other motel units were made in later years as part of playsets, but none were so large and elaborate as the Kiddie Brush example.

Playtown Hot Dog and Hamburger Stand. The original box identifies this wood structure as Set No. 530 by Playtown Products Co. Inc. of New York. The plaster and wood accessories illustrated on the box are the same as those shown with this set. ($150-175). *Courtesy of Lois L. Freeman.*

Ideal Diner. The plastic diner had a removable roof which provided access to the interior. Inside was a well-equipped counter with advertised specials written on the wall above. Four red stools were provided for diners. ($75-125). 4" high x 7" wide x 5.5" deep. *Courtesy of Ruth Petros.*

Plasticville "Diner Kit, No. DE-7." The box retains its original price tag of 89 cents. Made by Bachmann Brothers in the mid-1950s, the kit consisted of five plastic pieces which snapped together. The operable door welcomed O-scale compatible patrons to dine. ($25-30). 3" high x 9" wide x 3.25" deep. *Photograph by Suzanne Silverthorn.*

Rich "Bar B-Q." The Masonite barbecue by Rich Toys of Clinton, Iowa provides four stools for patrons at the service counters. It is back-opening with an operable front door. The door is the same as that used on many of the Rich dollhouses. ($175-200). 12.5" high x 21" wide x 11.25" deep (at base). *Courtesy of Mary Harris.*

Plasticville "Motel No. 1621." The box is marked "Bachmann Bros. Inc. Philadelphia, U.S.A. Scaled to O and S Gauge." The plastic motel is typical of the late 1950s with its salmon and white color scheme. Nine pieces snap together to form the motel with three operable doors. The paper flowers are easily lost and often missing from the set. ($20-25). The box measures 9.75" x 5.25" x 1.5". The motel is 2.25" high x 9.25" wide x 5" deep. *Courtesy of Gary Mosholder.*

"Friendly Folks Motel." Kiddie Brush and Toy Company, also known as Susy Goose, of Jonesville, Michigan manufactured the #777 motel in 1954. It was made of lithographed tin and shipped, unassembled, in a brown cardboard box which measured 18" x 33" x 3". The cover of the box featured a drawing of the motel, printed in blue and red, and noted that it was "Advertised in Life." A boy and girl are shown playing with the motel.

This unusual toy had an office with check-in counter and two motel rooms, each with their own bath. The office had a built-in lithographed counter with a plastic telephone and cash register. The set also contained oversized registration forms, big enough to substitute as sheets for the guest beds. There are three, free-standing metal and plastic signs advertising the motel's special features which included "Luxury-Rest Mattress," "Autronic Television," "Pure-Air Conditioning," "Warm-Air Radiant Heat," and "Lux-O Towels." ($450-500 with original box). 15" high x 32" wide x 18" deep. *Courtesy of Marcie Tubbs. Photograph by Bob Tubbs.*

The Susy Goose motel had a lithographed interior. One of the rooms is equipped with a lithographed kitchenette on one wall. Each of the motel rooms contained identical furniture but in contrasting colors, one set in ivory and the other in green. The plastic furnishings for each room included a double bed, television, armchair, luggage stand, baby crib, sink, toilet, two pillows, and stool.

There were six plastic figures, including a man, woman, girl with doll, boy and two babies. The father was a little over 3" tall and had hands that were made to fit the plastic suitcase handles. The guests arrived in a 9.5" long plastic car. *Courtesy of Marcie Tubbs. Photograph by Bob Tubbs.*

Entertainment

Theater and Television

Theaters have a special magic for children who have always loved to entertain each other and their parents. Several German companies, including Gottschalk and Christian Hacker, made toy theaters around the beginning of the twentieth century. Their toys were made of wood and painted or covered with lithographed paper. *The Universal Toy Catalog of 1924-26* shows a lithographed Opera, with that word printed above the stage in English, which came with pasteboard figures, scenery, and a book.

Montgomery Ward advertised a lithographed cardboard theater by McLoughlin Brothers in their 1903 catalog. It sold for 85 cents and had "American Theater" printed across the top of the curtain. It included a backdrop for the play "Little Red Riding Hood" along with three different scenes and figures to be cut out.

Tynietoy, of Rhode Island, made a high quality wood theater circa 1930s. It was named the "Peter Pan Theater" and could be taken apart for storage. It included lights, a drop curtain, and scenery. Tri-ang, of England, made an interesting wood theater around the same time, with battery-operated footlights and a velvet curtain. Another English company, Spears, made a cardboard Little Tots Theater as well as a Punch and Judy Puppet Theater.

With the development of motion pictures, stages were often replaced by movie screens and this was reflected in the toy world. The 1911 Bliss catalog shows a "Moving Picture House" marked "Tiny Town." It was said to be lithographed in five colors and to include a reel of pictures. Marx issued a movie theater made of metal as part of their Hometown series during the 1930s. It came with a paper "movie" which could be wound onto wood reels and viewed through a cut-out window. Many of the other motion picture theater toys were made of cardboard. Some were in book form, to be punched out and assembled. In 1959, Remco produced an unusual "Drive-In Movie Theater" complete with small cars, a projector, and film strips.

Television began making an impact on American culture in the 1950s. The Admiral Television Studio and Shirley Temple's TV Theater were both cardboard sets which allowed children to pretend to produce a television program.

German "Opera." This elaborate opera house is believed to have been manufactured by Moritz Gottschalk or possibly Christian Hacker, circa 1880s. It included a velvet curtain. 29.75" high x 26.25" wide x 20" deep. *Courtesy of Toy and Miniature Museum of Kansas City. Photograph by Tom Moulis.*

"Opera" Theater. This circa 1900 theater is probably German. It has lithographed stage scenery and a curtain that winds up. 24" high x 22" wide x 8.5" deep. *Courtesy of Mineral Point Toy Museum. Photograph by Carol Stevenson.*

Lithographed Opera House. Believed to be French, this musical opera house features a music roll in the back with a handle. The scene changes in front as the handle is turned. The lithographed pediment above the stage is richly detailed with a scene of a fairy with elves and a rabbit. The "wings" of the theater depict opera patrons in box seats. The dolls shown are not original to the piece. 30" high x 25" wide x 18" deep. *Courtesy of Gloria Hinkel and Beverly J. Thomes, Delaware Toy Museum.*

Lithographed theater. The base of the theater is made of wood and designed as a storage area for extra props. Scenes from fairy tales are lithographed on the pediments and sides of the stage. ($500-700). 20" high x 24" wide x 14" deep. *Courtesy of Ruth Petros.*

Spear's "Punch and Judy" Theater. The circa 1920s boxed set contains a folding cardboard puppet theater of lithographed cardboard and 8 puppets. The cardboard puppets have an attached wire which can be used to move one of their arms. The box is marked "Spear's Games" and "Made by J.W.S. & S. Bavaria." ($100-125). 11.5" high x 8" wide x 3" deep. *Photograph by Patty Cooper.*

"Fold-A-Way Theatre." The original envelope includes the name of the manufacturer, Fold-A-Way Toys of Chicago, Illinois. The circa 1932 set included three scripts and numerous cardboard props and characters. It is believed that the front was colored by a child. ($120). *Courtesy of Jim and Shirley Cox.*

The assembled "Fold-A-Way Theatre" included a stage with box seats on each side and an orchestra pit. Children could put on three different plays, "Little Red Riding Hood," "Cinderella," and "Little Black Sambo." *Courtesy of Jim and Shirley Cox.*

"The Theatre Game." The boxed set had changeable scenery for three plays, "Little Red Riding Hood," "Cinderella," and "Robin Hood." The stage is made of cardboard. The script for each play was printed on the back of the scene for another play. Each character had a cardboard stand and was labeled on the back. ($150). Theater is 7.5" high x 9.75" wide x 4" deep. *Courtesy of Marge Powell.*

When set up, the stage of the Theatre Game had a three-sided backdrop and cardboard characters for performing each of the three plays. *Courtesy of Marge Powell.*

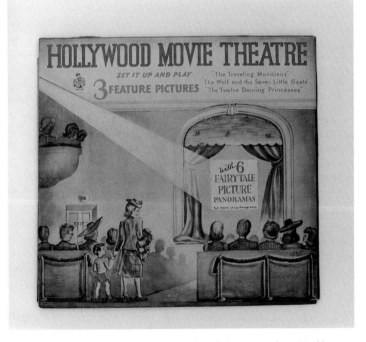

"Hometown Movie Theatre." Unlike others in the Marx Hometown series, the theatre is lithographed on the back and sides rather than the interior. There is a cut out section through which a paper "movie" can be viewed. The movie is made of a long piece of printed paper rolled onto two spools which can be turned to show the pictures. This one features "Bobby's and Betty's Trip to China." The pictures on the left side of the theater show movie patrons at the ticket window. ($175-250). 3.25" high x 5" wide x 2.75" deep. *Photograph by Patty Cooper.*

"Hollywood Movie Theatre." According to the information on the original box, this set was made by Rudolph J. Gutmann and the J.E. Schilling Company of New York, New York. It was copyrighted 1944. When setting up for play, a child could choose from three different feature pictures, "The Traveling Musicians," "The Wolf and the Seven Little Goats," or "The Twelve Dancing Princesses." ($75-125). *Courtesy of Elaine Price.*

It's Showtime

Theater fun for young "stars"

An unusual drive-in theater was advertised in the 1959 Sears catalog. The "Movieland Drive-in Theater" included a projector, screen, parking lot, six filmstrips, and six metal cars. It sold for $4.89. *Courtesy of Marge Meisinger. Photograph by Suzanne Silverthorn.*

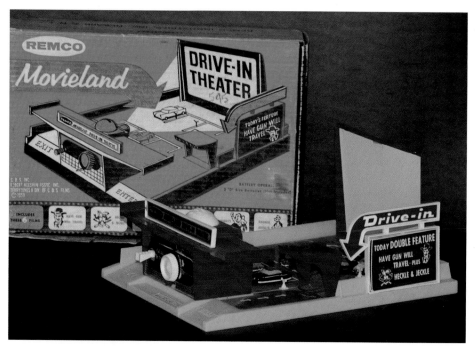

"Remco Movieland Drive-In Theater." The plastic theater came with six filmstrips, copyrighted 1959 CBS Inc. Terrytoons, Robert Keeshan Associates. The films which could be projected onto the movie screen included "Have Gun Will Travel," "Heckle and Jeckle," "Mighty Mouse," "Dink Duck," and one other. ($175-250). 9.5" high x 14" wide x 7" deep. *Photograph by Suzanne Silverthorn.*

"Admiral Television Studio." The cardboard television studio was made of heavy paper in 1953. It came, unassembled, in the envelope shown. Unlike earlier movie or theater toys, this was an up-to-date television studio complete with television camera, cameraman, lights, and microphone.

The set included a 32 page script book for four plays: "Peter Pan," "The Lonesome Pig," "Flight to Mars," and "Sky King in the Dynamite Bend Hold-up." The figures and props which accompanied the scripts were printed in full color. (Unpunched $200-250). *Courtesy of Jim and Shirley Cox.*

"Shirley Temple's Magnetic TV Theater." The boxed set by Amsco toys was advertised in the 1959 Sears catalog for $4.89. The set contained everything needed to stage "The Three Bears," "Red Riding Hood," and "Sleeping Beauty."

The metal-framed toy was designed to look like a television. Children could operate the 16 figures using magnets. Two different backdrops were provided along with a "TV title screen." The set was made as a tie-in to the television program "Shirley Temple's Storybook" which was broadcast on NBC beginning in 1958. ($100-125). 15" high x 18" wide x 10" deep. *Courtesy of Mary and Werner Stuecher.*

Circuses and Zoos

Children love animals and have always been entertained by circuses, both real ones and miniature versions. Probably the most collectible toy circuses are the Humpty-Dumpty sets made by the A. Schoenhut Company of Philadelphia. The circus could be purchased a few pieces at a time or as a complete package with tent. The 1903 Montgomery Ward catalog offered sets of three to eleven pieces ranging in price from 85 cents to $2.25. The circus animals and figures were mostly made of wood but several of the performers were made with bisque heads. A new edition of the Humpty Dumpty circus was made in 1952.

Two very collectible circuses were produced by the Louis Marx Company in the early 1950s. One set was called "Super Circus" and the other named "The Big Top." The "Super Circus" was a tie-in to the television program featuring Mary Hartline which was then airing on ABC. Both of these sets are highly sought by collectors and very expensive when found in complete condition.

Although toys based on zoos are rare, they fit nicely with a circus collection because some of the same animals were made for both sets. Several zoos were made by the O. & M. Hausser company, of Germany, to house their Elastolin animals which were made of composition type materials.

Schoenhut "Humpty Dumpty Circus." Schoenhut first offered a circus around 1902. The tents were made in at least two different sizes and could be purchased separately or with animals. The largest tent was made of fabric with a wire frame, supported by a dowel. (Tent only $600.00). 36" high x 35.75" wide x 24.5" deep. *Courtesy of Gene Harris Antique Auction Center.*

Schoenhut Circus Figures. Several of the Schoenhut Circus performers are shown in front of one of the original boxes. (Box measures 12" x 8"). The figures shown have glass eyes and jointed, wood bodies which indicate that they are some of the early ones made by the company. The animals with glass eyes are more difficult to find and much more expensive. The clowns and acrobats are approximately 8" tall. *Courtesy of Mineral Point Toy Museum. Photograph by Carol Stevenson.*

"Ready-Cut Zoo." The maker of the Ready-Cut sets is still unknown, but a village by the same company was advertised in the 1931 Montgomery Ward catalog. The box is marked "No. 5" and "Printed in U.S.A." It contains nine animals, seven cage backs, two cage roofs, seven cage enclosures, and one sign, all made of cardboard, printed on one side. ($75). The largest cage is 3.5" high x 5" wide x 2.25" deep. The box measures 5" x 15" x 1". *Photograph by Patty Cooper.*

"Circus Animal Cutouts." This boxed set by Platt & Munk Co., Inc. is marked #261 and contains over 100 pieces including circus animals, wagons, cages, clowns, and farm animals. ($35-50). *Photograph by Suzanne Silverthorn.*

Elastolin Zoo. The O. & M. Hausser company made these buildings in wood and the composition material known as Elastolin. The animals are also Elastolin. The set is marked "Made in Germany" and was probably made just before World War II. ($500). The buildings are approximately 5" high x 9" wide x 3.5" deep. *Courtesy of Ruth Petros.*

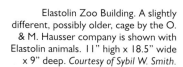

Elastolin Zoo Building. A slightly different, possibly older, cage by the O. & M. Hausser company is shown with Elastolin animals. 11" high x 18.5" wide x 9" deep. *Courtesy of Sybil W. Smith.*

"Bild-a-Set 3 Ring Circus-Carnival." The box is marked "D.A. Pachter Co., Chicago. Copyright 1943." It contained five heavy cardboard sheets to punch out and a sheet of paper with pre-gummed flags. Like the farm made by Pachter, this set contained pieces that could be assembled with thin wood or cardboard dowels to allow the carnival rides to "roll, turn, or revolve." The original price was $1.00. The circus set contains 25 different animals, 2 cages, three rides, and various circus acts. ($100-125). The ferris wheel is 9" high. The box is 12" x 15". *Photograph by Patty Cooper.*

The Marx Super Circus set was advertised in the 1952 Sears catalog for $5.89. The set was based on the television show "Super Circus" with Mary Hartline which was on ABC from 1949 to 1956. The set included metal midway signs, 35 circus people, 21 circus animals, 10 wild animals, a barker's booth, popcorn wagon, platforms, pedestals, barrels, rings, bars, ladders, etc. The steel tent was 9.25" high x 24.75" wide x 10.25" deep. *Photograph by Suzanne Silverthorn.*

Marx "Super Circus." The tent and two side shows were made of lithographed metal. The set included many plastic animals, acrobats, clowns, and circus props. ($500-750). *Courtesy of Keystone Toy Trader.*

"Big Top Woodette Circus Edition No. 3." This kit was advertised in the 1945 Ward's catalog. Set No. 3 contained several boxes of wood pieces which could be assembled into animals and painted. The boxes themselves became the cages, ticket window, etc. The box notes that the toys were designed by Mary Stoddard. The set was manufactured by Woodettes of Chicago copyrighted in 1945 by the Dupligraph Jr. Company. ($50-75). The box is 12" x 12". *Photograph by Suzanne Silverthorn.*

In 1952, Montgomery Wards sold a Marx Circus set called "The Big Top" which appears to be very similar to the Super Circus. It sold for $5.89. The complete set included a lithographed metal tent and "Side Show" platforms. According to the Wards catalog, the accessories included plastic performers, animals, and spectators, "even a father leading the usual crying child to make it seem just like a real circus." A similar set was sold by Aldens, the same year, and their catalog states that there were over 75 pieces in all. *Courtesy of Betty Nichols. Photograph by Suzanne Silverthorn.*

VI. Mass Transit

Railroad Stations

At the end of the nineteenth century, when the alternative was a horse-drawn carriage, most people traveled by train when they needed to reach a destination quickly. The growth of the railroad industry occurred at the same time that toys were first being mass-produced. Inevitably, children were intrigued by railroads and wanted to play with their own toy trains. Toy manufacturers in Germany created elaborate trains and wonderfully detailed train stations. These early stations are rare and usually command high prices.

Both Marklin and Gottschalk produced train stations in Germany, beginning in the latter part of the 1800s. The early Gottschalk stations were made of wood covered with lithographed paper, much like their "Blue Roof" dollhouses. Some were even furnished with the same type of pressed cardboard furniture supplied for the company's dollhouses.

The Marklin Company, which also produced toy trains, made the most elaborate stations out of hand painted tin. Many of the Marklin stations came with numerous accessories including people, luggage, baggage carts, ticket windows, newspaper stands, and furniture.

In the United States, the toy train stations were far less elaborate. During the 1920s, Chein made several simple stations of lithographed steel. The A. Schoenhut company offered wood and embossed fiberboard stations in three different sizes with roofs that could be lifted to provide access to the one-room structures.

The Louis Marx Company marketed several different metal train stations over the years. Their most collectible ones date from the 1930s. The 1936 Sears catalog featured the Marx Glendale Depot which included a platform, electric lights, a baggage truck, and a signal which lowered when a train was on the track. During the same period, Marx made a Grand Central Station which was sold as part of a set with an airport and bus station.

Several American companies, who specialized in toy trains, also made stations and accessories. These included American Flyer and Lionel. Both companies made stations in lithographed metal.

In the 1940s, other U. S. companies began producing toy railroad stations. Built-Rite (Warren Paper Products) made inexpensive cardboard stations with pieces which had to be punched out and assembled. The number of pieces in each set varied but might have included a station, platform, signals, or other accessories.

During this same period, Keystone issued a talking railroad station, made of pressed hardboard. It featured a hand cranked phonograph record and a loudspeaker to let the passengers know departure times and destinations.

By the 1950s, several companies produced railroad buildings out of plastic in various scales. Bachmann Brothers (Plasticville), Marx, and Skyline all made inexpensive kits which could be assembled into fairly realistic looking structures.

Toy trains became less popular in the 1960s. Although train sets continued to be made, they were more often purchased as hobby toys for adults than as Christmas presents for children.

Marklin Railroad Platform. This circa 1902 train station platform is listed as #2044 in the catalogs of the German firm of Marklin. It is made of hand painted tin. The accessories include figures, luggage, a cigar stand, and carts. This is the only complete original example known to exist. ($26,000-27,000). *Courtesy of Kirk F. White.*

Marklin Railroad Station. Shown as #02015 in the circa 1905 Marklin catalogs, this hand painted tin railroad is still in mint condition. It includes many figures, outdoor seating, and a weather vane atop the dome of the roof. 13.5" high x 16" wide x 12.25" deep. *Courtesy of Kirk F. White.*

Marklin Railroad Station. The roof of the Marklin station lifts off to provide access to two furnished rooms. The inside of the station includes a ticket booth and waiting room. *Courtesy of Kirk F. White.*

Gottschalk "Leipzig" Station #2964. This circa 1900 Gottschalk railroad station is made of lithographed paper over wood in the classic "Blue Roof" style. It is furnished with Gottschalk pressed cardboard furniture in the smallest scale also used in dollhouses. ($2800-3500). 13.5" high x 17" wide x 7" deep. *Courtesy of David Pressland.*

Mason & Converse Train Station. This lithographed paper over wood train station was made by Mason & Converse circa 1880s. The original train included an engine, tender, passenger car, and gondola. 9" high x 14" wide x 8.75" deep. *Courtesy of Carl and Linda Thomas, Jr.*

Chein "Toytown Ticket Office." There is a lithographed telegraph window on the left side and an American Railway Express Baggage window on the back. In the 1920s, Chein made several railroad stations and a filling station, using the same blank but different lithography. The other known stations were marked Grove, Oakland, Parkville, and Glendale. ($85 in condition shown; $200 in excellent condition). 5" high x 5.5" wide x 4" deep. *Photograph by Patty Cooper.*

Schoenhut Railroad Station. These stations were pictured in the Schoenhut catalogs from 1917 until 1923. They were made in two different colors (gray or brown) and three sizes. The brown ones, like this one, were probably the later models. They were made of wood and embossed cardboard with glass windows and opening doors. The roof lifts off for play access. ($650-800). 8.25" high x 14" wide x 7.25" deep. *Courtesy of Lois L. Freeman.*

Marx "Glendale Depot." As a train neared the station, the red light flashed and the gate went down. The original set included a 6" steel baggage truck, trunk, suitcase, bench, and hand cart. Sears sold the station for $1.00 in 1936. ($900 complete). 5.5" high x 13.5" wide x 10" deep. *Courtesy of Charles L. Gilbert.*

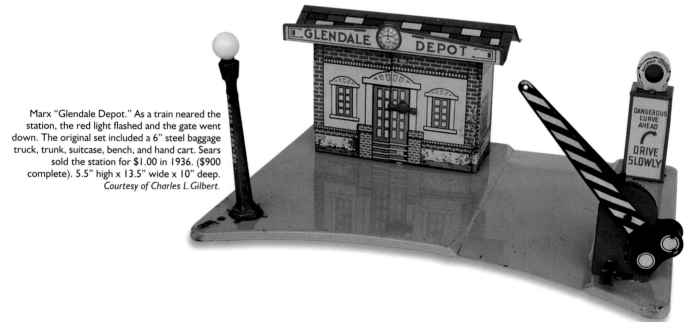

Marx "Union Station." Sears advertised a set of three Marx buildings in their 1938 catalog. They included the Union Station shown here, a Bus Terminal, and a City Airport for 89 cents. The train station came with a "MarLine" train, also made by Marx. The crossing gate could be raised and lowered. The station is marked "Marx Toys. Made in U.S.A." ($700-800 complete). 3.5" high x 12" wide x 6.75" deep. *Courtesy of Mineral Point Toy Museum. Photograph by Carol Stevenson.*

A circa late 1930s catalog from the American Flyer Company pictured five different buildings: Central Station, Kenilworth, Terminal Station, Freight Station, and Switch Tower House. *Courtesy of Mineral Point Toy Museum. Photograph by Carol Stevenson.*

Marx "Grand Central Station." Marx made a series of slightly larger buildings, circa 1937, which included an airport, a bus station, fire station, and a Universal Auto Repair. The lithographed metal station was very Art Deco in style. ($400-500). 3.5" high x 16.75" wide x 10.75" deep. *Courtesy of The Early Adventure.*

American Flyer Station No. 96. The number is marked on the side of this lithographed metal station. It appears to be very similar to the Kenilworth Station shown in the catalog above. This station was advertised in the 1938 catalog of the N. Shure Company. ($200-250). 5.5" high x 9.5" wide x 5.5" deep. *Courtesy of Mineral Point Toy Museum. Photograph by Carol Stevenson.*

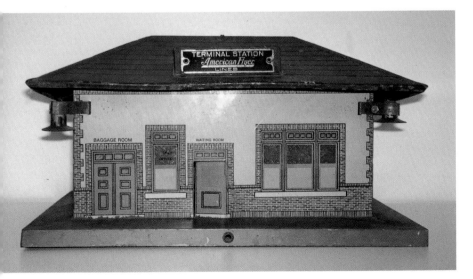

American Flyer "Terminal Station" No. 97. This metal lithographed station was shown in the American Flyer catalog circa late 1930s. It is slightly larger than the others pictured. ($200-250). 7.5" high x 12" wide x 7" deep. *Courtesy of Mineral Point Toy Museum. Photograph by Carol Stevenson.*

"Lionel City" #124 Train Station. A circa 1930s train station by Lionel is made of embossed metal. The O scale station featured lights and operable doors. ($150-175). 10" high x 13.5" wide x 9.25" deep. *Courtesy of Jim Ferguson, "Almost Antiques." Photograph by Patty Cooper.*

Unmarked American Flyer Station. Although unmarked, this circa 1930s lithographed tin station is believed to have been made by American Flyer. ($200-250). 5.25" high x 9.5" wide x 5.5" deep. *Courtesy of Mineral Point Toy Museum. Photograph by Carol Stevenson.*

Lionel "Winnertown" Train Station. The lithographed metal station is marked Lionel. It was first sold in 1939 and was pictured in the John Plain catalog for that year. This example is missing its base. The station was also issued as a whistling station in 1939. ($50-75 in condition shown). 3.5" high x 5.5" wide x 3.75" deep. *Courtesy of Marilyn Pittman.*

Hornby Station and Platform. This small scale lithographed metal station was made in England as part of the Hornby series by Meccano Ltd. ($100-125). *Courtesy of Mary Harris.*

Hornby Signal House. Part of the same series by Meccano Ltd., of England, this two story signal house is shown with Esso pumps by Lesney (Matchbox) and Britain's figures. ($100-125). *Courtesy of Mary Harris.*

Built-Rite "Union Station." The circa 1930s Warren Paper Products Set No. 19 has its original box. It is made of cardboard with slot and tab construction. Included are two figures which fit into slots behind the ticket windows. ($150). 8.5" high x 13" wide x 10" deep. *Photograph by Patty Cooper.*

Built-Rite "Railroad Accessory Set." Set No. 1010 by Warren Paper Products of Lafayette, Indiana, is shown with its original box. The company made this same style station for many years in several different sets. The station was part of a "Railroad Accessory Set and Scenery" set advertised in the October 1949 issue of Children's *Activities* for $2.25. It included cardboard parts to make a bridge, freight packages, and figures. A larger set included a signal tower, three billboards, signs, and 60" of scenery. (As shown $25; MIB $150). 7.5" high x 17" wide x 10.5" deep. *Photograph by Suzanne Silverthorn.*

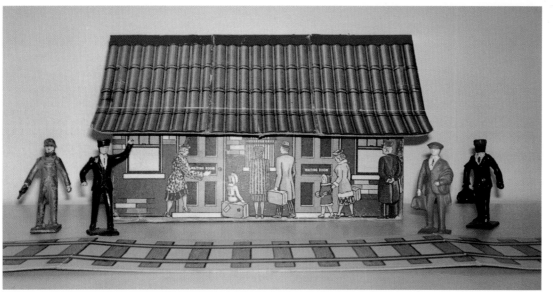

"Lincolnville" Railroad Station. The cardboard station was marketed by The J. L. Wright Company, also known as Lincoln Logs, of Chicago. This is Set No. 30, made by Morris Paper Mills, Morris Illinois. The name "Lincolnville" is marked on the end of the building. It came with a paper track 14" long and lead figures 2.25" tall. The Lincoln Logs firm produced at least one other toy railroad station, according to their advertising in 1938. ($200-250). 5.25" high x 8" wide x 3" deep. *Courtesy of Mineral Point Toy Museum. Photograph by Carol Stevenson.*

Keystone "Talking Railroad Station" No. 418. The station is complete with its original box. The Masonite and Tekwood building was advertised in the 1952 Sears Christmas catalog for $2.79. The talking mechanism worked by turning a handle to activate the stylus speaker unit which announced the names of cities. The speaker unit came in a separate box and it is very unusual to find an example with this feature intact. ($275-300). 6" high x 17" wide x 7.5" deep. *Courtesy of Lois L. Freeman.*

Marx "Grade Crossing Signal Man." This railroad accessory by Louis Marx was advertised in the 1953 Sears catalog for $3.79 and sold for many years. As the train neared the crossing, the man came out of the building and the guard rail went down. (MIB $300-350). 4.5" high x 7" high x 6.5" deep. *Courtesy of Jim Schaut.*

"Union Station." This totally enclosed station is made of a Masonite with plastic windows. Although the building is unmarked, its metal windows have a distinctive middle piece which wraps around the frame to the inside. Several of the dollhouses made by the Rich Toy Company also have this feature.

Since Rich made gas stations, barns, and garages, as well as dollhouses, it seems likely that the company would also have produced a railroad station. The Rich dollhouses that have this type of window were made in the 1940s. On the bottom of the station, it is marked in pencil "#313/1.98." There is also a sticker which reads "Schoonmalar & Son, Inc." ($100-125). 8" high x 15" wide x 9" deep. *Photograph by Suzanne Silverthorn.*

Marx "Glendale" Station. This circa 1950s lithographed metal station was produced by Marx for many years. It was featured in the 1955 Sears catalog, with no accessories, for $1.85. By the late 1950s, it was offered as a whistling station. It is totally enclosed. ($100-125). 6" high x 20.5" wide x 10" deep. *Photograph by Suzanne Silverthorn.*

Marx "Girard Whistling Station." The lithographed steel station was advertised in the 1958 Sears catalog for $4.29. With the push of a button, a train whistle could be heard. (MIB $300-400). 5" high x 9" wide x 5" deep. *Courtesy of Jim Schaut.*

"Plasticville Station." This set, by Bachmann Brothers, circa 1956, included a train station, signal tower, and accessories. Although these buildings were sold to accompany an O gauge train, they were really too small in scale. The car pictured is marked Lionel and was originally loaded on a railroad car made by that company. (Complete set $50). Station is 6" high x 7" wide x 5" deep. *Courtesy of Jeff Zillner, (childhood toy), Photograph by Suzanne Silverthorn.*

Freight Terminals

Real freight was hauled by trucks as well as trains and several companies produced terminals to be used with toy trucks. Rich Toy Company made at least two different models out of Masonite circa 1950s. Marx made a lithographed steel terminal in 1952. In 1961, T. Cohn (Superior) introduced a metal combination service station, truck stop, and freight terminal. It retailed for $4.98. This type of toy remained popular into the early seventies as Brumberger offered a Tiny Town Truck Terminal made of lithographed pressed wood and designed to be used with the Tiny Tonka trucks available during that time.

"Rich Truck Terminal." The Deco-style freight terminal is made of Gypsum hardboard. It has a central door which can be lifted to provide access for the trucks. There is storage space on the second floor and a clock with movable hands. The overhang on the right side is missing on this example, but the one on the right features a very Art Deco guard rail. A metal pole on the left appears to have been intended to raise and lower a ramp so the trucks could slide out of the building. The freight house is 11" high x 7" deep and is attached to a base that is 24" wide and 13" deep. ($75-100 in condition shown). *Photograph by Patty Cooper.*

Rich Toys "Freight Office." The circa 1940s truck terminal is made of Gypsum type hardboard. The round Rich Toys decal is on the floor of the building, just inside the "office" door. The front and side doors are operable. ($200-250). 7" high x 13" wide x 11" deep. *Courtesy of Ben DeVoto.*

A lithographed metal freight terminal by Marx was advertised by Sears for several years during the 1950s. Their 1957 Christmas catalog illustrated a 57 piece set for $4.89. The set included five plastic figures, three plastic trucks, dummy scale, three plastic baggage wagons, six wooden barrels, 24 empty food cartons, and more. *Photograph by Suzanne Silverthorn.*

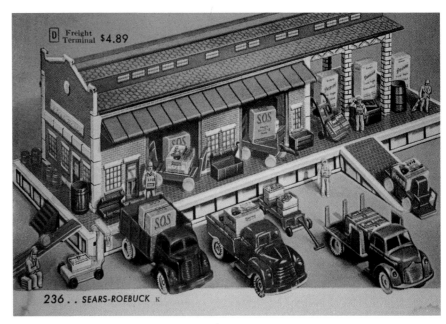

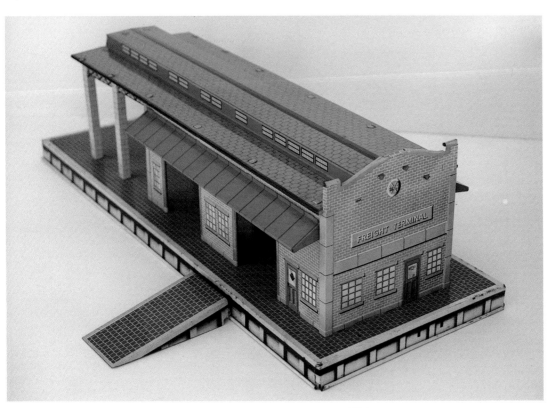

Marx "Freight Terminal." The lithographed metal truck terminal included a loading platform, offices, storage areas, and a loading ramp. ($100-125). 8.5" high x 28" long x 10.75" deep. *Photograph by Suzanne Silverthorn.*

129

T. COHN NO. 845 HIGHWAY SERVICE STATION, TRUCK STOP AND FREIGHT TERMINAL

Multi-play station featuring a complete service station with modern cars, pumps, attendants play truck-terminal with trucks, ramp and cargo. All metal parts are lithographed. All cars, cargo and freight accessories are of unbreakable polyethylene. 6 in carton; wt. 20 lbs.

No. 845 — Per Dozen **$75.60**
(Retail Price, $4.98)

The 1961 catalog of the Dallas based Cullum and Boren Company advertised a T. Cohn Highway Service Station, Truck Stop, and Freight Terminal. The number 845 set included a lithographed metal terminal with plastic cars, cargo, and freight accessories. *Photograph by Suzanne Silverthorn.*

Brumberger "Tiny Town Truck Terminal #795." The circa 1970s building was made of pressed wood. The front doors opened and the top lifted to provide play access. The inside of the terminal was also colorfully lithographed. It was designed to be used with trucks the size of the Tiny Tonka models, but none were included with the set. ($100-125). 7" high x 19" wide x 10" deep. *Photograph by Suzanne Silverthorn.*

Bus Stations

Bus transportation was fairly common during the mid-1900s. Toy bus stations are rare, but were made by at least two different companies. Marx made two variations in lithographed metal. The Marx Greyhound Bus Terminal was advertised in the 1937 Sears catalog and included two buses. A smaller Marx bus station was advertised in the 1938 Sears catalog as part of a three-piece set which included a train station and airport.

Keystone made three different bus stations out of pressed hardboard in the 1950s. One was similar to their train station and included a record with loudspeaker. Another had a large base with a circular driveway for the buses. The third was a combination service station, parking garage, and bus terminal, reminiscent of small towns where bus service was offered as part of another business.

NEW 97c

20-Inch Greyhound Bus Terminal (2 Buses)

Ultra modern big metropolitan bus stations in New York and Chicago have nothing on this handsome building for looks and detail. And busy! Wait'll you see! 2 steel buses, about 4¾ in. long, you can roll easily in and out of the two large garages to discharge and take on passengers.

The whole main floor, built on a strong steel base, is lined with colorful interesting shops, waiting rooms, ticket offices, lobbies, etc., realistically printed on metal. There are 2 dummy gas pumps, 2 dummy signs. Base also definitely marked with travelling lane and sidewalks. **Station over-all, 20¼x11x4½ in. high.** A sturdy toy that will provide hours of educational fun.
49 V 5862—Shpg. wt., 3 lbs......97c

4 dummy lamp post
Suspension bridge s
boats under the big
49 V 5863—Sh

REVERSES BY ITSELF

A Greyhound Bus Terminal by Marx was advertised in the 1937 Sears catalog for 97 cents. The set came with two steel buses about 4.75" long. The steel base was lined with shops, waiting rooms, ticket offices, and a lobby. There were also two gas pumps and two signs. The bus station, with its two large bays, was similar in design to the airport, fire station, repair shop, and railroad station made by Marx during the same time. *Courtesy of Marge Meisinger. Photograph by Suzanne Silverthorn.*

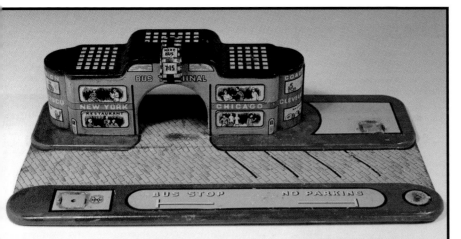

Marx "Bus Terminal." This small, lithographed metal terminal by Marx was advertised in the 1938 Sears catalog. It was part of a three piece set which also included a train station and an airport. The bus station originally had a gas pump, stop and go signal, and a bus. ($75-100 in condition shown). 3.5" high x 12" wide x 6.75" deep. *Photograph by Patty Cooper.*

"Keystone Bus Terminal." The circa 1952 terminal was equipped with the same type of loud speaker system that was used on the Keystone Railroad Station. Unlike the railroad station, the bus terminal was mounted on a large base. It was made of Masonite. ($350 without bus). 6" high x 23" wide x 14" deep. *Courtesy of Toys and More.*

"Keystone Bus Terminal." A circa late 1950s bus terminal was made of Masonite pressed board and mounted on a large base to provide room for buses. The set included a plastic stop light, two parking meters, and a plastic bus. A large clock was mounted on the roof and a time table listed the arrivals and departures. ($200-250). 6" high x 24" wide x 18" deep. *Photograph by Patty Cooper.*

Keystone Combination "Bus Station, Service Station and Parking Garage." The circa late 1950s, multi-purpose structure is reminiscent of small towns where bus service was part of another business. The "Bus Station Waiting Room" sign is often missing from this set. The parking garage has an elevator operated by crank. Cars may also exit the garage via a ramp at the rear. Access to the service/sales room is through the open back. The door to the service area folds open. The building is made of Masonite pressed wood. ($200). 9" high x 23" wide x 13.5" deep. *Photograph by Patty Cooper.*

Airports

Toy airports have been far more popular with children than bus stations. As air travel became more common, toy companies began producing toy planes and airports. The Louis Marx Company led the way, once again, by introducing several models in the 1930s. One series was produced in the same mold but with different finishing touches. Basically, they consisted of a metal building on a metal base. Most featured three or more airplanes and some sort of gimmick—either a searchlight, airplanes on a revolving arm, or a lighted runway.

Other toy airports of the 1930s were simple metal hangars which housed a metal airplane. Dowst (Tootsietoy), Marx, and Wolverine all made toys of this type. Wyandotte also made a small metal airport with lots of runway space for landing toy planes.

Built-Rite (Warren Paper Products) produced several cardboard airports during the 1930s and early 1940s. These sets featured wonderful graphics and are becoming increasingly popular with collectors.

A simple wood airport was marketed by Arcade in 1941 to house two of the company's metal airplanes. This airport is far more difficult to find than the Marx models of the 1930s. Rich made two variations of a Masonite "Skyway Airport." Both had a large central bay for planes with offices on each side. The earlier one had Art Deco style, curved celluloid windows on each end whereas the later one was squared on the ends with plastic, mullion windows.

In the 1950s, Bachmann Brothers (Plasticville) produced a plastic airport unit that included two buildings, a landing strip, airplanes, and cars. The Plasticville Airport Administration Building was one of their most complicated structures with 19 plastic parts and glow-in-the-dark lights. Their competitor, Skyline, issued an airport in 1950 which used magnets to control the movement of the vehicles.

Toy airports produced after the 1960s emphasized a quantity of vehicles over the architecture of the airport. Often, the buildings were little more than the cardboard boxes in which the planes were packaged. Today, collectors are often most interested in the early structures which reflected the design trends of their time. A complete metal airport from the 1930s, in its original box, will command a high price.

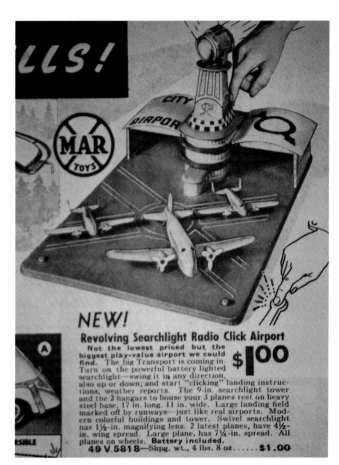

A Marx City Airport was advertised in the 1937 Sears catalog for $1.00. This set included a battery operated search light that could be clicked to provide landing instructions. The set also came with three metal airplanes, the largest with a wingspread of 7.25". *Courtesy of Marge Meisinger. Photograph by Suzanne Silverthorn.*

Marx "City Airport." The circa 1937 Marx airport included a large runway area and very modern terminal building. ($350-400). 11" wide x 17" deep. *Courtesy of The Early Adventure.*

89¢

Airport with Five Planes

Laid out like a real Airport—2 hangars, administration building tower and landing field with runways. 17 by 7¼ in. Brightly colored metal. 2 metal airplanes on revolving arm fly a long time on one winding around tower. Also included are 3 pull-type steel planes—largest one 6 in. long.

48 T 3910—Ship. wt. 5 lbs.
Set...................................89¢

A very similar Marx airport was advertised in the 1939 Montgomery Ward catalog for 89 cents. In addition to the three planes on the ground, this version had two more planes which revolved around the tower. The revolving planes, which were operated by a winding mechanism, replaced the search light on the earlier version. *Courtesy of Marge Meisinger. Photograph by Suzanne Silverthorn.*

Marx "Electric Lighted City Airport." Still another version had battery operated lights on the runways, two towers on the roof (one holding an American flag and the other a metal windsock), and a beacon light in the middle of the roof. The set came with several airplanes. (MIB $1000). 11" wide x 17" deep. *Courtesy of Thrilling Toys of Yesteryear.*

Marx "City Airport." This small lithographed metal airport is one of the circa 1938 series which included the Union Station, Blue Bird Garage, and Bus Terminal. The City Airport included a gas pump and two small gray planes. ($125-150). 3.5" high x 12" wide x 6.75" deep. *Photograph by Suzanne Silverthorn.*

"Tootsietoy Airport." The circa late 1930s metal hangar, by Dowst, originally came with two Tootsietoy airplanes, one black and one a red Ford Tri-motor. ($1000). 2.75" high x 6" wide x 4.75" deep. *Courtesy of Charles L. Gilbert.*

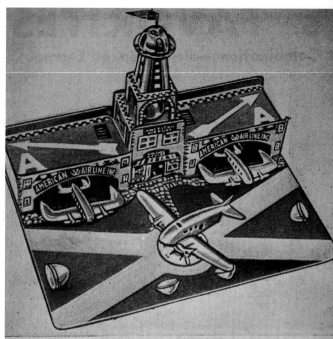

MUNICIPAL AIRPORTS

16x11⅝x10⅞ in., 4-color litho, heavy gauge steel, litho landing lights, red and green control light with lever, beacon light on tower, revolving wind sock, ticket office, weather bureau, radio station, drug store, etc. lithographed on sides. Complete with two 7¼ in. steel airplanes and 2 electric light bulbs. Battery not included.

62-7671—1/12 doz sets in box............ **Doz sets** **8.00**

The 1936 Butler Brothers catalog advertised an airport by Wyandotte. It was made of four-color lithographed, heavy gauge steel. The set included landing lights, control light with lever, beacon light on the tower, and revolving windsock. The advertising copy stated that it came with two 7.25" steel airplanes (although three are shown in the illustration) and two electric light bulbs. *Photograph by Suzanne Silverthorn.*

Wyandotte "City Airport." This is apparently the same airport shown in the 1936 Butler Brothers advertisement, although several parts are missing on this example. The central portion of the building houses a ticket office with a hangar on each side, both for American Airlines, Inc. The main part of the toy contains the runways. The lithographed sides show a dispatcher's office and a repair shop. On the back there are printed windows showing a drugstore, newsstand, waiting room, and restaurant. There is no interior lithography. It is marked "Wyandotte Toys. Made in USA" inside a circle. ($75-100 in condition shown). 4.5" high x 16" wide x 11.25" deep. *Photograph by Patty Cooper.*

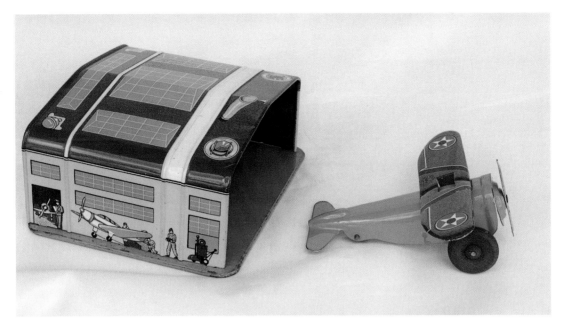

Marx Hangar. A circa 1940s lithographed metal hangar by Marx also included an airplane. The plane was 5" long with a 6" wingspan. It had wooden wheels and a metal propeller. (Hangar with plane $350-450). 3.25" high x 7" wide x 5.75" wide. *Courtesy of Charles L. Gilbert.*

The 1936 Butler Brothers catalog contained an advertisement for a Built-Rite Municipal Airport. The Built-Rite toys were made by Warren Paper Products. *Photograph by Suzanne Silverthorn.*

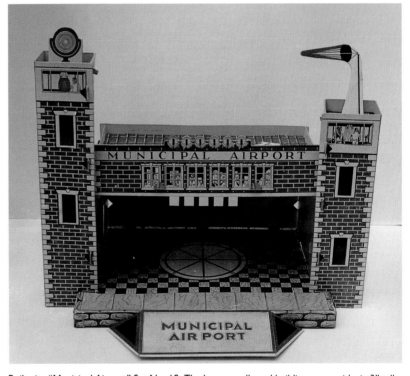

Built-rite "Municipal Airport" Set No. 18. The heavy cardboard building came with six 3" tall figures. It was offered in the 1935 Sears catalog with a Tootsietoy plane and automobile for 59 cents. ($200-250). 11.25" high x 15" wide x 12" deep. *Photograph by Patty Cooper.*

135

Built-Rite "United Air Lines" Airport
Set No. 26. The colorful graphics on
this boxed set are typical of Warren
Paper Products toys. ($150-175).
Box measures 15.75" x 10". *Courtesy
of George Mundorf.*

Rich Toys "Skyway Airport." The circa 1940s structure was
made of pressed wood. The "Airport Office" is on the left side
with a "Lunch Room" on the right. Both have plastic windows.
It is an open-backed structure with only one, undivided space.
A paper label on the front reads "Rich Toys/Clinton, Iowa."
The plane in the photograph is a Dent Ford monoplane.
(Building only $300-350). 7" high x 26.5" wide x 11" deep.
Courtesy of Bill and Stevie Weart.

Rich Toys "Skyway Airport."
A very similar, possibly earlier
version, of the Rich airport is
much more Art Deco in style. It
has rounded clear plastic
windows on each corner and a
paper label in the center. This
example is missing the fuel
pumps. ($100-150). 7" high x
26.5" wide x 11" deep.
Photograph by Patty Cooper.

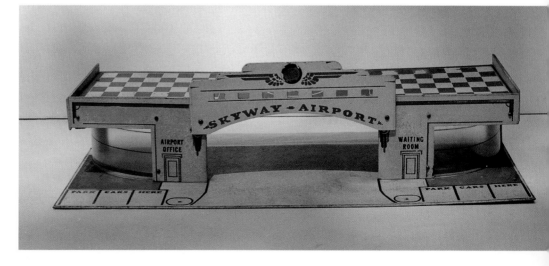

"Arcadia Airport." This wood airport was featured in the 1941 Arcade catalog. It included a steel wind sock and overhead awning. The large door could be opened to admit the two cast iron planes. The planes are 7.75" long and have a wingspan of 7". (Airport only $1000-1200. With planes $1600-2000). *Courtesy of Bill and Stevie Weart.*

"Superior Airport." The lithographed metal airport by T. Cohn was made in the 1950s. The set came with plastic accessories which included two airplanes, an airport bus, gasoline truck with hose, and a crash truck with hose. There was a crane mounted on the roof. ($300-350). The base measures 24" wide x 16" deep. *Courtesy of Jim and Beverly Cox, Sussex Antique Toy Shop.*

Plasticville "Airport Administration Building AD-$."
The circa 1954 building by Bachmann Brothers has 19 plastic parts. It featured glow in the dark lights to guide incoming planes. ($75). 8.5" high x 9.75" wide x 7" deep. Box measures 11" x 5.75" x 2". *Courtesy of Gary Mosholder. Photograph by Jacob Dohm.*

Plasticville "Airport Hangar Kit AP-1." Five plastic pieces snap together to form the circa 1950s hangar by Bachmann Brothers. The windsock is often missing from the set. ($35-40). 4.5" high x 8.75" wide x 7.5" deep. *Courtesy of Gary Mosholder. Photograph by Jacob Dohm.*

"Ideal Airport" #CS 152. The lithographed metal airport is mounted on a cardboard base. It is marked on the top "Made in U.S.A. by Ideal Toy Corporation, Hollis 13, N.Y." The sides of the building picture a marine helicopter, a U.S. Air Force plane, and several military personnel. The plastic airplanes pictured are a B-45 Tornado and an XF 86 Saber. It is believed to have been made in the 1950s or early 1960s. ($125-140). 2.5" high x 7" wide x 6.5" deep. *Photograph by Suzanne Silverthorn.*

VII. The Automobile

Private Garages

As the automobile replaced the horse and buggy, stables and barns began to evolve into shelters for the new machine. The early cars were complex and valuable investments which needed to be protected from the elements. At first, many cars shared space with the horses. When it became clear that automobiles were more than a passing fad, the stalls and hay racks were removed to create more room. As automobiles became more common, the garage was born. The first were separate buildings with little architectural distinction. Like stables, they were usually relegated to the back of the lot. Home magazines often provided suggestions for camouflaging the eyesores. By the 1920s, garages began to reflect the architecture of their owner's homes, with similar roof lines and exterior siding. These garages often had sets of double doors which swung or folded open to admit a vehicle. As automobiles became an indispensable part of modern life, they began to be built closer to houses until eventually the two structures merged and private garages as separate structures all but disappeared.

Children have always loved to play with toy vehicles. Miniature automobiles were popular almost as soon as the first car was invented. If real automobiles needed housing, then toy cars did, too. By 1912, Bing, a German manufacturer, was offering a cardboard garage complete with mechanical automobile. Like their real-life counterparts, these private garages were usually free-standing structures, separate from houses. During the 1920s, various toy metal garages were marketed with two cars to place inside the structure. Sears sold such a set, also made by Bing, in 1921. The mechanical cars included a roadster and a limousine. The package sold for 98 cents. *The Universal Toy Catalog of 1924-26* shows similar metal garages by at least two other German companies. German toy manufacturers, including Moritz Gottschalk and Christian Hacker, also sold wood garages which nicely complemented their dollhouses.

Several manufacturers of toy vehicles marketed garages made of heavy paper or cardboard as containers for their metal cars. Arcade sold such a package in 1923. The company added wood garages to their line in 1930 and by 1934, the firm was offering two different styles of wood garages to be used with various dollhouses. Dowst sold a Tootsietoy folding cardboard garage, with two doors, along with a set of four metal vehicles, in 1925.

Several companies which produced dollhouses made garages to match. Built-Rite (Warren Paper Products) produced a cardboard private garage printed in the same brick pattern as at least one of their dollhouses. Tynietoy marketed a wood garage to complement

their upscale dollhouses and the Rich Toy Company offered a garage made of pressed wood along with its circa 1940 line.

After World War II, many companies made garages of either metal or plastic. Marx and Courtland produced metal garages while Ideal, Wyandotte, Payton Products, and Renwal made plastic cars and garages. These products were popular throughout the 1950s.

Garages as separate structures seem to have survived a little longer in the toy world than in real life. Perhaps because toys were marketed according to gender, companies felt a need to provide separate housing for boys' vehicles. However, by the 1960s, separate toy garages had disappeared, reflecting the earlier marriage of private garages with houses in real life. This change was seen in the inclusion of garages as a special feature of dollhouses produced by many companies as early as Schoenhut, Tri-ang, and Gottschalk in the 1930s. Garages were frequently found on the more deluxe lithographed metal dollhouses made by Marx and T. Cohn in the 1950s.

Hacker Garage. This early 1900s paper over wood garage has been attributed to Christian Hacker of Nuremberg, Germany. The roof on this building has paper in the same design as many of the Hacker dollhouses. Although this toy is labeled "garage," it houses early fire fighting equipment. The vehicle rolls down the sloping floor when a knob is pushed which lets the door spring open. A bell rings at the same time. (Building only $1500-2000). 14.5" high x 12" wide x 12" deep. *Courtesy of Bill and Stevie Weart.*

Bing Garage. The lithographed metal garage and car were made by Bing of Germany. The garage was pictured in the 1924 Sears catalog along with two metal cars. ($500+ with one car; $650-700 with two cars). 4.75" high x 8.25" wide x 6.5" deep. *Courtesy of Charles L. Gilbert.*

Gottschalk Garage/Stable #6814. An unusual combination garage and stable by Moritz Gottschalk of Germany was probably made circa 1920s. Although not legible in the photograph, the sign above the doors on the right reads "Auto Garage." There are sets of double doors on each side with space to house two automobiles. The center section has two stalls with metal hay racks for horses. A loft, with opening door, provides hay storage with a pulley for lifting the bales. ($750). 14.5" high x 16.25" wide x 9.75" deep. *Courtesy of Judith Armitstead.*

Gottschalk Garage. This wood, two-car garage was made by the German firm of Moritz Gottschalk circa 1920s. It has a cardboard roof and is part of the series known to collectors as "Red Roofs." The paper flooring has a parquet pattern much like the floor papers in the company's dollhouses. (Garage only $500-600). 14.25" high x 21.25" wide x 18" deep. *Courtesy of Lois L. Freeman.*

Schoenhut Garages. Two garages by the A. Schoenhut Company of Philadelphia are made of wood and cardboard embossed to represent block. The circa 1927 buildings have cardboard roofs with an embossed shingle pattern. (Garage with car $500 each). 6.5" high x 5" wide x 7.25" deep. *Courtesy of Lois L. Freeman.*

Arcade "Garage." This one-car garage is similar to the example pictured in the 1934 Arcade catalog. It contains a single opening door. The iron Model T Ford is also an Arcade product. (Garage only $650-750). 6.5" high x 7" wide x 8" deep. *Courtesy of Bill and Stevie Weart.*

Tynietoy Garage No. 41. This wood one-car garage was produced by Tynietoy of Providence, Rhode Island, circa 1930s. It was probably made to be used with the firm's dollhouses. ($850-900). 10.5" high x 10.75" wide x 16.25" deep. *Courtesy of Joan and Gaston Majeune, Toys in the Attic.*

A lithographed metal Magic Garage by Louis Marx was advertised in the 1935 Montgomery Ward Christmas catalog. It sold for 59 cents and came complete with a metal roadster. The garage was 4.5" high x 6.5" wide x 7" deep. A similar "Electric Eye Garage" was sold by Marx in 1936. *Photograph by Suzanne Silverthorn.*

Marx Garage. This metal garage was advertised in the 1935 Montgomery Ward Christmas catalog for 20 cents, complete with a metal Chrysler car. ($100). 2.5" high x 3" wide x 5" deep. *Courtesy of Charles L. Gilbert.*

Built-Rite No. 7. The Warren Paper Products Company produced this one-car garage circa 1936. The garage was intended to be used with the cardboard dollhouses produced by the company. ($50). 8" high x 7.5" wide x 8" deep. *Photograph by Patty Cooper.*

Wyandotte two-car garage. The heavy gauge, lithographed steel garage by Wyandotte is shown complete with its two original cars. The gas pump lithographed on the side indicates that perhaps it was supposed to be a filling station as well but the doors are more like those of a private garage. This garage was pictured in the 1936 catalog of Butler Brothers of Minneapolis. The wholesale price was $2.00 per dozen. ($350 and up with cars). 3.25" high x 3.75" wide x 4.5" deep. *Courtesy of Charles L. Gilbert.*

"Dickie's Garage." The wood gas station appears to have been commercially made, but it is unmarked. There is a cut-out window on one side and a door at the rear. A knob on the front left originally controlled an electric light bulb inside. It is approximately 1" to the foot in scale. ($60-75). 11.5" high x 16" wide x 22" deep. *Courtesy of Lois L. Freeman.*

Wood and fiberboard garage. Perhaps made to accompany a circa 1940s dollhouse, the manufacturer of this garage is unknown. A lever on the right side opens the garage door. ($45-50). 4.25" high x 8.5" wide x 7.5" deep. *Courtesy of Marcie Tubbs. Photograph by Patty Cooper.*

Rich One-car Garage. The Rich Toy Company of Clinton, Iowa made most of their buildings of Gypsum board. This circa 1940 example was probably meant to accompany one of the company's dollhouses. The plastic window panes are missing. ($50-65). *Photograph by Patty Cooper.*

144

Courtland garage. The door of this lithographed metal garage by Courtland pops open when hit by the car. Like the garage, the windup tin car is from the late 1940s. (Garage $75-95, car $75). 7.5" high x 7.5" wide x 10" deep. *Courtesy of Marcie Tubbs. Photograph by Bob Tubbs.*

Marx "Honeymoon Garage." The lithographed steel garage has the words "Honeymoon Garage" under the Marx logo in the peak of the front gable. The garage originally came with two 9" steel, spring wound cars. The set sold for 59 cents in the 1935 Sears Fall/Winter catalog. ($125). 4.5" high x 7.25" wide x 6.5" deep. *Photograph by Suzanne Silverthorn.*

Marx "Automatic Door" Garage. The lithographed steel garage was advertised in the 1952 Alden's Christmas catalog with a metal police car. Together they sold for $1.89. The same year, Sears sold the garage with two plastic cars for $1.89. The door opens "automatically" when hit by a car. The inside of the garage is also lithographed. ($75-95). 6" high x 9" wide x 9.5" deep. *Photograph by Suzanne Silverthorn.*

Marx One-car Garage. The door of the lithographed metal garage folds horizontally to admit a car. It was made by the Louis Marx Company circa 1950 and bears the company's logo on the peak of the front gable. ($75). 7.75" high x 8.25" wide x 10.25" deep. *Courtesy of Gene and Arliss Morris. Photograph by Gene Morris.*

Marx Two-car Garage. This two-car version by Louis Marx is brightly lithographed inside and out with garden tools and other items normally found in a garage. It makes a delightful companion to the company's dollhouses. The door opens from the bottom. ($85-95). 8" high x 12.5" wide x 15" deep. *Courtesy of Nanci Moore. Photograph by Roy Specht.*

Lithographed Two-car Garage. The unmarked lithographed metal garage has a spring and latch door. Although the manufacturer is unknown, the style of the building suggests it was made circa 1950s. It would have made a nice accessory for the metal dollhouses sold during that time. ($60). 6" high x 9" wide x 9" deep. *Courtesy of Marcie Tubbs. Photograph by Bob Tubbs.*

Eagle Garage. The Canadian firm of Eagle made this lithographed tin and fiberboard one-car garage in the 1950s. It is shown with a Reliable lawn mower from the same period. (Garage $65). 4.5" high x 7.75" wide x 9" deep. *Courtesy of Marcie Tubbs. Photograph by Bob Tubbs.*

Cardboard Garage. Made of cardboard with double tin doors, this garage is unmarked and the maker is unknown. The idyllic lithography, with bluebirds nesting in the front gable and a mother playing with her pig-tailed daughter, evokes memories of the 1950s. ($50-55). 7" high x 10" wide x 9.75" deep. *Courtesy of Becky Norris. Photograph by Don Norris.*

Renwal No. 195 "Garage With 2 Autos." The circa 1950s MIB plastic garage is pictured with two Renwal mechanics. (Boxed set $100-125, mechanic $300). *Courtesy of Marcie Tubbs. Photograph by Bob Tubbs.*

Renwal Garages. Two circa 1950s Renwal plastic garages are shown with their original cars. Both have hipped roofs. Like other Renwal products, the garages were available in a variety of color combinations. (Garage and car $40-50). 1.5" high x 3.75" wide x 5.25" deep. *Courtesy of Gene and Arliss Morris. Photograph by Gene Morris.*

Renwal Garage. Another style of garage by Renwal, circa 1950s, has a gabled roof and double doors. ($30-40). 3.5" high x 5" wide x 6.5" deep. *Courtesy of Ruth Petros.*

Wyandotte Garage. A circa 1950s plastic garage by Wyandotte includes two cars made by the same company. ($25-35). 1.75" high x 2.75" wide x 2.5" deep. *Courtesy of Gene and Arliss Morris. Photograph by Gene Morris.*

Payton Products garage. The unusual rounded double doors give this garage an Art Deco look. It was made by Payton Products, Inc. and included two cars. (MIB $50-75). 2.75" high x 5" wide x 7.5" deep. *Courtesy of Gene and Arliss Morris. Photograph by Gene Morris.*

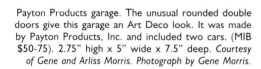

Ideal garage. This MIB plastic garage was made by the Ideal Company circa 1950s. The garage door opens to admit two plastic cars, also by Ideal. ($100-125). 3.25" high x 5" wide x 6" deep. *Photograph by Suzanne Silverthorn.*

Commercial Garages, Service Stations, and Car Washes

Many of the same toy companies produced commercial garages which provided a wonderful setting for housing and playing with a collection of small vehicles. These included parking garages, repair shops, and new car dealerships. As in real life, many of these functions were often combined in the same toy structures. It is also difficult to draw a distinction between commercial garages and services stations. Sometimes service stations were labeled as garages. So many toy service stations have been produced during the last 75 years that a collector could assemble quite a large collection of only these miniature structures.

One of the earliest examples of a toy commercial garage was made by the R. Bliss company in the early 1900s. Like the firm's dollhouses, the garages were made of wood with a lithographed paper covering. Parker Brothers was another American company which issued a commercial garage circa 1910. Their cardboard garage came with three metal cars and, according to its sign, was intended to house cars that were for sale or hire. Converse made wood automobile garages in several sizes, circa 1912. By 1938, Marx was marketing a lithographed metal building called the "Universal Auto Repair Shop." It sold for 89 cents in the Sears catalog.

Other companies, like Chein, made commercial garages during the 1930s. Milton Bradley offered a small garage as part of

their Bumpalow series during this same decade. By the late 1930s and early 1940s, Built-Rite was producing very interesting cardboard garages and sales rooms, some very Art Deco in style. The Rich Toy Company manufactured more substantial garages and service stations of Masonite circa 1950.

One of the most prolific companies was Keystone of Boston who produced pressed board parking garages and service stations during the 1940s and 1950s. The Keystone stations were made in seemingly endless variety, with differences in size and style almost unnoticeable except to a dedicated collector. They offered several play features including gas pumps that could pump water and plastic cars with hoods that could be lifted. The De Luxe Game Corporation made similar stations of Tekwood, including one that played music. Many of the De Luxe stations were sold through Sears under the Happi-Time label.

Lithographed metal service stations were made by Marx, T. Cohn, Wolverine, and others. Some were little more than service islands while others were elaborate structures with elevators and ramps which allowed the roof tops to be used as parking lots for toy vehicles.

Like all toys, garages and service stations are most valuable when found in their original boxes, complete with accessories. Stations which are currently most in demand when found in that condition include the many Marx metal stations from the 1930s, the Arcade wood models, and the other early stations including those made by the Rich and Keystone.

Lithographed "Garage." Made of lithographed paper over wood, this unmarked garage is printed in the subtle shades often found on toys by the R. Bliss Company. The front of the garage opens for play. The door marked "Office" is lithographed in place, but the double doors of the "Garage" open to admit a toy automobile. The car and figure are not original to the structure. ($1800-2000). 15" high x 14" wide x 9.5" deep. *Courtesy of Bill and Stevie Weart.*

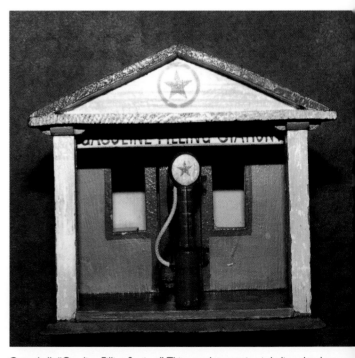

Gottschalk "Gasoline Filling Station." This wood gas station is believed to have been made by the German firm of Moritz Gottschalk. It has the red roof and outlined windows typical of the buildings the company made circa 1920s. It was apparently made for the American market as it is labeled in English and uses the word "gasoline." It has one wood gas pump. ($1500-2000). 7.5" high x 8" wide x 10.5" deep. *Courtesy of Bill and Stevie Weart.*

150

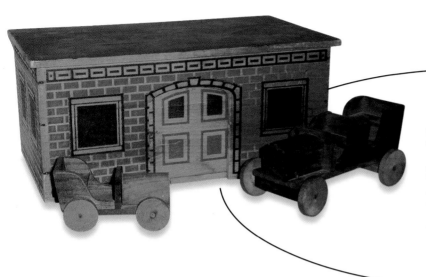

Converse Automobile Garage #761. Another version of this garage was pictured in the 1912 Morton E. Converse catalog. It was available in three sizes including a two-story model with three cars. This version came with the two vehicles shown and originally had an "Automobile Garage" sign which spanned the width of the roof. The Converse company applied the ink design directly on the wood. ($700-800). 5" high x 14" wide x 6" deep. *Courtesy of Leslie and Joanne Payne.*

The 1922 Montgomery Ward catalog advertised a metal lithographed service station which appears to use the same blank as the small Chein railroad stations. It came with an 8" long friction-powered automobile. Together, they sold for $1.89. The station was 5.5" high. *Photograph by Patty Cooper.*

Chein Service Station No. 426. The lithographed metal service station and garage was made by J. Chein & Company of New York in the late 1930s. One end opens to admit a vehicle. ($275 -300). 4" high x 6.75" wide 3.25" deep. *Courtesy of Christmas Morning. Photograph by Ben Stevens.*

Hullco "Toygas Station." The original box of this circa 1920s gas station identifies the manufacturer as Hullco of New York. The Hullco station was made of paperboard and had lithographed tin gas pumps. (MIB $500). 8" high x 13" wide x 11" deep. *Courtesy of Christmas Morning. Photograph by Ben Stevens.*

"Playgas Garage." Another circa 1920s paperboard station is missing the pumps but has a lithographed customer at the service window. ($100-150). *Courtesy of Marge Powell.*

Gibbs Service Station. This circa 1920s station is made of lithographed tin and has **wood** gas pumps. ($800). 7" high x 8.5" wide x 11.5" deep. *Courtesy of Christmas Morning. Photograph by Ben Stevens.*

Bumpalow Garage. Shown complete with its original box, this "Easy Builder Toy" was part of a series of buildings made by Milton Bradley in the 1930s. The building is made of flat pieces of laminated chipboard which can be fitted together using the precut slots and tabs. It includes a service area, office, and gas pumps. ($375-390). 5.75" high x 10" wide x 6" deep. *Courtesy of Christmas Morning. Photograph by Ben Stevens.*

Marx Service Station. An early lithographed tin service station by Louis Marx has one gas pump. A similar station was advertised in the 1929 Sears catalog with two pumps, a friction motor racer, and a bus for 48 cents. ($500-600). 3.75" high x 6" wide x 5.25" deep. *Courtesy of Christmas Morning. Photograph by Ben Stevens.*

"Britelite Filling Station." This lithographed tin service island was produced by Marx circa 1930s. The upright oil and grease display stand provided housing for batteries which powered the lights atop the pumps. ($350-450). 6.25" high x 9.25" wide x 3.25" deep. *Courtesy of Jim and Shirley Cox.*

"Marx Roadside Rest Service Station." This station was advertised in the September 1936 Butler Brothers catalog. The metal set included a roadster car, two electric lighted gas pumps, portable oil wagon, water can, two counter men (who resembled Laurel and Hardy), cash register, and stools for the diner. (MIB $1100-1600). 13.5" wide x 10" deep. *Courtesy of Thrilling Toys of Yesteryear.*

The Marx Sunny Side Service Station was advertised in the 1935 catalog of the Larkin Company of Buffalo, New York. The doors and windows of the metal station were operable. It came with a steel coupe, oil wagon, measuring can, water pail, and battery-operated lights. *Courtesy of Marge Meisinger. Photograph by Suzanne Silverthorn.*

Marx "Sunny Side Service Station." It is very difficult to find this Marx toy complete with the original box and accessories. (MIB $1000). 13.5" wide x 10" deep. *Courtesy of Charles L. Gilbert.*

Marx "Gull Service Station." The lithographed metal station was made by Louis Marx circa 1940. The set came with several vehicles, signs, and tires. The gas pumps could be lit by batteries. The gull style, with service bays on each side, is similar to an airport and fire station made by Marx during the same period. (MIB $900-1000). 16" wide x 11" deep. *Courtesy of Thrilling Toys of Yesteryear.*

155

Marx "Blue Bird Garage." The box of this lithographed metal station is marked "Universal Gas Service Station," but it is usually known to collectors by the name printed over the front entrance. It was one of a circa 1937 series made by Louis Marx which included a bus terminal, airport, and railroad station. ($450-600). 2.75" high x 11.75" wide x 6.5" deep. *Courtesy of George Handforth, Catsill Toys.*

Schoenhut "Gasoline and Service Station." This wood and fiberboard station was made by the A. Schoenhut Company of Philadelphia circa 1930s. The embossed cardboard roof is typical of buildings made by the company. Also pictured are three metal vehicles by Arcade. (Station only $800-1000). 4.25" high x 7.5" wide x 7.25" deep. *Courtesy of Bill and Stevie Weart.*

Arcade Service Station. A cast iron car, also by Arcade of Freeport, Illinois, is shown on the lift rack of the service station. This version has wood gas pumps, but the same station was also sold with cast iron pumps. The windows and other details are stenciled directly on the wood. (Station only $900-1100). 7.25" high x 12.5" wide x 12.5" deep. *Courtesy of Christmas Morning. Photograph by Ben Stevens.*

Arcade Gas Station. This wood Arcade gas station was advertised by Marshall Field and Company of Chicago in 1935. It sold for $1 with no vehicles. It had two gas pumps, a door that opened on the side, and stenciled details. An Arcade taxi is shown with the station. (Garage only, $1000-1200). 9" high x 8" wide x 12" deep. *Courtesy of Bill and Stevie Weart.*

Arcade "Super Service" Station. In addition to selling gasoline, this station offered parking on the roof. It was pictured in the 1941 Arcade catalog and was one of the last buildings made by Arcade as the company did not resume production after World War II. The wood station included three cast iron gas pumps and a cast iron car. (Garage only $1000-1200). 7.25" high x 12.5" wide x 9.25" deep. *Courtesy of Richard and Joan Ford.*

Built-Rite "Garage and Sales Room" No. 15. The cover of this MIB set is typical of the graphics used by Warren Paper Products in the 1930s. The illustration shows the word "Garage" in place of the "Reo" sign on the following example. The bottom of the box forms the base of the building. (MIB $400). *Courtesy of George Mundorf.*

Built-Rite "Reo" Garage and Sales Room No. 15. The circa 1930s cardboard structure is assembled using tab and slot construction. A catalog from Warren Paper Products shows this set with the word "garage" in place of the "Reo" sign. (MIB $400). 8.75" high x 13.75" wide x 9.75" deep. *Courtesy of Becky Norris. Photograph by Don Norris.*

Built-Rite Shell Service Station box. The bright graphics on the original box cover are typical of Warren Paper Products in the late 1930s. *Courtesy of George Mundorf.*

Built-Rite Shell Service Station. The assembled station was made of printed cardboard using tab and slot construction. ($400-450). 8.5" high x 17.5" wide x 13" deep. *Courtesy of Christmas Morning. Photograph by Ben Stevens.*

Rich Garage. The clearly marked building by Rich Toys of Clinton, Iowa has both a show room and service center. It was made of Gypsum board circa 1940s. The four metal vehicles are by Hubley and not original to the toy. (Garage only, $400). 8" high x 25" wide x 9.5" deep. *Courtesy of Bill and Stevie Weart.*

attractive box . . . makes an excellent gift.
49 N 7254—Shpg. wt. 2 lbs. 8 oz. . . . $1.98

Elevator really works!

De luxe Service Station with 6 plastic toy autos

Busiest gas station you ever saw! Many youngsters can play. $3.79
One can be in charge of the gas pumps, pretending to check their oil, fill 'em up, and pump up tires. Another can pretend to grease the cars on the grease rack. Someone must drive cars up the ramp to second floor parking lot. Another car is waiting to be taken up in the elevator. Just turn the knob up on the roof to raise the garage door. As door goes up, elevator comes down. Turn knob again—elevator carries cars up to the second floor for parking or repairs, while door closes once more. Overall size about 21¾x23x13 in. high. Made of Tekwood (3-ply fiber-board with wood center) and heavy fiber-board with wood framing. Set includes 6 plastic autos about 4¼ in. long, sturdy base and building, 4 signs, dummy air hose, cabinet, grease rack, 4 gas pumps with dummy hoses and lamp. Easy to assemble.
79 N 06460—Complete set. Shipping weight 5 pounds. $3.79

The first of a series of service stations by the De Luxe Game Corporation was advertised in the 1946 Sears Christmas catalog. The station was made of Tekwood (defined in the catalog as three-ply fiber-board with wood center and heavy fiber-board framing). It included an elevator, 6 plastic cars, air hose, grease rack, and 4 gas pumps. It is likely that the plastic cars were made by other companies. The station sold for $3.79. 13" high x 23" wide x 21.75" deep. *Courtesy of Betty Nichols. Photograph by Suzanne Silverthorn.*

New 18-piece super deluxe Service Station

Busiest, most modern gas station in Make-Believe Land!

- Big 2-floor building with elevator and sloping ramp for roof parking
- Elevator actually hoists car to second floor—as elevator goes up, door comes down automatically
- Store at rear with 2 counters
- True-to-life play gas pumps, air pump, greasing lift, tire racks
- 4 colorful, molded plastic autos —proportioned in size to station

Real elevator!

What youngster wouldn't be delighted at the chance to operate a big, de luxe service $4.79
station of his very own! Just like the real thing—gas pumps that really "fill 'em up" (with water), elevator that lifts auto to second floor, and greasing lift that really works. One youngster can pretend to check oil, sell gas, pump tires; another take charge of greasing; still another drive cars up ramp for parking on second floor or roof. Building with base 23x18x14½ in. high overall. Made of tekwood (3-ply wood-centered fiberboard). Set includes 1 sedan, 3 delivery trucks (2 have tanks you can fill)—all about 4½ in. long; air pump, attendant, and 3 gas pumps with 2 lamps—all of realistically molded plastic. Also includes dummy counters, oil cans, tire racks with tires and complete merchandise display in back. Complete station can be quickly set up.
79 N 06450—Shipping weight 5 pounds. . . . . Complete set $4.79

The 1947 Sears catalog pictured a De Luxe Service Station also made of Tekwood. It featured working gas pumps, an elevator, a grease lift, and roof top parking. Accessories for the station included 4 vehicles (2 had tanks to fill), air pump, and an attendant. The station sold for $4.79. 14.5" high x 23" wide x 18" deep. *Photograph by Suzanne Silverthorn.*

The Happi Time service station shown in the 1948 Sears catalog appears to have been made by the De Luxe Toy Corporation. This station featured a "De Luxe Laundry" and had the same type light as the De Luxe stations sold earlier by Sears. New features of this set were the laundry, which could hold water, and a battery operated light on the gas pumps. The station was made of Tekwood with plastic accessories which included an elevator, gas pumps that pumped water, attendant, grease rack, 3 tire racks with tires, 2 counters, and 3 plastic vehicles. The station sold for $4.89. *Courtesy of Betty Nichols. Photograph by Suzanne Silverthorn.*

"Happi Time" Service Station. Apparently identical to the station shown in the 1948 Sears catalog, this Tekwood building is believed to have been made by The De Luxe Toy Corporation. The lithographed stone and brick patterns are similar to other buildings believed to have been made by De Luxe. All of the accessories and the lights on the gas pumps are missing on this example. ($150-175). 14" high x 23" wide x 19" deep. *Courtesy of Jim Schaut.*

"Happi Time Service Station." Sold by Sears in 1949 and made of Tekwood, this station was probably made by De Luxe. The car wash was redesigned to be part of the building. The original station included an elevator, wood ramp, plastic gas pumps that held water, an attendant, and two vehicles (a delivery car and oil tanker). The station sold for $3.98. The gas pumps and most of the accessories are missing from the example shown. ($150-175). 11.75" high x 23" wide x 15.25" deep. *Courtesy of Jim Schaut.*

DE LUXE AUTO SERVICE STATION. The dream of every boy comes true when they receive one of these beautiful and well constructed service stations. Built of strong Tekwood construction thruout, it is gaily painted white with red and green trim. Large acetate display windows look just like the real thing, but will not break. A completely equipped garage, filling station, lubritorium, car laundry and parking garage combined. Overall dimensions 23"x19" and 14" high. Fully equipped with ramp to roof, and an elevation that actually works. Two electrically lighted gas pumps that hold and dispense water (imitation gas) to the tank of a plastic touring sedan. Also a separate car laundry service station that really washes, an air pump, a gasoline truck, and a fully equipped auto washroom containing counters and eight tires on racks. To top it all there is a mechanic and a metal hydraulic lift that raises and lowers cars. Mounted on sturdy base. **All for $6.00, postpaid.**

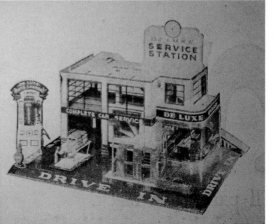

Another De Luxe Auto Service Station was advertised in the October 1949 *Children's Activities* magazine. It included all the features shown in the 1948 Sears Happi Time station advertisement and was priced at $6.00 postpaid. *Photograph by Suzanne Silverthorn.*

"Play Time De Luxe Service Station." This station appears to be identical to the one advertised in the 1949 *Children's Activities*. The only difference is the sign on top which read "Play Time," perhaps an indication that this station was made to be sold through another retailer. This model has an Auto Laundry, elevator, parking garage, lighted gas pumps, air pump, mechanic, hydraulic lift, and car. ($500-600). 14" high x 23" wide x 19" deep. *Courtesy of Toys and More.*

"Play Time Deluxe Service Station." This Tekwood station has the features of other De Luxe stations including the De Luxe Laundry, lift ramp, elevator, plastic gas pumps, and grease rack. The two story bow window with turret is a distinctive feature of this structure. ($500-600). 17" high x 23" wide x 12" deep. *Courtesy of Christmas Morning. Photograph by Ben Stevens.*

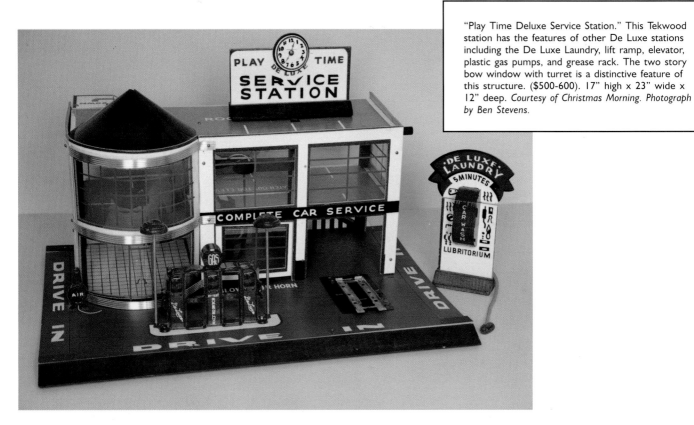

De Luxe "Firestone" Station. This circa late 1940s toy was made of Tekwood with a wood base, frame, and uprights. A paper which came with the station identified its maker as the De Luxe Game Corporation. The station included a grease rack, ramp, elevator, car wash on the side of the building, and gas pumps. ($200-250). 12.5" high x 23.5" wide x 16" deep. *Photograph by Suzanne Silverthorn.*

De Luxe "Firestone Complete Car Service." Another De Luxe station from the late 1940s indicates that the company may have done promotions for Firestone or made stations to be sold by the Firestone company. This Tekwood station uses the same gas pumps and lights as the earlier stations. There is an exit ramp, elevator, and separate sign. ($375-400). 15.75" high x 24" wide x 12.75" deep. *Courtesy of Christmas Morning. Photograph by Ben Stevens.*

New!.. Musical, electric-lighted Station

$4.59   Built of sturdy metal

HAPPI TIME   OUR OWN   TRADE MARK

Musical car-ramp inside station

Metal grease rack raises and lowers

Elevator automatically ejects auto

2 pumps dispense gas (water)

Priced low because of Sears large purchase . . . packed with a huge variety of fun and play features
Moving musical car lift tinkles "Whistle While You Work", lifts auto to roof . . . just turn crank
Automatic auto elevator . . . simply press lever and car is automatically raised and run out onto the roof
Display room has curved, transparent plastic front
Four plastic cars with easy-rolling wheels . . . 2 have gas (water) tanks that you can fill from pumps
Plastic auto laundry with flexible hose holds water for washing cars on metal grease-and-wash rack

• 3 plastic pumps, 2 dispense water from hoses

g enough to keep several youngsters happy at one
ne. One can run musical car ramp. Another can
e pumps that really "fill 'er up" (with water) or
sh cars on rack that raises and lowers . . . has pan
catch water. Third can hoist cars in elevator. Still
other can "drive" car to display room or "pump"

tires with dummy plastic air pump. Center plastic
pump lights up, uses penlight battery (not included).
Dummy floodlights and attendant of plastic. Lithographed metal station on Masonite Presdwood base
with rubber feet, 24x16x11 in. high overall. Wt. 7 lbs.
79 N 06475—Easy to set up, no tools needed $4.59

A De Luxe Happi Time Musical Service Station was pictured in the 1950 Sears Christmas catalog. This station had a base of Masonite and a lithographed metal station. When the car lift was used, the tune "Whistle While You Work" was played.

The station included an elevator, plastic auto laundry, grease and wash rack, display room, and 4 plastic cars. It sold for $4.57. In 1951, De Luxe produced a similar "Talking Service Station" that was also sold by Sears under the Happi Time label. It included a tape which said "Gas and oil, please" when a car was driven over it. *Photograph by Suzanne Silverthorn.*

"Happi Time Musical Service Station." By 1950, De Luxe began using litho-graphed metal for their stations with a Tekwood base. An elevator is provided to take cars to the roof top parking area and there is a ramp for them to descend. The office area has two chairs with metal tube legs and a matching table printed on one wall. All of the accessories and the musical feature are missing from this example. ($95-125). 11" high x 23" wide x 15.5" deep. *Photograph by Patty Cooper.*

Keystone "Washing-Lubrication-Parking." The circa 1940s Keystone garage was made of Masonite but, unlike most later Keystone buildings, the base was made of wood. The ramp, lift rack, air pump, and gas pump are also made of wood rather than plastic. The elevator on the right side is operated by a hand crank on the front of the building. ($200). 8.5" high x 23" wide x 14" deep. *Courtesy of Toys and More.*

A two-story Keystone Service Station was advertised in the 1948 Montgomery Ward Christmas catalog. The station was made of Masonite and wood. It included plastic gas pumps which could be used with water, a grease rack, and a car wash as well as a special car that could be filled with "gas." The price of the station was $4.49. *Courtesy of Betty Nichols. Photograph by Suzanne Silverthorn.*

"Keystone Service Station." Although very similar to the one advertised in the 1948 Montgomery Ward's Christmas catalog this example does not have a clock or printing over its service door or elevator. It features an elevator, car wash, grease rack, automatic door, and the special car. ($400-450). 8" high x 21.75" wide x 11.75" deep. *Courtesy of Toys and More.*

A one-story Keystone Garage was advertised in the 1949 Montgomery Ward Christmas catalog for $3.19. The station was made of Masonite Preswood and wood. It included a working elevator and gas tanks that could be filled with water. The wash pit had a pump that worked and the special car could have its "oil" drained.
20" wide x 9" deep. *Courtesy of Betty Nichols. Photograph by Suzanne Silverthorn.*

"Keystone Garage." This one-story version has a rounded window on the left and only one service door. It features a parking area on the left with a hedge and "car lubrication" sign at the back. The white plastic accessory in the foreground is marked "Penny meter." ($100-150). Building is 4.75" high x 8.25" wide x 5" deep. The base is 15.5" wide x 7.5" deep. *Photograph by Patty Cooper.*

"Keystone Garage." A garage, similar to this one, was shown in the December 1950 *Children's Activities* magazine for $5.25 postpaid. The model advertised had only one gas pump but otherwise they are the same. The station was made of Masonite and Tekwood and featured an elevator, gas pump that used water, air hose, grease rack, car wash, and a car that could be filled with "gas" or have its "oil" changed. The window frames are made of metal. ($300-400). 8" high x 24" wide x 11" deep. *Courtesy of George Mundorf.*

Keystone Service Station model #152. This small station still has its original box which designates its model number. The set included a plastic car which could be filled with "gas." The (now missing) hood could be lifted to check the oil. Although the celluloid gas pump is still attached to the base, the light shown on the box is gone. The garage door can be raised with the red knob. There is no lithography in the interior. ($175-200 with box). 5.25" high x 9.75" wide x 8" deep (at base). *Photograph by Patty Cooper.*

"Keystone Garage." The movable sign, with clock, on top of the garage, advertises this model as offering "complete car service." There are two opening garage doors providing access to the service area and roof top parking. A rounded plastic window on the right side provides a view into the sales area. The window frame above the garage door is plastic, unlike earlier models with metal windows. There is a plastic car wash with pump on the right side and a metal grease rack on the right. ($250-350). 8" high x 23.5" wide x 15.5" deep. *Photograph by Patty Cooper.*

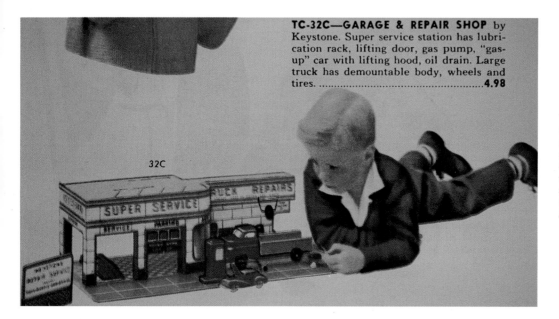

TC-32C—GARAGE & REPAIR SHOP by Keystone. Super service station has lubrication rack, lifting door, gas pump, "gas-up" car with lifting hood, oil drain. Large truck has demountable body, wheels and tires. **4.98**

The Keystone "Super Service" Shop was advertised in the 1953 Dayton Company catalog from Minneapolis. The station had a lubrication rack, lifting door, gas pump, car with lifting hood, and oil drain. A new twist was a truck which had a "demount-able body, wheels, and tires" so it could be repaired. *Courtesy of Marge Meisinger. Photograph by Suzanne Silverthorn.*

"Keystone Automatic Parking" Garage No. 213. The 1955 Keystone catalog described this garage as having "Rugged Tekwood Construction." It is all wood and fiberboard, with no plastic parts. A wood knob in the center of the roof operates a turn table inside which holds cars and moves them from the entrance to the exit. Another knob on the front of the roof operates a lever which pushes the cars out. The set was sold with six plastic cars. The slot in front of the clerk's window originally held numbered parking tickets which matched the numbers of the parking slots.. ($150-175). 4" high x 11.75" wide x 12" deep. *Photograph by Patty Cooper.*

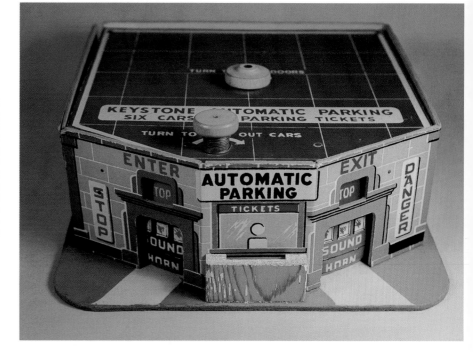

Keystone Service Station No. 219. This service station with clear plastic "wash pit" was also shown in the 1955 Keystone catalog. The building had two folding doors and a "new gas pump with recording dial." The set included a plastic car with "lifting hood." ($125-150). Base measures 24" wide x 16" deep. *Courtesy of Toys and More.*

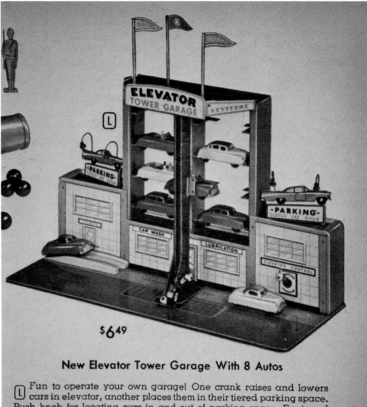

$6.49

New Elevator Tower Garage With 8 Autos

L Fun to operate your own garage! One crank raises and lowers cars in elevator, another places them in their tiered parking space. Push knob for locating cars in and out of parking space. Equipped with elevator, ramp, roof signs, pennants, 8 easy-roll cars.
48 T 2748 M—Abt. 24x9 in.; 15¼ in. high. Assembled. Wt. 6 lbs. 6.49

The 1957/58 Mihlbaugh catalog, from Sharon, Pennsylvania, advertised a Keystone station which was very similar to model No. 219. The later version had a fiberboard car wash and two gas pumps. The set sold for $4.98. *Courtesy of Marge Meisinger. Photograph by Suzanne Silverthorn.*

The Keystone Elevator Tower Garage was advertised in the 1957 Montgomery Ward catalog for $6.49. A crank could be used to move the eight cars up and down in the elevator and into their tiered parking spaces. 15.25" high x 24" wide x 9" deep. *Courtesy of Marge Meisinger. Photograph by Suzanne Silverthorn.*

"Tri-ang Minic Garage." The parking garage by Tri-ang of England has a sign on the side advertising space for "Model cars & lorries." It is made of wood with plastic doors and windows. There are two plastic gas pumps and an inside ramp which provides access to the second floor for toy vehicles. ($450-500). 10" high x 19" wide x 10.5" deep. *Courtesy of Jim and Shirley Cox.*

An advertisement for a Superior Service Station appeared in the Montgomery Ward Christmas catalog from 1949. The metal two-story station was made by T. Cohn. It included an elevator, gas pumps that used water, car wash, air reel, car ramp, and two plastic cars that could be filled with "gas" and then drained at the oil rack. The price was $4.29. *Courtesy of Betty Nichols. Photograph by Suzanne Silverthorn.*

Superior Service Station. The T. Cohn station advertised in the 1949 Ward's catalog was made of lithographed metal. A working elevator provided access to the roof top parking area. ($225-250). 10.5" high x 25" wide x 16" deep. *Courtesy of George Mundorf.*

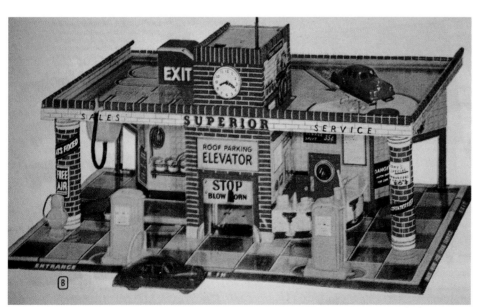

A similar Superior service station was advertised in the 1952 Montgomery Ward Christmas catalog. This T. Cohn metal station had posts at the outside corners and a snack bar on the right side complete with lithographed stools. The set included two plastic cars which could be filled with water from the pumps. It sold for $4.29. 10.25" high x 25" wide x 16.75" deep. *Photograph by Suzanne Silverthorn.*

172

Superior "Sky Park" Station. T. Cohn made a three-story version of their service station with roof top parking circa 1959. It featured a motor-driven elevator, plastic pumps, cars, trucks, accessories, and attendants. A vertical sign on the third story which said "Sky Park" is missing from this example. The original retail price was $9.98. ($200-250). 17.5" high x 25" wide x 15" deep. *Courtesy of Arliss and Gene Morris. Photograph by Gene Morris.*

Another version of the T. Cohn three-story garage was advertised in the 1959 Montgomery Ward Christmas catalog. The only difference between this one and the "Sky Park" model was the signage. *Courtesy of Marge Meisinger. Photograph by Suzanne Silverthorn.*

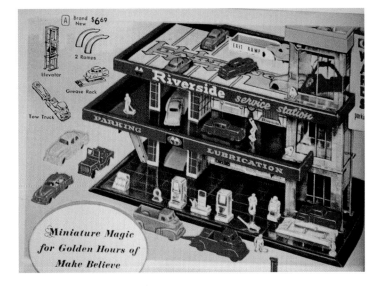

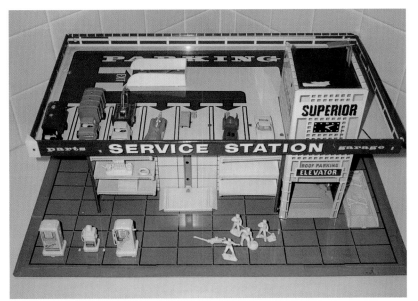

Superior Service Station. T. Cohn made several variations of this station circa early 1960s. Most had an exit sign on top and roof top parking accessible by an elevator or ramp. Accessories included attendants, jack, tires, and assorted tires. ($150-200). 13" high x 25" wide x 19" deep. *Courtesy of Diane Whipple.*

A metal Marx Service Station with "Sky-View Parking" was advertised in the 1950 Aldens Christmas catalog for $2.89. It included a metal elevator, metal ramp, oil rack, wash rack, and five plastic cars. *Photograph by Suzanne Silverthorn.*

Marx "Sky-View" Service Station. The metal service station advertised in the 1950 Aldens catalog was made of lithographed metal and offered roof top parking. (MIB $350). 11" high x 26" wide x 14.75" deep. *Courtesy of Jim and Beverly Cox, Sussex Antique Toy Shop.*

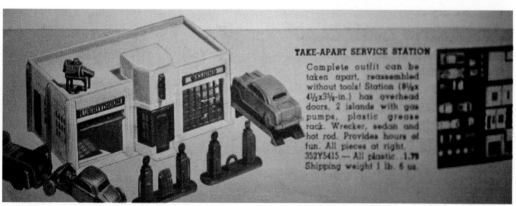

The Marx "Take-Apart" Service Station was advertised in the 1953 Aldens Christmas catalog for $1.79. The plastic station came with two islands of gas pumps, plastic grease rack, sedan, and hot rod. 3.5" high x 11.5" wide x 4.5" deep. *Courtesy of Marge Meisinger. Photograph by Suzanne Silverthorn.*

"Auto-Laundry." This small lithographed tin structure was believed to have been made by Marx for either Sears or Firestone, circa 1950s. *Courtesy of Jim and Shirley Cox.*

Marx "Mid-Town Garage" and "Car Wash." This lithographed metal structure consists of two walls and a roof with opening doors on each end. One of the doors says "Garage" and the other "Lubritorium." There is a plastic skylight through which vehicles can be viewed. ($50-75). 3.25" high x 6" wide x 9" deep. *Photograph by Patty Cooper.*

Marx Service Station with "Take A-Part Car." The early 1950s plastic service station came in several different colors. The set included two cars, one of which could be taken apart. It also contained a lift rack, gas pumps, engine stand, and five figures. It appears to be the same as the station advertised in the 1953 Aldens catalog. ($125-150). *Courtesy of Toys and More.*

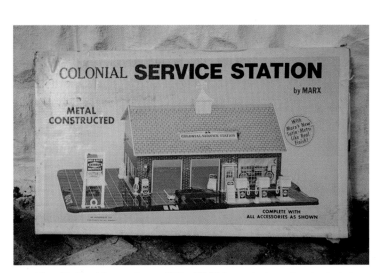

Marx "Colonial Service Station." The 1968 lithographed metal station includes a lubrication rack, tire rack, oil rack, two cars, and other plastic accessories. (MIB $250-275). 8.25" high x 26.5" wide x 15.5" deep. *Courtesy of Jim and Beverly Cox, Sussex Antique Toy Shop.*

The 1959 Sears Christmas catalog advertised a Happi-Time service station with tall parking garage for $7.98. This set was made by Marx and is like their own Midtown Service Station. *Courtesy of Marge Meisinger. Photograph by Suzanne Silverthorn.*

Marx "Midtown Service" Station. The circa 1959 lithographed steel building has a steel base. The set included an electric operated elevator, pumps with canopy, "real" car wash, attendants, cars, and other accessories. (MIB $300-350). 14" high 29.75" wide x 16" deep. *Courtesy of Toys and More.*

Marx/Distler "Electronic Filling Station." The circa 1950s station is made of lithographed metal and came with a plastic and metal car. The set was made by Distler and sold through Marx in the United States. The batteries recharge the motor in the car to simulate refueling. (MIB $450-600). *Courtesy of Christmas Morning. Photograph by Ben Stevens.*

Cragston/Alps Mobilgas Service Station. The circa 1950s metal station came with a "mechanical automobile." (MIB $450). *Courtesy of Jim Schaut.*

Line Mar "Cities Service Station." The set included a lithographed metal station and car. The electric motor from the station revved up the car's engine. The station on the box cover was featured in the 1957 Aldens Christmas catalog for $2.98. (MIB $150-200). 3.5" high x 10.5" wide x 5.5" deep. *Courtesy of Christmas Morning. Photograph by Ben Stevens.*

Buddy L Texaco. The circa 1957-60 building is made of lithographed metal and the accessories are plastic. It includes opening garage doors and a service ramp lift. ($550-600). 6.25" high x 24" wide x 18" deep. *Courtesy of Christmas Morning. Photograph by Ben Stevens.*

Sears "Servicenter." This station was shown with a sign which said "Servicenter" in the 1973 Sears catalog. It was made to be used with Matchbox cars which were not included with the set.

The station includes a grease rack that goes up and down, a turntable for car inspection, a drive- through car wash, and a ringing gas pump. The station is made of plastic and metal. (Station only $50-75). 5" high x 11.75" wide x 8" deep. *Courtesy of Suzanne Silverthorn (her childhood toy).*

"Matchbox Series Service Station MG-1." The plastic BP station was sold without accessories. The pumps, signs, and Matchbox vehicles were purchased separately, but at the same time, in the 1950s. (MIB $150). 4.5" high x 9" wide x 6.5" deep. *Courtesy of Bill Dohm (his childhood toy).*

Brumberger "Tri Level Service Station." The station was made of composition wood and plastic in 1971. There were ramps which provided access to all three levels for the six plastic cars included in the set. The toy was sold in the J.C. Penny's catalog for $4.99. (MIB $100-125). 17.25" high x 25" wide x 14" deep. *Courtesy of Toys and More.*

Wolverine "Shell Service Station." The circa 1970s Colonial style station was made of lithographed steel with two operable doors. Wolverine advertised the same style of station with different gas pumps as a Texaco station in 1975. The tow truck and car were the same with both stations. The plastic accessories included service ramp lifts, air pump, tire display, jack, and signs. (MIB $300-350). 11.75" high x 24.5" wide x 15" deep. *Courtesy of Christmas Morning. Photograph by Ben Stevens.*

VIII. Defense and Exploration

Since the beginning of humankind, people have had disagreements over possessions, ideas, and territory. These conflicts have led to individual fights as well as to more organized warfare. Humans have designed all kinds of structures to defend themselves from enemy attack. From the Great Wall of China to the fascinating European castles to the more primitive American forts, fortresses were built to protect inhabitants from invasion.

Probably the most popular defense toy has been the castle. Toy fortresses were commercially produced in Germany as early as the middle of the nineteenth century and their production continued into the middle of the twentieth century. Early German companies who sold castles included Moritz Gottschalk, Marklin, and Paul Leonhardt. Many of these castles were designed with storage space in their bases for toy soldiers. Tri-ang, the English company owned by Lines Brothers, also made castles in the early part of the twentieth century.

In America, Built-Rite (Warren Paper Products), Rich Toys, Keystone, and Louis Marx all offered toy castles during the 1930s through 1950s. Built-Rite marketed at least three different cardboard castles, some complete with cardboard soldiers. Rich made four different models of pressed hardboard toy fortresses for boys. In addition, they made a Colleen Moore castle in two sizes. This was an affordable toy modeled after the elaborate castle owned by the movie star and was used to raise money for charity. The Colleen Moore castles were more likely to house Tootsietoy dollhouse furniture than soldiers. Keystone produced a simple castle type fort made of wood with an affixed cannon. The prolific Marx company issued several lithographed metal castle play sets during the 1950s. These included the Prince Valiant Fort in 1954 and the Robin Hood Castle in 1956.

American companies in the early part of the twentieth century produced several toys modeled after the military forts and armories found in the United States. The R. Bliss Company and W.S. Reed used lithographed paper over wood and cardboard to produce highly detailed structures that were affordable to the middle class. These forts often came with wood cannons which could be used to knock over lithographed soldiers. In 1903, Schoenhut advertised a cardboard armory which opened to show lithographed scenes of a drill room, parade ground, and camp. It included eight composition soldiers.

In the late 1940s and early fifties, toy manufacturers began making a variety of forts which recreated periods in American history. Many of these were related to popular television shows with a western theme. T. Cohn introduced a lithographed metal Fort Superior Trading Post in 1951. It included metal stockade fencing and plastic figures. The famous Louis Marx firm produced many lithographed metal forts including various Fort Apache and Rin-Tin-Tin play sets. They also made an Alamo Fortress, Revolutionary War, and Civil War playsets that included lithographed buildings, tents, and enough plastic soldiers to stage a pretend battle.

More modern forts were produced just before and after World War II. Keystone made a series of "Exploding Forts" which collapsed when shot by the accompanying tank. The Keystone Company also issued at least four variations of a Coast Defense Fort, in different sizes and price ranges. Some included wood ships or airplanes which could be launched with a spring-loaded device. During the 1950s, Louis Marx made several U.S. Armed Forces sets with lithographed metal headquarters and a variety of plastic tents, soldiers, tanks, and airplanes. During this same time, T. Cohn made a U.S. Naval Base which included a giant revolving crane and plastic ships.

By the 1960s, when the United States was involved in the unpopular war in Viet Nam, military playsets became less fashionable and were mostly discontinued. But during this same period, the United States began committing more of its resources to space exploration. When the Soviet Union launched Sputnik in 1957, the excitement generated by the "space race" led to the production of space related playsets. Some of the early space toys were based on imaginative exploits such as those on the CBS television program "Tom Corbett, Space Cadet." Louis Marx began producing playsets that were more realistic. Most of their sets were based on Cape Canaveral, but each new issue was slightly different and modeled after real space missions such as Project Mercury. Later Marx sets reflected the renaming of the space facility to Cape Kennedy.

Toy castles, forts, and space stations are highly valued by collectors today, both as settings for toy soldiers and for the part of history they represent.

Reed "No. 19 Fort Grant." This lithographed paper over wood fort by the Whitney S. Reed Company is very similar to a fort which was advertised in the 1889 Montgomery Ward catalog. Both were designed so that the box in which the fort was packed became the base of the structure. A wood cannon was provided to assault the fort (or perhaps to defend?).

A smaller No.10 1/2 Fort Grant was advertised in the Reed catalog for 1897-98. It was 10" high and came with only four soldiers. The box of the fort shown here is 18" x 4" x 6.75". The assembled fort is 10" high (not including flags) x 21.5" wide x 6.75" deep. *Courtesy of Linda and Carl Thomas, Jr.*

Reed "U.S. Armory." Another lithographed paper over wood fort by W.S. Reed has been identified as #34. The set includes twelve lithographed soldiers and a cannon. ($2500-3500). 13.75" high (without flags) x 33" wide x 13" deep. *Courtesy of Linda and Carl Thomas, Jr.*

Bliss "Fort Sumter." The circa 1890s lithographed paper over wood fort by R. Bliss can be stored neatly in its hinged box. When the box is opened, the bottom becomes the base of the fort and the top becomes the second tier. The soldiers lithographed on the fort itself appear to be wearing Civil War era uniforms while the four movable soldiers guarding the top are dressed in clothes from an earlier era. The set also includes a lithographed paper over wood cannon. ($2500-3500). 18" high x 17.5" wide x 3" deep. *Courtesy of Linda and Carl Thomas, Jr.*

Bliss Fort #530. This lithographed wood fort is clearly marked "R. Bliss Company," with the logo used by the company circa 1901. The number 530, printed along the edges of the lithographed papers, helps confirm this vintage since the dollhouses shown in the 1901 Bliss catalog are also numbered in the 500s. The front of the tiny structure opens to reveal one room. The door which is inset into the front is also operable. The turret on the right is a solid cylinder, inaccessible to soldiers or children. A fort much like this one has been seen with turrets on both sides. ($1500). 8.75" high x 8.75" wide x 4.5" deep. *Courtesy of Sibyl W. Smith.*

The interior of Bliss Fort #530 is richly lithographed with a battle scene depicting figures which can not be mistaken for anything but toys. The printed soldiers all have wooden bases and their leader rides a horse on wheels. *Courtesy of Sybil W. Smith.*

Lithographed German Fortress. This richly lithographed paper over wood fort has no markings. It is believed to have been made in Germany circa 1900-1910. ($350-500). 10" high x 9" wide x 7" deep. *Fort and photograph from the collection of Ruth Petros.*

Lithographed German Fortress. A slightly larger lithographed paper over wood appears to be from the same manufacturer as the previous one. It is unmarked but believed to be circa 1900-1910. ($500-700). 11" high x 11" wide x 8" deep. *Courtesy of Ruth Petros.*

German Fortress. The base of this castle/fort is consistent with painted wood forts known to have been made by the German firm of Moritz Gottschalk. (800-1000). *Courtesy of Carol Miller.*

Gottschalk Fortress No. 5730. The style of this fort and the presence of a four -digit number under its base allow it to be attributed to Moritz Gottschalk with a high degree of probability. It is stamped "Made in Germany." The base of the fort contains storage space for the removable buildings. There is also a trap door through which unwary invaders may find themselves in the dungeon. ($450-600). 13" high x 17.25" wide x 13.25" deep. *Photograph by Patty Cooper.*

German Fortress. Probably made by Moritz Gottschalk, this larger fort has a textured base similar to the previous one. The numbers penciled on the bottom appear to read #501 - G-1. It has two trap doors. The pieces can be stored in the base. ($1600-1800). 25" high x 27" wide x 21" deep. *Courtesy of Leslie and Joanne Payne.*

Gottschalk Fort No. 5518. The four-digit number and the words "Made in Germany" are stamped under the base of this painted wood fort. A similar fort numbered 5259, was advertised in the Gottschalk section of *The Universal Toy Catalog* of 1924. A hinged trap door at the top of the ramp provides access to a storage compartment in base. The bottom is also hinged. ($450-600). 13" high to top of tower x 13.5" wide x 9" deep. *Private collection. Photograph by Patty Cooper.*

Pressed Wood Fort. The manufacturer of this unmarked, pressed wood fort is unknown. It features an operable portcullis. ($200-300). *Courtesy of Ben DeVoto.*

185

Tri-ang Castle. On the back of the base is a round metal label which reads "Triangtois. The World's Best Toys." Tri-ang was the trademark of Lines Brothers of England and this label was used in the 1920s.

The castle is made of wood with a flocked base. The main castle building, walls, and towers are painted with bushes and flowers, like many of the Tri-ang dollhouses. A light bulb is mounted inside the back castle arch, with a metal contact switch on the back of the castle. The ramp is made of heavy cardboard. ($600-750). The base measures 12" wide by 10" deep. *Courtesy of Linda Hanlon.*

Rich Toys Fort. Like the Rich dollhouses, this fort is made of Gypsum board except for the red tops of the turrets, which are wood. The back of the sliding door is stamped "Made in U.S.A. Rich Toys. Clinton, Iowa." The fort is trapezoidal in shape and open at the top. A Rich fort was advertised in the 1939 Edward K. Tryon Company catalog. ($350-400). 9.25" high x 20" wide x 7" deep. *Courtesy of Mineral Point Toy Museum. Photograph by Carol Stevenson.*

Rich Toys Castle. In the mid-1930s, the actress Colleen Moore toured the country with a Hollywood-designed toy castle to raise money for children's charities. The Rich Toy Company, which had already manufactured a number of toy forts, recognized an opportunity to market a fiberboard version of Miss Moore's famous castle. The original Colleen Moore Castle is now housed at the Museum of Science and Industry in Chicago. The Rich castles came in two sizes. The larger one had multiple (although two-dimensional) turrets and exterior balconies deep enough to accommodate dolls. It contained a total of eight rooms plus a two-story courtyard at the front of the castle. ($750-1000). 20" high x 30" wide x 19" deep. *Courtesy of Mineral Point Toy Museum. Photograph by Carol Stevenson.*

Rich Toys Castle. The smaller version of the Colleen Moore castle is still an impressive piece of toy architecture, although most of the details are silk screened rather than three-dimensional. Both versions are extremely difficult to find. ($400-500). 17" high x 24" wide x 13" deep. *Courtesy of Kathy Garner.*

The smaller version of the Colleen Moore castle by Rich Toys contained five rooms. Although the ceilings are very high, many collectors furnish their castles with Tootsietoy furniture by Dowst because of the limited floor space and size of the door openings. It is believed that the castles were sometimes sold with Tootsietoy furniture. The interior walls, like those in many Rich dollhouses, were plain brown, but the windows and doors of the castle had silk-screened frames. *Courtesy of Kathy Garner.*

A 1937 advertisement from the Larkin Company of Buffalo, New York, offered a Built-Rite Army Camp for $2.00 in coupons. The original set was made of heavy cardboard. It came with 6 olive drab pup tents; 4 trench sections with attached dugouts; and 108 soldiers, each 3" high. Note the Keystone Exploding Fort shown on the same page. *Courtesy of Marge Meisinger. Photograph by Suzanne Silverthorn.*

Built-Rite Fort. Warren Paper Products of Lafayette, Indiana manufactured this cardboard fort. The precut pieces were assembled by fitting tabs into slots. The bottom of the box became the base of the fort. ($85-100). 8" high x 11.75" wide x 8.75" deep. *Courtesy of Becky Norris. Photograph by Don Norris.*

A more elaborate Built-Rite Fort was advertised in the 1943 Montgomery Ward catalog for $1.79. The 110-piece army set included 8 vehicles, "more than 90 fighting men," and "a pistol for the General." Rubber bands could be shot from the gun, but happily for parents, none were included with the set. *Photograph by Suzanne Silverthorn.*

Built-Rite Fort Set No. 25. Although the box top pictures soldiers and airplanes, none were part of the set. When assembled, the bottom of the box becomes the base of the fort. Eight additional cardboard pieces fit together, using tabs and slots, to form the walls, second floor, ramp and tower. The double front doors are made to open. According to the box, the set was copyrighted in 1940 by the Warren Paper Products Company of Lafayette, Indiana. ($100-125). 10.75" high x 13.5" wide x 9.5" deep. *Photograph by Patty Cooper.*

Keystone Exploding Fort. A similar Keystone exploding fort was advertised in the 1938 catalog of the N. Shure Company. The forts originally included a tank with shells which could be released with a spring mechanism. If a shell hit the red metal disk visible below the doors of the fort, a lethal-looking mousetrap mechanism was released which caused the pieces of the fort to fly apart. The tank is missing from this set. The two cannons provided to defend the fort were not designed to actually work. ($100-125). 5.25" high x 14" wide x 5" deep. *Photograph by Patty Cooper.*

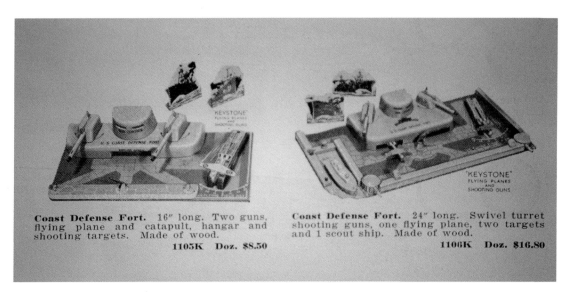

Coast Defense Fort. 16″ long. Two guns, flying plane and catapult, hangar and shooting targets. Made of wood.

1105K   Doz. $8.50

Coast Defense Fort. 24″ long. Swivel turret shooting guns, one flying plane, two targets and 1 scout ship. Made of wood.

1106K   Doz. $16.80

The 1941 wholesale catalog from Carson Pirie Scott & Company of Chicago pictured two different versions of the Keystone Coast Defense Fort. Both included guns, planes which could be ejected, and shooting targets. At least three other versions of this fort are known to have been made. *Courtesy of Marge Meisinger. Photograph by Suzanne Silverthorn.*

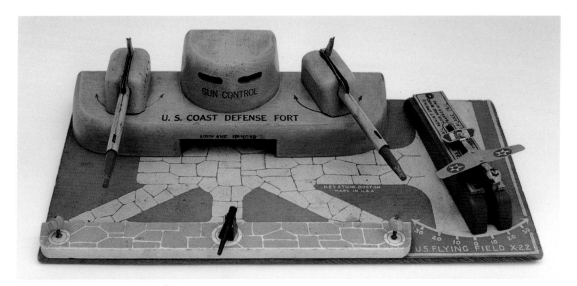

Keystone U.S. Coast Defense Fort. The Keystone Manufacturing Company of Boston made this fort of pressed board and wood with a few metal pieces. For such a simple toy, it offered a lot of action. Both of the swivel turret shooting guns could project a wooden missile, the spring-loaded devise could launch the metal plane, and two wood spotlights were designed to swivel in search of enemy aircraft. ($100-150). 3.5″ high x 16″ wide x 8″ deep. *Photograph by Patty Cooper.*

Keystone Fort No. 531. This fort was solidly built of plywood and wood. A wood cannon, mounted on a swivel base, could shoot cannon balls from the roof of the fort. A detachable chain barricaded the entrance. The front towers have holes which originally held flags. The same fort was also available with battery operated lights on each side of the entrance. A paper label near the cannon reads "Keystone Mfg. Co., Boston, Mass." ($100-125). 10" high x 12.75" wide x 6.75" deep. *Photograph by Patty Cooper.*

Keystone Shooting Frontier Set. The boxed Keystone set included a log western fort with a mountainous backdrop. The covered wagon, with cloth canopy, and the stagecoach were made of sturdy pressed board and had operable wheels. A toy rifle, marked "U.S. Cavalry," was included with rubber bullets which could be used to knock over either Indians or cowboys. ($150-200). *Photograph by Patty Cooper.*

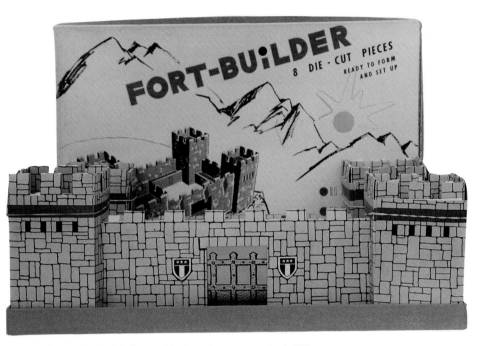

"Fort Builder" set by R.E. Dwyer. This boxed set is copyrighted 1950. It contains eight die-cut cardboard pieces which form the structure. The bottom of the box forms the base of the fort. ($40-50). 7" high x 22" wide x 15" deep. *Photograph by Suzanne Silverthorn.*

"Midgies: The Complete Mobile Miniature Army." Jaymar Specialty Company of New York, produced this boxed wood and cardboard army set circa late 1950s. ($100-125). *Courtesy of Gene and Arliss Morris. Photograph by Gene Morris.*

"Fort Superior." The lithographed fort by T. Cohn was also a trading post. The buildings had colorful details both inside and outside. The two-story building was open-backed and contained three rooms. The rolled edges on the metal stockade fencing allowed the pieces to be connected and the same device made the front gates operable.

   The original set included plastic horses, cowboys, Indians, wagons, ladders, and a cannon said to really fire shells. It was advertised in the 1951 Billy and Ruth catalog for $4.98. ($150-175). The trading post is 8" high x 11" wide x 7.5" deep. *Photograph by Patty Cooper.*

TC-33E

TC-33E PRINCE VALIANT MEDIEVAL FORTRESS (5-13 years) by L. Marx—a play set featuring the youngsters' favorite, Prince Valiant! Steel fortress 23" x 13¾", 8¼" high. Drawbridge,

The Marx "Prince Valiant Medieval Fortress" was advertised by The Emporium of San Francisco in 1954. The steel fortress was 8.25" high x 23" long x 13.75" deep. It included a drawbridge, 5 Prince Valiant figures, 30 knights, 9 horse, and 2 cannons for $6.50. *Courtesy of Marge Meisinger. Photograph by Suzanne Silverthorn.*

"Prince Valiant Castle Fort." The cover of the boxed set says that it came with figures, horses, and cannons, but does not state how many. ($450-500). *Courtesy of The Early Adventure.*

The Robin Hood Playset by Marx was sold through the Montgomery Ward catalog in 1956. The lithographed metal set included 90 pieces and sold for $5.72. It was similar to the Prince Valiant Fortress, but had conical peaks to the towers. The plastic figures included Robin, fair maid Marian, Friar Tuck, Little John, and the Sheriff of Nottingham, as well as thirty-three Merrie Men and twenty armored knights. Other pieces included six armored horses, deer, trees, and "medieval accessories." A smaller castle with only thirty-five pieces was advertised on the same page for $3.97 and additional figures could be purchased in a set of twenty-two. *Courtesy of Marge Meisinger. Photograph by Suzanne Silverthorn.*

Big 147-piece Army Training Center
Howitzer, Machine Gun Actually Shoot

If pieces were bought separately, set would cost over $10. Over 95 Vinyl **plastic soldiers** in various poses: on parade, marching with rifles and flags. Also combat soldiers firing bazookas, charging with rifles and bayonets, firing rifles, throwing hand grenades, bearing stretchers, etc. Accurately detailed for realistic effect. Two stretchers also included. **Big Headquarters Building** measures 11x7x6 inches. Constructed of durable metal. Realistically lithographed. All edges turned for strength and safety. Very easy to set up. **Plastic Furniture for Headquarters** includes desk, swivel chair, army switchboard, rifle rack, crate, wastebasket, map table, file cabinet, bench and side chairs. **Army field equipment** includes 5-inch howitzer and 3¼-inch machine gun which actually ejects dummy bullets. Other equipment: Rifle on tripod, tents, stacked rifles, bazooka gun, flag, trees, half track, scout car, etc. 16 sections of fence. Soldiers, equipment all to scale. $589
79 N 05920—Shipping weight 5 pounds . . . . Big value 147-pc. set $5.89
22-piece Set of Extra Soldiers (not illustrated) in a variety of positions.
49 N 5976—Set of 21 soldiers 1 nurse. Add·set to 79 N 05920 above. Shpg. wt. 10 oz. . . . . 88¢

Left: Sears advertised a 147- piece Marx Army Training Center in their 1952 catalog for $5.89. The set included a lithographed metal building with over 95 plastic soldiers in various poses. Plastic furniture for the headquarters building included a desk, swivel chair, army switchboard, rifle rack, crate, wastebasket, map table, file cabinet, bench, and side chairs. A 5-inch howitzer was included which actually shot dummy bullets. Other field equipment included rifles, tents, a bazooka gun, flags, trees, half track, scout car, and sixteen sections of fence. An extra set with twenty-one soldiers and a nurse could be purchased for 88 cents. *Photograph by Suzanne Silverthorn.*

Below: The 1957 Sears Christmas catalog advertised a Marx U.S. Armed Forces Training Center which used the same building design, but had slightly different lithography. The 165-piece set sold for $5.84. There were over 100 plastic soldiers, approximately 2" tall. The set also included three launching platforms with nine rockets to launch. There were twenty-two pieces of field equipment, a jet plane, a combat car, camp accessories, flagpole with flag, and sixteen sections of fence. *Photograph by Suzanne Silverthorn.*

Marx "U.S. Armed Forces Training Center." The lithographed metal building had details printed inside and outside. (As shown, $50-60; MIB set $300-325). 6" high x 11" long x 7" deep. *Photograph by Suzanne Silverthorn.*

194

The Marx Revolutionary War Playset was advertised in the 1957 Sears Christmas catalog. The 140-piece set sold for $5.77. The Colonial Headquarters building was a "2-story lithographed steel building" which measured 7" high x 10.5" long x 4.5" deep. In a gesture to fairness, there were thirty-six Colonial soldiers and thirty-six Redcoats. The British had the advantage of fourteen Indian braves helping them attack. The plastic figures, in fighting poses, measured approximately 2.25" (54mm) tall.

There was an extensive array of plastic accessories. Furnishings for the house included a table, ladder-back chair, two benches, rocking chair, three stools, spinning wheel, cauldron, and a butter churn. Outside, there was a chopping block, woodpile, anvil, campfire with pot, well, two lanterns, two powder kegs, musket stack, three trees, two tree stumps, stretcher, flagpole, six sections of fence, and two stone walls. A heavy cannon and two light canons could shoot miniature shells and had the requisite ramrod, bore swab, shot tray, shot, and shells. *Photograph by Suzanne Silverthorn.*

The Marx Fort Apache Set was advertised in the 1958 Sears catalog. The 130-piece set sold for $5.79. A similar set with 100 pieces was shown in the 1957 Sears catalog and their 1959 catalog offered a set with 135 pieces. The sets included a lithographed steel headquarters (6" high x 11" wide x 6" deep), a 9" high gate blockhouse, additional plastic blockhouses, plastic figures approximately 2.25" (25mm) high, horses, cannons, powder kegs, anvil, well, camp fire, Indian braves with horses, and teepees. Smaller sets were advertised by other retailers. *Photograph by Suzanne Silverthorn.*

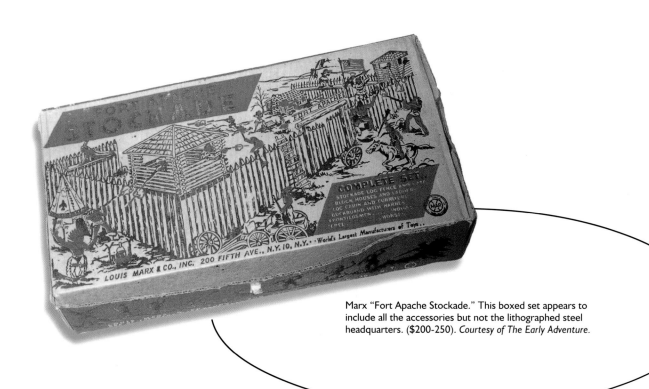

Marx "Fort Apache Stockade." This boxed set appears to include all the accessories but not the lithographed steel headquarters. ($200-250). *Courtesy of The Early Adventure.*

Marx "Fort Apache Play Set." A different style lithographed headquarters is shown on this box cover. A similar set, called "Rin-Tin-Tin Fort Apache Set" was advertised in the 1957 catalog of Kilpatricks of Omaha for $5.98. That advertisement described the headquarters building as lithographed steel featuring "the Post Commissary, Blacksmith Shop, Headquarters Sign." The Kilpatricks' set included Rip, Rusty, Rin-Tin-Tin and twenty cavalrymen, as well as Indians with a teepee. The boxed set shown appears to have the same main pieces, but no Rin-Tin-Tin tie-in. ($250-300). *Courtesy of Jim Schaut.*

The Blue and the Gray

180-piece Set $5.98

So realistically detailed you can almost feel the tension as these great armies face one another on this long-ago battlefield. In the distance President Lincoln and Gen. Grant survey the scene, while Gen. Lee readies his troops. **Troops:** 48 Union soldiers, 48 Confederate soldiers, 6 rider figures . . plastic, about 2½ inches high. **Confederate Headquarters** mansion, 11 in. long . . steel and plastic . . easy to assemble.

Union Headquarters: Field tent, 3 pup tents . . a shell shooting cannon, a caisson with shooting field piece, and a trench mortar . . 4 cavalry horses, 2 harness horses, one dead horse (4 in. long). **Accessories:** include flags, trees, drum, ammo box, barricades, buckets, boulders, flagpoles, bridge, dispatch table, broken wheels, sandbag emplacement, etc. All 3 dimensional plastic. 79 N 05984—Shipping weight 6 lbs. . . . $5.98

446 SEARS

"The Blue and The Gray" play set by Marx was advertised in the 1959 Sears catalog. The 180-piece set sold for $5.98. On the Union side were plastic figures of Lincoln and Grant, forty-eight soldiers, a field tent, three pup tents, a cannon, a caisson, a trench mortar, four cavalry horses, two harness horses, and one dead horse. With General Lee in charge, the fourty-eight Confederate soldiers defended their headquarters, a lithographed steel mansion. Accessories shared by both sides included flags, trees, drums, ammunition box, barricades, buckets, boulders, flagpoles, bridge, dispatch table, broken wheels, and sandbag emplacement. Several different sizes of this set were made in different years. *Photograph by Suzanne Silverthorn.*

Marx Blue and Gray Play Set. The main piece of the Civil War playset was the lithographed southern mansion being used as a headquarters building. ($100-125). House is 6" high x 11" wide x 7" deep. *Photograph by Suzanne Silverthorn.*

The 1959 Sears catalog also offered the Marx "Battle for Freedom in Colonial Days" play set. Twenty-four plastic Redcoats marched on a village of twenty-four Colonials. The plastic figures were approximately 2.5" high. There were two lithographed steel cabins, each 4.5" high x 4.5" deep x 8.5" long and a plastic blockhouse with sections of stockade fencing. There were twenty other accessories including cannons, trees, benches, rifles, stools, powder kegs, lanterns, spinning wheel, churn, anvil, pile of logs, chopping block, well, rocking chair, and hitching post. *Photograph by Suzanne Silverthorn.*

Gee Bee Fort. The original plain brown corrugated cardboard box reads: "F 3 Fort. A Gee Bee Toy, Hull England." It is a western type fort made of wood and fiberboard. The circa 1960s fort was purchased with unmarked plastic figures which could not reliably be attributed to Gee Bee Toys. ($100-150). 8.5" high x 23.75" wide x 17" deep. *Photograph by Patty Cooper.*

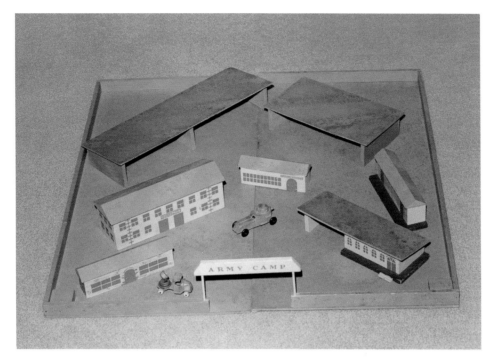

F.A.O.Schwarz Army Camp. The box of this set unfolded to form the grounds of an army camp complete with wood barracks, hangars, and administration buildings. The vehicles were made by Dowst (Tootsietoy). The buildings measure approximately 4" deep x 9" long. *Courtesy of Ben DeVoto.*

The 94-piece Rex Mars Space Port, made by Marx, was advertised in the Alden's 1953 Christmas catalog for $5.79. The main building and fencing were metal, but the other pieces were plastic. On the front gate is printed "Rex Mars/Planet Patrol." The building was 11" high x 12" wide x 6.25" deep. A space code clicker mounted on the roof could be used to send secret messages.

The Port equipment included instruction chart, flight file, two desks, four benches, instructor's table, chair, control panel unit, ladder, fuel storage tanks, radar unit, telescope, camera, ray gun, searchlight, relay tower, supply warehouse, gravity charger, and space rocket car. There were also two flying saucers, a launching platform, three rocket ships. catapult platform, and sixty space people. *Courtesy of Marge Meisinger. Photograph by Suzanne Silverthorn.*

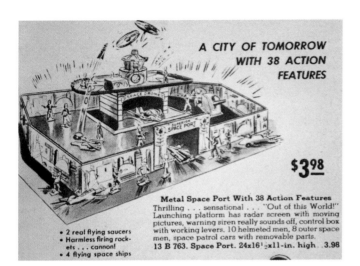

A CITY OF TOMORROW
WITH 38 ACTION
FEATURES

$3.98

• 2 real flying saucers
• Harmless firing rockets . . . cannon!
• 4 flying space ships

Metal Space Port With 38 Action Features
Thrilling . . . sensational . . . "Out of this World!"
Launching platform has radar screen with moving
pictures, warning siren really sounds off, control box
with working levers. 10 helmeted men, 8 outer space
men, space patrol cars with removable parts.
13 B 763. Space Port. 24x16½x11-in. high . .3.98

A Superior metal Space Port by T. Cohn was pictured in the Niresk
Industries, Inc. catalog from Chicago in 1954. The set included 38 action
figures, warning siren, launching platform, rockets, and space patrol
cars. The play set sold for $3.98. It measured 11" high x 24" wide x 16"
deep. *Photograph by Suzanne Silverthorn.*

Superior Space Port. This incomplete set includes pieces produced by T. Cohn
circa 1954 for their Superior Space Port. The bright graphics, typical of T. Cohn,
are evident on these pieces. ($50 and up). *Courtesy of The Early Adventure.*

200

A Marx Cape Canaveral set was shown in the Montgomery Ward catalog in 1959. There were over 100 pieces in the set which sold for $7.29. The headquarters building and fence were metal while the other pieces were made of plastic. The set included several launching pads, missiles, satellites, plastic figures, and an "Official U.S. Air Force Booklet" explaining "space-age terms." *Courtesy of Marge Meisinger. Photograph by Suzanne Silverthorn.*

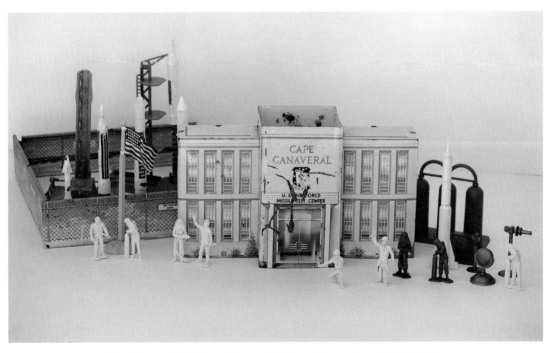

Cape Canaveral. This incomplete set is similar to the one pictured in the 1959 Montgomery Ward catalog. Marx frequently offered different sized sets of playsets that could be sold for a variety of prices. The metal building measures 7" high x 12" wide x 4" deep. (Incomplete set $75 and up. MIB set $400 and up). *Photograph by Suzanne Silverthorn.*

Marx "Project Mercury Cape Canaveral Play Set." A similar set was pictured in the 1962 Sears Christmas catalog. It sold for $4.97. It consisted of fifty pieces including flying saucer launchers, Atlas missiles, sixteen technicians, and another launching gantry. The astronaut was to be placed in the capsule and the helicopter was to be used to rescue the astronaut when he landed.

All of these innovations were based on what was happening in the real Project Mercury space program. The metal building measured 12" high x 12" wide x 4" deep. (MIB $550 and up). *Courtesy of The Early Adventure.*

Marx "Carry-All Cape Kennedy Play Set." This 1968 set reflects the name change of the Cape to honor President John F. Kennedy after his death. This is model #4625 and sold for $7.59 when new. The new type of metal case opened to contain the playing area for the Marx play sets. The case replaced the buildings in the earlier space sets. ($100 and up). *Photograph by Suzanne Silverthorn.*

The Toy Companies

American Flyer

American Flyer was established in Chicago by William O. Coleman and William Hafner in 1907. (Later, Mr. Hafner began Hafner Manufacturing, another maker of toy trains). It was originally known as the Edmonds-Metzel Hardware Company but, by 1910, the name was changed to The American Flyer Manufacturing Company. The firm produced toy trains and accessories until 1938 when the company was sold to A.C. Gilbert of New Haven, Connecticut. The Gilbert Company also made Erector Sets. In the 1950s, the company was second only to Lionel in sales. However, the popularity of toy trains declined and by 1967 the bankrupt company was purchased by Lionel.

Arcade

The Arcade Company was founded in 1885 in Freeport, Illinois as the Novelty Iron and Brass Foundry. They produced various household and industrial items and in 1888, they began manufacturing toys. By the turn of the century, Arcade was well-known for their cast iron banks, trains, stoves, and other toys. Their toys were designed to look like their full-size counterparts, thus, inspiring the company slogan "They Look Real."

Arcade produced high quality furniture to furnish every room of a dollhouse. Many of the pieces were scaled replicas of popular name brands of the 1920s including Crane, Hotpoint, Kohler, and Boone. Cardboard room settings were sold to display the furniture along with at least two models of dollhouses. The largest Arcade dollhouse was nine feet wide and contained ten rooms.

The same high quality and attention to detail can be seen in the cast iron cars, trains, and airplanes produced by Arcade. In order to give more play value to these items, the company offered several different styles of gas stations, airports, garages, and fire stations in wood. These buildings were marketed with the cars, trucks, and airplanes.

In 1946, Arcade was purchased by the Rockwell Manufacturing Company of Buffalo, New York and toy production ceased.

Auburn

Auburn Rubber was founded in 1913 in Auburn, Indiana, as the Double Fabric Tire Corporation. The company made their first toys in 1935. The toy division closed in 1968 after moving to Deming, New Mexico in 1960. The firm marketed a miniature Auburn Dollhouse during the 1950s. The dollhouse came in small room units which could be connected to make a complete house. The rooms were made of plastic and cardboard. They included a living room, kitchen-dinette, utility room-playroom, and bedroom-bath. Auburn also produced a toy farm and many products that were used with various toy buildings including farm animals, tractors, and other equipment.

Bachmann Brothers (Plasticville U.S.A.)

Bachmann Brothers originated as early as the 1830s when the company made ivory cane handles and combs. By 1907, they were using an injection molding process to manufacture frames for eyeglasses. After World War II, the company began producing their line of "Plasticville" accessories for model train layouts. These were sold in the form of inexpensive kits with component pieces which could be snapped together to form fairly realistic looking buildings. The Plasticville architecture reflected the styles of the 1950s and 1960s. They produced almost every conceivable kind of structure including houses, churches, barns, railroad buildings, motels, apartment buildings, airports, stores, banks, diners, schools, hospitals, television stations, fire departments, gas stations, and a post office. These kits are still reasonably priced and it is possible for a collector to put together a whole town of Plasticville pieces.

The 1952 Montgomery Ward Christmas catalog advertised a variety of buildings by Bachmann Brothers (Plasticville USA). *Photograph by Suzanne Silverthorn.*

Bing

The German company, Gerbruder Bing, was formed by Ignaz and Adolf Bing in Nuremberg in the early 1860s. At first, they sold products manufactured by other companies, but they soon began producing their own line of metal toys. Although the firm made many different types of toys, the most successful was its line of trains. It also made mechanical toys, cars, and boats. Bing suffered financial difficulties during the Great Depression and many of their most popular lines were taken over by other companies. By 1934, the firm was out of business.

Tinplate toy buildings produced by Bing included garages and railroad stations. Bing toys have been found with the trademarks "G.B.N." and "B.W."

Bliss

The R. Bliss Manufacturing Company was based in Pawtucket, Rhode Island from 1832-1914. The company was founded by Rufus Bliss, in 1832, to make wood screws and clamps. By 1871, the firm was producing toys and in 1873, games were added to their production. In 1914, the toy division was purchased by Mason and Parker of Winchendon, Massachusetts.

The Bliss firm is especially famous for the dollhouses it began making around 1889. Most of the dollhouses were made of wood with an overlay of lithographed paper used to show the details of the houses. The early ones were Queen Anne in style with fishscale siding, ball-and-stick balustrades, bay windows, turned finials, and turrets. Usually the houses were marked "R. Bliss" above the front door. Beacause they so often marked their houses, whereas other companies did not, lithographed houses made in America are often referred to as Bliss without regard to their actual provenance.

The company also used lithographed paper over wood or cardboard to produce various barns and stables. The 1896 catalog featured three different farms called "The House That Jack Built" and two sizes of a "Rockyway Stable." Their 1911 catalog pictured four different models in several sizes. Many came with horses and wagons and/or carriages. The horses were probably of German origin.

In the 1895 Bliss catalog, a church made of blocks was advertised for sale. When assembled, the church was 21" tall. The base could be used as a case for the blocks when the church was disassembled. Included with the churches were sets of flat blocks which contained printed Bible verses.

Bliss produced several toy theaters, including an Opera House which was part of a three building set that also included a grocery store and a drugstore. The 1911 Bliss catalog advertised a moving picture show called "Tiny Town," which included a reel of pictures that could be "operated and shown at will."

Bliss also produced at least one lithographed paper over wood toy warehouse, a fort, three fire stations, and a commercial garage.

Brumberger

The Brumberger Company, located in Brooklyn, New York, produced several toy buildings during the 1970s. Sears featured a Chalet dollhouse made by Brumberger in their 1975 Christmas catalog. The house was furnished with plastic 1/2" to the foot scale furniture that appeared to have been made from the Superior (T. Cohn) molds. It is possible that Brumberger purchased T. Cohn during this period.

Brumberger made a Tiny Town Truck Terminal to be used with the Tiny Tonka trucks and a Brumberger service station. All of the buildings were made of a light wood or fiberboard material.

Built-Rite (Warren Paper Products)

The company that made Built-Rite Toys began as the Warren Paper Products Company. The firm was founded in Lafayette, Indiana in the early 1920s as a paper box manufacturer. By the early 1930s, they began producing a line of paper toys which were sold under the Warren Paper Products Company name. Later, the toy line was marketed under the Built-Rite trademark.

Built-Rite made toys for both boys and girls. Those marketed for boys included forts, railroad stations, farms, airports, garages, and service stations. For girls, the company made a number of dollhouses and two different sets of cardboard dollhouse furniture. The dollhouses ranged from one-room bungalows to houses with five rooms and a built-in kitchen. The scale of the dollhouses varied, some being small enough to be compatible with their other buildings and others large enough to accommodate the 3/4" to the foot furniture manufactured by Strombecker. All of the buildings came unassembled, with the bottom of the boxes often doubling as the foundations.

Built-Rite toys were frequently advertised in *Children's Activities* magazine in the 1940s and early 1950s, with coupons which could be used to order directly from the manufacturer. In the 1946 issue, a Built-Rite garage set was advertised for a prepaid price of $1.30. By 1950, the Railroad set was priced at $2.25. An advertisement from the December 1950 issue offered a service station for seventy cents and a dollhouse for $1.25.

With the increasing availability of the more durable plastic and metal playsets, in the 1950s, Built-Rite ceased production of most of their toy line except for puzzles and games. The company name was changed to the Warren Company in the mid-1970s.

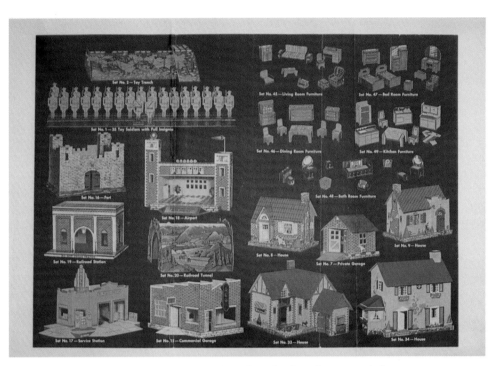

A flyer included with a boxed set by Warren Paper Products shows several of their early buildings, including an airport, service station, train station, fort, and several dollhouses. *Courtesy of Linda Boltrek. Photograph by Suzanne Silverthorn.*

The November 1947 issue of *Children's Activities Magazine* supplied a coupon for ordering a railroad station, game, or farm set by Built-Rite (Warren Paper Products). *Photograph by Suzanne Silverthorn.*

N.D. Cass

The N.D. Cass Company, located in Athol, Massachusetts, celebrated its one hundredth anniversary in 1996. The firm was founded by Nathan David Cass and it has been a family owned company throughout its history. Originally a manufacturer of suitcases, Cass soon began producing doll trunks, doll furniture, and dollhouses. Some of their earliest products, including a toy ark, were made of lithographed paper over wood, similar to those made by the R. Bliss company. The Cass dollhouses closely resembled those produced by the Converse Company, with architectural details directly applied to the wood rather than on paper. Both Cass and Converse produced dollhouses in the bungalow style popular in the early part of the 20th century.

Cass also made several other types of toy buildings. In 1914, Butler Brothers advertised a Cass grocery story measuring 9.25" high x 7.25" wide x 2.5" deep. It included a heavy cardboard counter, two shelves, and ten packages of grocery products. The same catalog featured a lithographed wood railroad car, by Cass, called the Circus Stock Car. It was available in three different sizes with four, six, or eight different animals cut out of wood. The cars ranged in size from 9" x 4.5" to 14" x 7". Converse also produced similar railroad cars which contained either farm or circus animals.

Chein

J.Chein & Co. was founded by Julius Chein in 1903. The New York City firm made steel toys and lithographed tin drums and banks. The firm has relocated twice, to Harrison, New Jersey in 1912 and to Burlington, New Jersey in 1949. In the 1970s, the company name was changed to Chein Industries, Inc. In 1985, the company was sold to Atlantic Products and the name changed to Atlantic Cheinco, a company which continued operating until filing bankruptcy in 1992.

Chein is best known for their wind-up toys, banks, and sand pails. Although the company was in business for a long time, only a few of their toys could be considered part of a toy community. These include several different mechanical amusement park rides such as roller coasters, merry-go-rounds, ferris wheels, and roller coasters. A one-car garage, with variations in the lithography, was produced to house their many windup cars and, in the 1930s, there were several models of a small, one-room train station, variously named Grove, Oakland, Parkville, and Glendale. The same blank was used for a car garage. In addition, Chein made at least two different versions of a larger automobile garage.

T. Cohn, Inc. (Superior)

T.Cohn, Inc., located in Brooklyn, New York, produced many collectible toy buildings beginning in 1948. They used the tradename "Superior" on many of their products. T. Cohn became one of the first companies to manufacture a modern metal dollhouse when their new design was featured in the 1948 Montgomery Ward Christmas catalog. The firm continued to produce various metal houses into the early 1960s. At that time, the company began making dollhouses out of Gypsum wood.

T. Cohn made several different kinds of toy buildings in lithographed metal. In 1952, they made a Fort Superior Trading Post western play set and, in 1954, they introduced the Superior Space Port. Other toy buildings included airports, garages, barns, and military related structures, including a naval base. They also manufactured several different models of metal service stations, similar to those made by Marx.

T. Cohn was purchased by Brumberger some time in the late 1960s or early 1970s. The Brumberger Company sold dollhouses with plastic furniture made in the Superior molds.

Converse

In 1878, Morton E. Converse and Orlando Mason formed a partnership to manufacture wooden toys, utensils, and boxes. Mason & Converse was located in Winchendon, Massachusetts and among their early toy products were wagons and rocking horses. In 1884, Converse formed his own company under the name Morton E. Converse Co. In 1898, the name of the firm was changed to Morton E. Converse and Son. During the 1890s, the firm was said to be the largest wood toy manufacturer in the world.

Converse was especially known for the dollhouses it produced. At first, the houses were made of wood covered with lithographed paper but, by 1909, the company began printing its designs directly on wood. Most of the houses were bungalow types with faux stone foundations. Some of the houses were richly lithographed both inside and out. Many of these were marked with the company name as part of the floor pattern. Other houses, believed to be Converse, are unmarked and because of their close resemblance to dollhouses produced by Cass, it is difficult to attribute them with accuracy.

In addition to dollhouses, Converse produced wood barns complete with two-dimensional wood animals that fit into slotted bases. Some of the barns were elaborate structures with sliding doors and individual stalls inside. Others were simple, open-fronted sheds.

A small farm set was advertised in the 1912 Sears catalog as the "Sunnyside Stock Farm." According to the catalog, it included a farm house, barn, garage, greenhouse, fencing, and seven assorted wooden animals "all nicely embossed on wood." The buildings were designed to nest one inside the other for storage. It sold for ninety-five cents.

In 1921 Sears advertised a Converse farm set, which included the barn and animals, for $1.33. Among the many barns produced by Converse, over the years, were those marked "Red Robin Farm" and others named "Roosevelt Stock Farms."

A page of the 1912 Converse catalog, reproduced in *Antique Toy World* magazine, shows three different sizes of an "Automobile Garage." The tallest was

13.75" high and came with three wooden autos, the smallest was only 5" high and came with one auto. Converse was purchased by Mason Manufacturing Company of South Paris, Maine, in the early 1930s.

Courtland

Courtland Manufacturing Company was begun by Walt Reach in 1944 for the production of cardboard toys. After the war, he began making lithographed tin toys. The company was first located in Camden, New Jersey, and later moved to Philadelphia. The firm closed in 1951.

Courtland is best known for their toy trucks, however the firm also manufactured several toy buildings, including fire stations and garages.

De Luxe Game Corporation

The De Luxe Game Corporation was located in Richmond Hill, Long Island, New York. The firm manufactured toys during the 1940s and 1950s. Their products included games, bowling alleys, blackboards, doctor and nurse kits, paint kits, and sewing kits. They also made a series of toy buildings which included service stations, dollhouses, and a fire station. Several barns and stores have been found which are believed to have been produced by the company.

The De Luxe toy buildings were made of Tekwood, a three-ply material with a wood center and cardboard outer layers. The first service stations were produced in 1946 and advertised in the Sears Christmas catalog for that year. Sears continued to carry the De Luxe stations through 1951. Some of the stations bore the Sears "Happi Time" label instead of De Luxe. All of the stations included working parts, such as gas pumps that pumped water and elevators which moved. Many featured an unusual separate car wash. The service stations from 1950 and 1951 had Tekwood bases, but the buildings themselves were made of lithographed metal. These Happi Time stations included some unusual innovations. The 1950 station was called a "Musical Service Station" because it played "Whistle While You Work" when the car lift was operated. In 1951, De Luxe advertised their "first and only Talking Service Station." It contained a tape which said "Gas and oil, please" when a car was driven over it. In addition to the Sears catalog, the De Luxe service stations were advertised in *Children's Activities* magazine.

Dowst (Tootsietoy)

The Dowst Brothers Company, located in Chicago, had its beginning in 1878 when brothers Charles and Samuel published a trade publication called "Laundry Journal." Around 1900, the company began making metal miniatures to be used as premiums. Soon they enlarged the business to include party favors. Eventually, they were responsible for producing many of the metal Cracker Jack prizes.

In 1922, Dowst began manufacturing a line of cast metal dollhouse furniture in approximately 1/2" to the foot scale. The colorfully enameled furniture reflected popular designs of the 1920s. The furniture was named "Tootsietoy" after "Toots," one of the Dowst granddaughters. This name was later used on all the Dowst toys, including die cast cars, trucks, airplanes, and other vehicles.

After the company began making dollhouse furniture with some success, the Dowst Brothers expanded, merging with Cosmo Manufacturing Company in 1926. The new firm was called Dowst Manufacturing Company.

Like many other companies, Dowst marketed a few toy buildings to accompany their cast metal toys. A Spanish mansion dollhouse as well as several other more modest cardboard houses were sold by the company to house their furniture. Wayne Paper Products Company of Ft. Wayne, Indiana, probably produced many of these houses. Dowst marketed several airports, train stations, and garages for their vehicles.

In 1961, the company acquired the "Strombecker" trademark and changed their name to the Strombecker Corporation.

Gibbs

The Gibbs Manufacturing Company of Canton, Ohio was originally a maker of wooden items including barrels and tubs. Lewis Gibbs was the original owner.

The company's first toy was produced as a give-away for the political campaign of William McKinley, a Canton native. Most Gibbs toys were wood or tin, sometimes with lithographed paper for decoration. Gibbs made both toy service stations and garages of lithographed metal.

Moritz Gottschalk

The German firm of Moritz Gottschalk was located in Marienberg, Saxony, and produced a wide variety of toys over more than seven decades. The Gottschalk company dominated the dollhouse market from the 1880s until the late 1930s when, with the advent of World War II, toy production in Germany was changed forever.

The firm also marketed a large number of other toy buildings. These included shops, rooms, fortresses, warehouses, theaters, railroad stations, stables, and garages. The early Gottschalk structures were made of lithographed paper over wood. Most of the buildings manufactured from the 1880s through the 1910s had blue roofs and before these toys were attributed to Gottschalk, collectors often called them "Blue Roofs." Sometime around 1920, the company discontinued the use of exterior lithographed papers and began painting the exterior walls, usually a shade of yellow. These newer designs had pressed cardboard window mullions and red roofs. Some of the Gottschalk buildings featured working elevators.

It is believed that Gottschalk ceased toy production during the war, but resumed making some toys throughout the 1950s.

Grey Iron Company

The Grey Iron Company was founded in Mount Joy, Pennsylvania in 1840. At that time, it was called the Brady Machine Shop. In 1881, the name was changed to the Grey Iron Casting Company, Limited. By 1903, the firm was making toy banks, stoves, cap pistols, and trains. By 1917, the company was also producing toy soldiers.

Of interest to toy building collectors is the series the company made circa 1940-1941. Included were four different playsets made of cardboard with iron people and accessories. The sets were called "On the Beach," "American Family at Home," "American Family Travels," and "American Family on the Ranch." The cast iron adult figures are approximately 2.15" to 2.5" tall. These sets are very difficult to find in original boxed condition because World War II ended production of the series.

Grey is still in business as the John Wright division of Donsco and makes mechanical banks and horse drawn vehicles.

Christian Hacker

Christian Hacker of Nuremberg, Germany, produced exquisite dollhouses as well as toy kitchens, warehouses, and shops from the mid-1800s through 1914. The company was best known for its three story dollhouses with mansard roofs. These houses were made in several pieces and could be taken apart for shipping or storage. One of the company's butcher shops, from the early twentieth century, came complete with meat, knives, a butcher, and a cash booth. Instead of using lithographed paper for architectural details, the Hacker company made their toy buildings from wood with applied wood trim, turned balusters, and three-dimensional balconies. Some of the Hacker products were marked with a crown-topped shield containing the initials "CH."

O. & M. Hausser (Elastolin)

Elastolin was a composite material made of plaster, sawdust, and glue over a wire base. Otto and Max Hausser of Ludwigsburg, Germany began their company in 1904 and produced a variety of tinplate toys. However, it wasn't until 1926 that they began using the new material which became the company's trademark. Both before and during World War II, toy soldiers were produced of Elastolin to accompany tinplate military toys. The Marklin Company purchased Elastolin figures for their train sets. The composite material was used until 1955 when it was replaced by plastic and wood. No tinplate toys were made by the company after 1957. Toy buildings known to have been made by Hausser include farm sets and zoos designed to house their Elastolin animals. Some of the these are shown in the *Universal Toy Catalog 1924-26*.

Ideal

The Ideal Company had its beginning in the early part of the century when it was founded by Morris Michtom. After several name changes, it became the Ideal Novelty and Toy Company in 1912. The firm was located in both Brooklyn and Hollis, New York. They manufactured high quality dolls for many decades and their lines of plastic dollhouse furniture are highly prized by collectors.

Ideal manufactured many different kinds of toy buildings including barns, airports, a car wash, and a diner. During the late 1960s, their "Super City" series included a Heliport Set, Skyscraper Building Set, Town and Country Set, Skyport Set, Landscape Set, and Roadway Accessory Set.

The Ideal company was sold to the Columbia Broadcasting System in 1983 and was merged with the network's Gabriel toy line.

Jaymar

Most collectors are familiar with the toys made by Louis Marx and Company, but less is known about the Jaymar Specialty Company which was also associated with the Marx family. This company was financed by Louis Marx in the 1920s and was headed by his father, Jacob. The new Specialty Company became a successful organization for the Marx family. In order for it not to be in direct competition with the larger Louis Marx firm (which specialized in metal and plastic toys), its products were to be made of either wood or cardboard. The Jaymar company did not make many toy buildings but the firm did produce at least one railroad village made of cardboard. They also produced some items to be used with toy buildings, including dollhouse furniture and military sets.

The Judy Company

The Judy Company of Minneapolis, Minnesota, made farm sets circa 1940 through the 1950s. The buildings were made of cardboard and were quite similar to Built-Rite. Some sets had rubber animals, which look somewhat like those made by the Auburn Rubber Company. Others, smaller in scale and perhaps made earlier, had crude wood animals and vehicles. The design of the vehicles, despite the difference in materials and size, were the same, mostly flat, with red trucks and blue cars. According to a flyer found with a 1946 farm set, the company's other products included puzzles, story toys, "match-ettes," alphabets and numerals, as well as a farm set numbered 106, apparently smaller. The buildings and animals are not marked.

Keystone

The Keystone Manufacturing Company was founded in Boston in the early 1920s by Chester Rimmer and Arthur Jackson. The original name of the company was Jacrim and they produced movie projectors.

From the mid 1930s until the 1950s, Keystone also manufactured dollhouses and other toy buildings. The dollhouses were constructed of Masonite and most were decorated both inside and outside. The exterior walls were printed with clapboard siding, shutters, plants, trees, and shrubs. Inside, many of the houses had printed "wallpaper" and pictures on the walls. Some of the earlier houses had plain brown walls, with no decoration.

Like their dollhouses, the company's other toy buildings were made of Masonite and wood. They were produced in amazing variety. The gas stations have been found in numerous sizes, with subtle design changes from year to year. There were several different fire stations, railroad stations, at least three bus stations, parking garages, and several barns. They may be the only company known to have made a lumber yard. Keystone made several different forts, from medieval looking castles to exploding models to at least four designs of coast defense forts.

Many of the sets were designed to hold water which children could use to pretend to milk the cow, fill gas tanks, or put out fires. The railroad station was equipped with a recording device which called out the names of the stations. Most of the buildings included other accessories to enhance play. The sets sold for around $5.00 in the late 1940s.

In 1953, Keystone sold its toy division to concentrate on the camera and projector market.

Kiddie Brush and Toy Company

The Kiddie Brush and Toy company was founded in 1930 by Paul A. Jones, Sr. and John Doty in Bryan, Ohio. Like the Ohio Art Company, also located in Bryan, the Kiddie Brush Company used lithographed metal for many of their toys. The company moved to Jonesville, Michigan in 1932 when Jones bought out his partner's interest. The company's earliest toys were housekeeping pieces which included a metal carpet sweeper, floor mops, brooms, and a duster. The trade name "Susy Goose" came into use after the firm moved to Michigan. Although this name is probably best known in connection with several Barbie (Mattel, Inc.) toys, the Kiddie Brush and Toy Company used it for several toy buildings.

The oldest building made by the company appears to be the Susy Goose dollhouse which was featured in several mail order catalogs during the late 1930s. It was made of pressed hardboard.

The Friendly Acres Dairy Farm set was first issued in 1949. It featured a lithographed steel barn with fencing and animals and retailed for $2.89. The animals were unusual because each set contained cows of distinctly different breeds which offered a degree of realism.

Their most unusual toy building was the Friendly Folks Motel. It was advertised in the 1954 Montgomery Ward catalog. The lithographed metal motel contained two guest rooms and an office, furnished with 1/2" to the foot scale plastic furniture and people along with child sized check-in sheets. Because this is one of the few toy motels ever made, it is considered highly collectible.

Lesney (Matchbox)

The Lesney London firm was founded in 1947 by Leslie and Rodney Smith, whose first names were combined in naming the company. Their small die-cast cars were first issued in 1953. The car designs were based on those used by real automobile manufacturers. The trade name "Matchbox" referred to the size of the box in which the cars were packaged. The toys proved to be so popular that an American division was founded in 1964.

To accompany the small cars, the firm marketed several toy buildings. These included service stations, garages, a fire station, and several different Matchbox "cities."

The company was sold by the original owners to Universal International of Hong Kong in 1982

Lincoln Log (See Wright, J. L.)

Line Mar

During the 1950s, many metal toys were produced in Japan under the Line Mar name. The products were then sold by Louis Marx and Company. Included in this line of toys was a metal service station which used the Cities Service logo. It came with a metal car that obtained power from the station motor.

Lionel

Lionel Corporation, the famous maker of model trains, was founded by Joshua Lionel Cowen in 1903. In order to give the trains more interest, the New York firm also marketed many train accessories. These included various train stations and signal booths.

The Ives Company became part of Lionel in 1931 and Gilbert was purchased in 1967. Because of the decline of the railroad industry in the United States, toy trains also lost their appeal for children. The Lionel firm closed in 1969, but many of the Lionel products continued to be made by Fundimensions, a subsidiary of General Mills.

Marklin

Gebruder Marklin & Cie was founded by Theodor Marklin and his wife Caroline in Goppingen, Germany in 1859. At first they made tinplate kitchenware. The firm expanded their toy line to include toy boats, carousels, zeppelins, and trains. They also produced railroad stations to accompany their train sets. These metal stations, dating from the early 1900s, are now the most collectible and expensive of all train accessories. It is very hard to find these early stations complete.

Reprints of company catalogs show that Marklin made a few other toy buildings, including a school room, public swimming pools, and castles. The street lights made by Marklin for railroad layouts make a wonderful accessory for any early twentieth century toy building.

Marklin is one of the few German toy manufacturers to have survived both wars. By the mid-1930s, Marklin began to concentrate almost exclusively on their model railroad products. Although the company was involved in some war-related production during World War II, the plant escaped any direct damage. Soon after the war ended, they started producing model trains again, this time with an increasing number of plastic parts. The Marklin company has been in continuous production since its establishment and today is largely known for its HO scale railroads.

Marx

The company that became known as Louis Marx and Company, Inc. was begun shortly after World War I when its founder, Louis Marx, purchased toy molds from the Strauss Manufacturing Company. As a former employee of Ferdinand Strauss, Marx was familiar with their production of lithographed tinplate mechanical toys. The new company made some minor changes in the toys before they were marketed under the Marx name. The Louis Marx Company proved successful and remained in business for over fifty years. Marx produced more toy buildings than almost any other company. They began manufacturing toy buildings in the 1920s and continued to make them until the early 1970s when the company was sold to Quaker Oats.

The earliest Marx dollhouse-type toy, produced in the 1920s and early 1930s, was a series of small metal "Newlywed" rooms. Both the rooms and furniture were made of lithographed metal. The rooms were simple boxes, open at the front and top, with brightly lithographed floors and walls. They were sold in individual boxes as well as in a cardboard box, printed to look like a dollhouse, which contained four of the rooms. The same concept was used to produce a series of "Hometown" buildings which included a fire station, police station, theater, and several stores.

During the 1930s, Marx manufactured many more metal toy buildings including several versions of garages, service stations, airports, bus stations, railroad stations, and fire stations. These items are some of the most sought after Marx collectibles.

In 1938, Marx produced another small metal dollhouse, a bungalow type with two-rooms and a garage. Sears sold this house furnished with the tiny Midget Tootsietoy furniture. By the late 1940s, Marx was manufacturing the larger metal dollhouses most commonly found today. These contained five or more rooms and were in either 1/2" or 3/4" to the foot scale.

Many other toy buildings were produced by Marx in the 1940s, and it was during this time that the toys were expanded into playsets which included at least one building along with many plastic accessories. These sets were heavily advertised in the catalogs of major retailers, especially Sears. The following is a list of Marx playsets shown in the catalogs used by the authors in researching this book. It should be noted that Marx changed the names of various sets over the years.

1950: Ranch (house with furnishings and extras)
1951: Army Training Center
1952: Big Top Circus
1952: Tom Corbett's Space Academy
1952: Big Top Circus
1952: Fort Dearborn Stockade
1952: Freight Rail Terminal
1952: Roy Rogers Double R-Bar Ranch
1952: Bar M Ranch
1952: Super Circus with Mary Hartline
1952: Fort Dearborn
1952: Mineral City - Roy Rogers and Dale Evans
1952: Army Training Center (New)
1952: Western Town
1952: Roy Rogers Double R Bar Ranch Rodeo
1953: Roy Rogers Rodeo Ranch
1953: Captain Space Solar Academy
1953: Futuristic Space Port
1953: Medieval Castle
1953: Western Town
1953: Rex Mars Space Port
1954: Prince Valiant Medieval Fortress
1954: Captain Space Solar Academy
1954: White House Kit
1955: Army Air Force Training Center (two story building)
1955: Super Service Station

1956: Fort Apache (still part of line in 1975)
1956: Construction Camp
1956: Robin Hood Castle
1956: Rin Tin-Tin Fort Apache
1956: Captain Gallant Foreign Legion Set
1956: Lone Ranger Ranch Set
1957: Roy Roger's Western Town
1957: Revolutionary War Set
1957: Wyatt Earp Dodge City Western Town
1958: Roy Rogers Mineral City
1958: Cape Canaveral Rocket Research
1958: Battleground Set with Missile Launcher
1958: Walt Disney Zorro Garrison
1958: Arctic Explorer Set
1958: Wyatt Earp Dodge City
1959: Historic Wells Fargo
1959: Robin Hood Castle with Catapult
1959: Battle for Freedom in Colonial Days
1959: Alaskan Frontier
1959: Cape Canaveral with Sound Effects
1959: Rifleman Ranch Set
1959: Fort Pitt Play Set
1959: Battle of the Blue and Grey
1959: Army Training Center with PX
1960: Dodge City
1962: Roy Rogers Double R Bar Ranch

Although many of these sets continued to be made for many years with minor changes, the popularity decreased and new designs were more limited after 1960. Some of the sets from the 1960s include: Ben Hur (1962), The Alamo (1962), Strategic Air Command Base (1964), and Garden Mark Farm Set (1966). In the 1970s, the company designed new containers so that the sets were made as part of a suitcase type carrier and the extra pieces could be stored in the case when not in use. Ft. Cheyenne, Kennedy, and a Medieval Castle were all marketed in this fashion.

Since each of these Marx playsets contained so many pieces, it is difficult to obtain a complete set. Therefore, the original boxed sets are at a premium. Several of the early sets have been reproduced including Fort Apache, Cape Canaveral Missile Center, King Arthur's Castle, and the Davy Crockett Alamo Set.

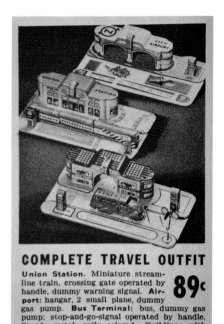

COMPLETE TRAVEL OUTFIT

Union Station. Miniature stream-
line train, crossing gate operated by
handle, dummy warning signal. Airport: hangar, 2 small plane, dummy
gas pump. **Bus Terminal:** bus, dummy gas
pump; stop-and-go-signal operated by handle.
Sturdy metal, gaily colored. Buildings with
base average 12x6¾x3¼ in. high.
49 V 5741—Shipping wt., 3 lbs......**89c**

89c

A Sears, Roebuck and Company catalog from
1938 offered a three piece set of buildings by
Louis Marx. The set included a small Union
Station, airport, and a bus terminal. Marx also
made a service station using this design.
Photograph by Suzanne Silverthorn.

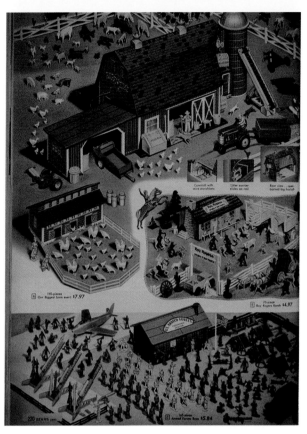

A Happi Time barn, chicken house, U.S. Armed Forces Training
Center, and Roy Rogers Ranch were all made by Louis Marx and
advertised in the 1957 catalog of Sears, Roebuck and Company.
Photograph by Suzanne Silverthorn.

Matchbox (see Lesney)

McLoughlin

The McLoughlin Brothers Company of New York was famous for producing brightly lithographed books, games, and toys beginning in the late 1850s. The company started making dollhouses as early as 1875. Most of these houses were folding cardboard models. The firm also made cardboard theaters, including one advertised by Montgomery Ward in their 1903 catalog for 85 cents. It featured the story of "Little Red Riding Hood."

Also pictured in the 1903 Montgomery Ward catalog, was a McLoughlin "New Pretty Village" which contained eight buildings and twenty-four figures. Several variations of the village were produced over the years. In 1920, the McLoughlin firm was purchased by Milton Bradley, who continued to produce many of the McLoughlin products.

Mettoy Company Ltd.

This British company was founded by Henry Ullman and made tinplate toys from the 1930s through 1960s. According to an article in *Plastic Figure and Playset Collector*, Mettoy made lithographed metal hospitals in two different sizes, circa 1960s, a City Heliport, and Fort Cheyenne. They also produced a service station marked "Joytown." Mettoy also made lithographed tin dollhouses which were open-backed with plastic chimneys and doors, somewhat similar to those made by Marx in the 1960s.

Milton Bradley

The Milton Bradley Company was founded in Springfield, Massachusetts in 1860. Later, the firm moved to East Longmeadow, Massachusetts. Milton Bradley was a lithographer and his famous games were a result of his printing business. Milton Bradley was always interested in education and many of the products marketed by the firm were educational toys. When Bradley died in 1911, his company was the most important game manufacturer in the United States. The firm bought the McLoughlin Brothers Company in 1920. The company remained a family owned business until 1984 when it was purchased by Hasbro.

After purchasing the McLoughlin Brothers Company in 1920, Milton Bradley continued to produce many of the McLoughlin toy buildings, including folding dollhouses and several sets of lithographed sheets that could be cut and folded to create three-dimensional villages. They also made a Toy Town Post Office.

Bradley manufactured several construction toys as well as the series of Bumpalow buildings issued in the 1930s. They were made of laminated chip board and included houses, gas stations, schools, and stores, sold both separately and as a village.

Moline (Buddy L)

The Moline Pressed Steel Company was begun in 1910 in East Moline, Illinois. It was founded by Fred A. Lundahl to produce steel parts for trucks and farm equipment. Through the years, the firm has had several name changes and is now known as the Buddy L Toy Company.

The firm began manufacturing toy trucks and other steel toys in the 1920s. In order to enhance the play value of their toy trucks, the company produced some toy service stations. A metal "Texaco" station was issued in the late 1950s which was made with plastic accessories.

Ohio Art

The Ohio Art Company, located in Bryan, Ohio, is well known for the high quality metal toys which the company manufactured over many decades. The firm was founded in 1908 by Henry S. Winzeler who formed the company to produce metal picture frames. Ohio Art eventually added toys to its line and by 1920 they were manufacturing the tin tea sets that remained popular for several decades. They also produced sand pails, watering cans, and drums that are highly collectible today. Ohio Art ceased toy production from 1942 to 1944 in order to manufacture items for the war effort. When they began producing toys once again in 1945, the company's product line expanded rapidly.

Ohio Art produced several toy buildings. In 1949, they issued a very small metal dollhouse which collectors often refer to as "Midget Manor." It was only 5.25" high by 6" wide and 2" deep. The house was furnished with tiny plastic furniture.

Several different styles of metal barns were marketed by Ohio Art during the 1950s and 1960s. Most of the barns were named, making these items easy to identify. The names included "Meadow Lane Farms," "Rolling Acres Farm," "Springdale Farms," "Sunnyfield Farms," and "Valleyview Farm." The barns came complete with animals and some farm machinery. Ohio Art is still in business and is best known as the maker of Etch-a-Sketch.

D.A. Pachter Company

Little information has been found on this company, other than that provided on the cover of a boxed Circus-Carnival set. The company's address was given as Merchandise Mart, Chicago, Illinois. In 1943, (the copyright date given on the box) the company was offering eight different playsets under the tradename Bild-a-Set. These included two different train sets, a construction set, three military sets, and a farm, in addition to the Circus and Carnival set. All appear to have been made of cardboard which could be punched out of perforated sheets. Thin wood dowels served various functions, such as axles on the tractors and ferris wheels or poles to hold the merry-go-round ponies. The Bild-a-Set products

215

closely resemble Built-Rite and may be distinguished by a difference in scale and the use of the wood dowels. Most of the sets were priced at $1.00 and could be ordered directly from the company. The Bild-a-Set stock farm was also sold through the Spiegel catalog in 1945.

This flyer was included in a boxed circus set by D.A. Pachter who made Bild-a-Sets. *Photograph by Patty Cooper.*

Parker Brothers

George S. Parker founded Geo. S. Parker and Co. in 1883 in Salem, Massachusetts. By 1885, he was selling eight different games in his catalog. In 1888, the firm's name was changed to Parker Brothers when his brother, Charles Parker, joined the firm. Although most of the company's products were game related (Flinch, Pit, Rook, and Monopoly), they also manufactured several items for the toy community, including the Little Toy Town Grocery Store.

General Mills purchased the company in 1969 and it became known as Kenner-Parker Toys in 1985. The game division continued to change hands until the production of the games was moved to the Milton Bradley factory in Springfield in the early 1990s.

Plasticville (See Bachmann Brothers)

W. S. Reed

The Whitney S. Reed Company was founded in Leominster, Massachusetts in 1875. Primarily a manufacturer of other types of wooden toys, the company also made dollhouses and several toy buildings. The firm marked many of their toys "W.S.Reed Toy Company" with a patent date, but others are unmarked. In

1897, the company was sold and eventually renamed the Whitney Reed Chair Company, although they continued to manufacture toys.

W.S. Reed made dollhouses in a variety of sizes and styles. During the 1890s, the houses were small in scale with detailed lithographed exteriors. After the turn of the century, the design of the Reed houses changed so that the exterior papers showed a brick pattern but no other architectural details.

Besides dollhouses, the company produced a toy meat market, several grocery stores, a coal yard, a church, and an armory, circa 1900. Although most of these toys were small in scale, they produced a wholesale grocery that was 23" tall.

Renwal

The Renwal Manufacturing Company of Mineola, Long Island, New York, was founded in 1939 by Irving Lawner. ("Renwal" is the owner's name, backwards.) The company became famous for the plastic toys and dollhouse furniture that they marketed from the mid-1940s until the early 1960s. The Renwal Manufacturing Company was sold in the early 1970s.

Besides the dollhouse furniture, the firm marketed several toy buildings. A Little Red School House and Furniture set was introduced in 1947. The school house was made of cardboard while the furniture was plastic. A plastic private garage was sold, circa 1949, and housed two Renwal cars. They also made hospital nurseries and an animal hospital, which consisted primarily of boxes printed to provide a backdrop for the furniture, but of little architectural interest.

Rich

Maurice Rich Sr. and Edward M. Rich founded the Rich Company in 1921 in Sterling, Illinois. The firm originally manufactured tops for automobiles, but in 1923 they changed to toy production. In 1935, the company moved to Clinton, Iowa and became the Rich Toy Manufacturing Company. During the 1950s, they relocated to Tupelo, Mississippi, where labor was cheaper.

Rich produced several different types of toy buildings. The company's dollhouses were especially popular and remained a part of the toy line from the mid-1930s until the early 1960s. The houses were made of U.S. Gypsum hardboard and were similar to Keystone houses. Rich also made gas stations, garages, airports, freight terminals, and barns during the 1930s and 1940s. The toys were made of wood or wood products. In 1938, a Texaco Service Station was offered for the wholesale price of $1.47 and a red barn with white trim was sold for 70 cents by the All-American Products Corporation in Chicago.

The Chicago based All-American Products Corporation of Chicago pictured several Rich Toy Company buildings in their 1938 catalog. There are three dollhouses of pressed hardboard, a Texaco station complete with lunch counter, and a red barn with fence and animals. A Borden milk wagon is also shown, a clue that Rich may have manufactured the Borden barn shown in the Down on the Farm chapter. *Photograph by Suzanne Silverthorn.*

Saalfield Publishing Company

The Saalfield Publishing Company was founded by Arthur Saalfield in 1900 in Akron, Ohio. Saalfield published his first children's book in 1902. The firm then began producing paper dolls and painting books. Their most popular products were marketed in the 1930s when they held exclusive rights to publish Shirley Temple material.

The company was purchased by the Rand McNally Company in 1976. Because of Saalfield's interest in paper and cardboard materials, the firm produced several punch-out sets which could be assembled to make village buildings, playhouses, or farms.

Schoenhut

Albert Schoenhut founded the A. Schoenhut Company in Philadelphia in 1872. At first, the firm produced only toy musical instruments, but by 1903, they began making their famous Humpty Dumpty Circus. The circus was made with various sizes of tents with differing numbers of pieces in the sets. The circus animals were made of wood with joints which allowed them to be placed in a variety of poses. These included elephants, donkeys, lions, tigers, horses, dogs, hippopotamuses, rhinoceroses, giraffes, zebras, leopards, and camels, along with circus people, also made of jointed wood. Wagons and cages were part of some of the sets.

An 1903 *Playthings* advertisement, shown in *Dollhouses in America* by Flora Gill Jacobs, depicts a Schoenhut U. S. Armory complete with toy soldiers.

In 1917, Schoenhut began producing dollhouses made of wood and fiberboard. The fiberboard parts of the houses were embossed to give the appearance of stone walls and tile roofs.

At the same time, Schoenhut made railroad stations in three sizes, compatible in scale to their smaller dollhouses. The railroad stations, like the dollhouses, had embossed sides which resembled stone. They also manufactured some small fire stations, with several variations including one which was a tie-in to the Ed Wynn radio show.

The company made several different types of village sets. The Hollywood Home Builder series was offered in their 1930 catalog. There were six different houses, all named after a U.S. president. Each was packaged separately and meant to be built by the child. The Schoenhut Community Store Builder set was compatible with the Hollywood Home Builder. Eight different stores were available, including a cigar store, drug store, flower store, five & ten cent store, automobile dealer, bank, grocery, and movie theater. Each was sold separately. A much simpler Little Village Builder set contained the parts for five buildings to be assembled and painted. Schoenhut also produced a Midgetville with houses, a garage, airport, and fire station.

The A. Schoenhut Company went into bankruptcy in 1934, but two of the sons founded companies which carried on the Schoenhut name. O.Schoenhut, Inc. continued to make dollhouses, which somewhat resembled the earlier ones, for a brief time and the Schoenhut Manufacturing Company produced toy pianos for many years.

Stirn & Lyon

Stirn and Lyon made wood toys, dollhouses, stores, and games in New York City during the 1870s and 1880s. The dollhouses came in wood boxes which were used to form the base of the houses which had to be assembled by the owner. The houses were made of a thin wood and used a dowel and peg construction which was not very sturdy. A grocery store was also produced in 1882 using the same technique. The grocery store came stocked with various boxes. It is believed that Stirn & Lyon also produced a warehouse.

Strombecker

J.F. Strombeck and R.D. Becker incorporated the Strombeck-Becker Manufacturing Company in 1913. At first, the company produced many different kinds of wood handles. They began making their first toys in 1919, but they were not very successful until 1928 when they introduced a ten cent airplane.

In 1931, dollhouse furniture was added to the line and, in order to provide a place for the furniture, several different dollhouses were marketed by the firm. Although the houses were probably not made by the Strombecker Company, they were sold already furnished with Strombecker furniture under the company name. Several of the cardboard houses were made by Built-Rite.

The Strombecker Company sold a set of school furniture in the late 1930s. The boxed set contained a teacher's desk with opening drawers, a swivel chair, and four children's desks. Cardboard pieces included in the set could be cut out to furnish a school room.

The Strombeck-Becker Manufacturing Company name was sold to the Dowst Manufacturing Company (maker of Tootsietoy) in 1961. The original company continues to produce custom wood-working products under the Strombeck Manufacturing Company name.

Thomas

The Thomas Manufacturing Corporation produced interesting small plastic items that can be used to supplement the dollhouse furniture made by other companies. Islyn Thomas founded the company in 1944 in Newark, New Jersey. These toys included playground equipment, wagons, strollers, buggies, and dollhouse dolls. In the mid-1950, Thomas manufactured a school room complete with desks, pupils, teacher, and a teacher's desk, as a promotion for the Campbell Soup Company. Their products were marked with either "Acme" or "Thomas Toys" inside a circle.

Tootsietoy (See Dowst)

Tri-ang/Lines Brothers

The English Tri-ang firm was begun shortly after World War I by the three sons of Joseph Lines, co-founder of the famous G. & J. Lines Company. The two firms merged in 1931. Both of the companies were known for their popular dollhouses.

Tri-ang continued in business until 1971. In addition to dollhouses, Tri-ang manufactured several other kinds of toy buildings including stores, theaters, and gas stations.

Tynietoy

The dollhouses and furniture labeled Tynietoy have appealed to collectors since their introduction. Marion I. Perkins began making the miniature furniture around 1917. In partnership with Amey Vernon, Perkins opened the Toy Furniture Shop in Providence, Rhode Island around 1920. Soon dollhouses were added to the Tynietoy line. The wood houses came in several different designs from a two-room cottage to an eleven-room manor house. The two original partners were no longer producing these toys by 1942, although others sold the miniatures throughout the 1940s.

In addition to dollhouses and furniture, Tynietoy made a wood garage, to be used with the houses, a barn, and a Peter Pan Theatre.

Warren Paper Products (See Built-Rite)

Wolverine

The Wolverine Supply and Manufacturing Company was founded in 1903 by Benjamin F. Bain. The company was named after the Wolverine mascot of the University of Michigan. Although it began as a tool and die business, by 1913, the company was producing sand toys, and in the 1920s, the company began making housekeeping toys. In 1962, the company name was changed to the Wolverine Toy Company and in 1968, another change was made when the firm was acquired by Spang and Company. The company name was changed once again in 1986 after they moved to Arkansas and became Today's Kids.

The company produced several toy buildings during the 1930s. These toys were made of metal with accessories of different materials. Included were a post office, several grocery stores, drug store, a greenhouse called "The Little Gardener," and a bathroom.

A very nice Shell Service Station was sold by Wolverine during the late 1970s. The building was made of lithographed metal and the accessories were plastic.

The Wolverine company manufactured dollhouses from 1972 to 1990. The early houses were made of lithographed metal and most of the later houses were made of Masonite and plastic.

Wright, J.L. (Lincoln)

The most popular product of J.L Wright, Inc. (based in Chicago) was the Lincoln Logs that were produced for decades. The logs were designed by John Lloyd Wright in 1916. They were manufactured by the firm until the company was merged with Playskool in 1943. The Wright company advertised several Lincoln Logs sets that were sold as kits to be assembled into forts, barns, railroad stations, or settlers' cabins.

Lincoln also made already assembled buildings which were unrelated to their famous logs. These included a train station and a barn.

Right: Lincoln Logs were advertised in the December 1937 issue of *Children's Activities Magazine*. The illustration showed both buildings made with Lincoln Logs and pre-assembled buildings such as a train station and barn, which came with metal figures. *Photograph by Suzanne Silverthorn.*

Wyandotte

The Wyandotte company, located in the Michigan town of the same name, produced toys from the 1920s through 1956. The company is best known for transportation toys, but it also produced some doll buggies, games, and mechanical toys. The toy buildings produced by Wyandotte included metal fire stations, airports, and garages as well as plastic garages which were sold with their plastic cars. Wyandotte was purchased by Louis Marx in the 1950s.

Sources

Museums:

Angels Attic Museum
516 Colorado Avenue
Santa Monica, CA 90401
(310) 394-8331

Delaware Toy & Miniature Museum
Route 141
P. O. Box 4053
Wilmington, DE 19807

The Dollhouse and Miniature Museum of Cape May
118 Decatur Street
Cape May, NJ 08204

Kinney Pioneer Museum
P.O. Box 421
Hwy 18 West
Mason City, Iowa 50402-0421
(575) 423-1258

Mineral Point Toy Museum
Carol Stevenson, Curator
215 Commerce
Mineral Point, WI 53565
(608) 987-3160

Toy & Miniature Museum of Kansas City
5235 Oak Street
Kansas City, Missouri 64112
(816) 333-2055

Washington Dolls' House and Toy Museum
5236 44th Street, N.W.
Washington, DC 2015

Publications:

Antique Toy World
Antique Toy World Publications
P.O. Box 34509
Chicago, Illinois 60634

Plastic Figure & Playset Collector Magazine
Specialty Publishing Compay
P.O. Box 1355
LaCrosse, WI 54602-1355

Dealers:

Judith Armitstead
The Doll Works
P.O. Box 195
Lynnfield, MA 01940
(781) 334-5577

Pen Andrishok
3 Dogs Antiques
5656 400th Street SE
West Branch, IA 52358

Art of the Tin Toy, Ltd.
16, Hyde Park Gardens Mews
London W2 2NU England

Atticus Antiques
Cynthia Stuart Greene and Theresa Luttenegger
(319) 644-2852
4970 Morse Road
Iowa City, Iowa 52240
theresa@avalon.net

Lisa Boutilier
91B Brightwood Avenue
Worcester, MA 01604
(dollhouses and dollhouse furniture)

Calco
Linda and Carl Thomas, Jr.
345 Mountainview Avenue
Bluefield, WV 24701

Catskill Toy Company
16 Osborne Street
Monticello, NY 12701
New and Old Toys and Parts
(914) 791-6423

Childhood Memories Antiques & Collectibles
133 Cambridge
Pleasant Ridge, MI 48069

Christmas Morning
Antique Toy Mail and Phone Auction
Ben Stevens
1806 Royal Lane
Dallas, TX 75229-3126
(972) 506-8362

Continental Hobby House
Route 1, L.S. N9399
P.O. Box 193
Sheboygan, WI 53082
(920) 693-3371

Ben DeVoto
756 Craig Drive
Kirkwood, MO 63122
bendevoto@primary.net

Dolls House Antiques
Leslie and Joanne Payne
290 Summerhaven Drive North
East Syracuse, NY 13057

Charles Donovan, Jr.
11877 U.S. Hwy 431
Ohatchee, AL 36271
Specializing in Renwal toys.

The Early Adventure
445 Galliton Road
Belle Vernon, PA 15012
(412) 379-5833

Gene Harris Antique Auction Center, Inc.
203 S. 18th Avenue
P.O. Box 476
Marshalltown, IA 50158
(515) 752-0600

Fine antiques, toys, dolls, collectibles
Gary's Trains
Gary Mosholder
186 Pine Springs Camp Road
Boswell, PA 15531

Keystone Toy Trader
Bob Stevens
529 N. Water Street
Masontown, PA 15461
(723) 583-8234

Lucy Ellen Antiques
Jim& Shirley Cox
Redmond, WA 98052
(425) 885-5853

Ann Meehan
51 Pine Hurst Rd.
Portsmouth, NH 03801
Early antique dollhouses, furnishings,
and accessories 1850-1930.

Marilyn Pittman
Marilyn's Miniatures of Marshallville
P.O. Box 1246
Marshallville, OH 44645

Joe Russell
11 MacGregor Drive
Mahopac, NY 10541

Sussex Antique Toy Shop
107 Avenue L
Matamoras, PA 18336
(717) 491-2707
Toys from the teens through the fifties: pressed steel,
tin litho, plastic, and more.

Thrilling Toys of Yesteryear
64502 Joe Neil Road
Bend, OR 97701
(541) 383-1897

Toys in the Attic
Gaston and Joan Majeune
167 Phelps Avenue
Englewood, NJ 07631
(201) 568-6745
Dollhouses, shops, iron, tin, and paper lithographed toys.

William F. Weart
2222 Nottingham Road
Allentown, PA 18103
Specializing in cast iron automobile and horse drawn toys.
Also early American tin toys.

Kirk F. White
Box 999
New Smyrna Beach, FL 32170
(904) 427-6660Fax: (904) 427-7801

Bibliography

Ackerman, Evelyn. *The Genius of Moritz Gottschalk.*
  Annapolis, MD: Gold Horse Publishing, 1994.

Adams, Margaret, ed. *Collectible Dolls and Accessories of the Twenties and Thirties
  From Sears, Roebuck, and Co. Catalogs.* New York: Dover, 1986.

Antique Toy Collectors of America. *1896 Fall Catalogue of the R. Bliss Manufacturing Co.* Pawtuckett, R.I., R. Bliss Mfg., Co., 1896. Reprinted. 1986.

Antique Toy World. Chicago: Antique Toy World Publications, various issues.

Baeker, Carlernst et al. *Marklin: New Ways to Success, up to 1912.* New York:
  Hastings House, 1978.

Bagdade, Susan and Al. *Collector's Guide to American Toy Trains.* Radnor, PA: Wallace-
  Homestead Book
  Company, 1990.

Baker, Linda. *Modern Toys. American Toys 1930-1980.* Paducah, KY: Collector Books,
  1985.

Barlow, Ronald S, ed. *The Great American Antique Toy
  Bazaar.* El Cajon, CA: Windmill Publishing Co., 1998.

Bliss, R. Manufacturing Company. *1896 Fall Catalogue.* Pawtucket: RI: R. Bliss, 1896
  reprinted. Washington, DC: Antique Toy Collectors of America, Inc. 1986.

Brett, Mary. *Tomart's Price Guide to Tin Litho Doll Houses and Plastic Doll House Furniture.* Dayton, OH: Tomart Publications, 1997.

Butler Brothers. *Butler Brothers Fall Catalog.* New York: Butler Brothers, various
  issues.

Child Life Magazine. Boston: Child Life, Inc. Various issues, 1930s-1950s.

Children's Activities Magzine. Chicago: Child Training
  Association, Inc. Various issues, 1930s-1950s.

Donovan, Charles F., Jr. *Renwal: World's Finest Toys.* Ohatchee, Alabama: By the
  author, 1994.

Hare, Frank C, ed. *Plasticville: An Illustrated Price Guide.* Pittsburgh, PA.: IronHorse
  Productions, Inc., 1993.

Jaffe, Alan. *J. Chein & Co.: A Collector's Guide.* Atglen, PA: Schiffer Publishing Co., 1997.

Jacobs, Flora Gill. *Dollhouses in America.* New York: Charles Scribner's Sons, 1974.

Kerr, Lisa. *American Tin-Litho Toys.* Portland, OR:
  Collectors Press, 1995.

Kerr, Lisa. *Ohio Art: the World of Toys.* Atglen, PA: Schiffer Publishing, Ltd., 1998.

King, Constance Eileen. *Antique Toys and Dolls.* New York: Rizzoli International
  Publications, Inc., 1979.

King, Constance Eileen. *The Encyclopedia of Toys.* New York: Crown Publishers,1978.

L.H. Mace & Co. *Illustrated Catalogue and Net Price List 1907: Toys.* Washington,
  D.C.: Washington Dolls' House & Toy Museum, 1977. Reprinted. Flora Gill
  Jacobs.

Marshall Field & Company catalogs. Chicago, IL., various issues.

Mr. Gamage's Great Toy Bazaar. Introduction by Charlotte Parry-Crooke. London:
  Deny's Ingram Publishers, 1982.

Montgomery Ward. Catalogs. Chicago: Montgomery Ward, various issues.

O'Brien, Richard. *Collecting Toys No. 5.* Florence, AL: Books Americana, 1990.

O'Brien, Richard. *Collecting Toys No. 7.* Florence, AL: Books Americana, 1995.

Osborne, Marion. *Dollhouses A-Z.* Nottingham, England: By the Author, 29 Attenborough Lane, Chilwell NG9 5JP, 1986.

Osborne, Marion. *Lines and Tri-ang Dollhouses and Furniture 1900-1971.* Nottingham, England. By the author, 29 Attenborough Lane, Chilwell NG9 5JP, 1986.

Pinksky, Maxine A. *Greenberg's Guide to Marx Toys Volume I.* Sykesville, MD, 1988.

Pinksky, Maxine A. *Greenberg's Guide to Marx Toys Volume II.* Sykesville, MD, 1990.

Schroeder, Joseph J. Jr. *The Wonderful World of Toys, Games & Dolls 1860-1930.* Northfield, IL: Digest Books, Inc., 1971.

Schwartz, Marvin. *F.A.O. Schwarz Toys Through the Years.* Garden City, NY: Doubleday and Co., Inc., 1971.

Sears, Roebuck and Company Catalogs. Chicago: Sears, Roebuck and Company, various issues.

Snyder, Dee. "Time for School." *Nutshell News,* September 1989, pp. 36-37.

Snyder, Dee. "Colleen Moore's Doll Castle by Rich Toys. *Nutshell News.* February 1988, pp. 36-37.

Spero, James. Ed. *Collectible Toys and Games of the Twenties and Thirties from Sears, Roebuck and Co. Catalogs.* New York: Dover, 1988.

Spiegel Catalog. Chicago: Spiegel, Inc., various issues.

Stille, Eva. *Doll Kitchens 1800-1980.* West Chester, PA: Schiffer Publishing, Ltd.,1988.

Stirn, Carl P. *Turn-of-the Century Dolls, Toys, and Games.* New York: Dover Publications, Inc., 1990.

Tempest, Jack. *Post-War Tin Toys: A Collector's Guide.* Radnor, PA: Wallace-Homestead Book Company, 1991.

Terry, Tom. "Oh Doctor!" *Plastic Figure and Playset Collector,* April 1995, pp. 6-16.

Time-Life Books. *Encyclopedia of Collectibles: Dogs to Fishing Tackle.* Alexandria, VA: Time-Life Books, 1978.

Toy and Miniature Museum of Kansas City, Missouri. Kansas City, MO: The Museum,1992.

Tubbs, Marcie. "Dear Old Golden Rule Days." *Miniature Collector,* September 1996, pp. 30-33.

The Universal Toy Catalog of 1924/1926. (Der Universal Speilwaren Katalog.) Reprint edition. London: New Cavendish Books, 1985.

Wahlberg, Holly. "A House for the Automobile." *Old House Journal,* August 1998. Washington, DC: Hanley-Wood, Inc.

Whitehill, Bruce. *Games: American Boxed Games and Their Makers, 1822-1992.* Radnor, PA: Wallace-Homestead Book Co., 1992.

Whitton, Blair, ed. *Bliss Toys and Dollhouses.* New York: Dover Publications,1979.

Whitton, Blair. *The Knopf Collectors' Guides to American Antiques: Toys.* New York: Alfred A. Knopf, 1984.

Whitton, Blair. *Paper Toys of the World.* Cumberland, MD: Hobby House Press, 1986.

Whitton, Margaret, ed. *Dollhouses and Furniture Manufactured by A.Schoenhut Company, 1917-1934* (reprinted.) n.p., n.d.

Zillner, Dian. *American Dollhouses and Furniture From the 20th Century.* Atglen, PA: Schiffer Publishing, 1995.

Zillner, Dian and Patty Cooper. *Antique & Collectible Dollhouses and Their Furnishings.* Atglen, PA: Schiffer Publishing, 1998.